OXFORD
Children's
Encyclopedia

Volume 2

OXFORD
Children's
Encyclopedia

Comics to Ghana

Oxford University Press

Oxford University Press, Walton Street, Oxford OX2 6DP

Oxford   New York   Toronto
Delhi   Bombay   Calcutta   Madras   Karachi
Petaling Jaya   Singapore   Hong Kong   Tokyo
Nairobi   Dar es Salaam   Cape Town
Melbourne   Auckland
and associated companies in
Berlin   Ibadan

Oxford is a trade mark of Oxford University Press
© Oxford University Press 1991, 1994

This edition specially produced in 1994 for The Reader's Digest Association Ltd
Berkeley Square House, Berkeley Square, London W1X 6AB

1 3 5 7 9 10 8 6 4 2

ISBN 0 19 910163 9 (complete set)

Volume 2: 0 19 910165 5 (not for sale separately)

A CIP catalogue record for this book is available from the British Library

Printed in Spain by
Mateu Cromo, S.A. Pinto – Madrid

Editor	Mary Worrall
Design and art direction	Richard Morris
Cover design	Philip Atkins
Assistant editors	Jane Bingham
	David Burnie
	Tony Drake
	Deborah Manley
	Sarah Matthews
	Pamela Mayo
	Stephen Pople
	Andrew Solway
	Catherine Thompson
Copy preparation	Eric Buckley
	Richard Jeffery
Proof reader	Richard Jeffery
Index	Radmila May
Photographic research	Catherine Blackie
	Libby Howells
	Linda Proud
	Suzanne Williams

How to use the Oxford Children's Encyclopedia

There are three main ways of finding the information you want. You may search for the topics in the headings in the alphabetical sequence. You might think of another word which is close to the topic that interests you and search for that in the headings. Or you could use the index, which is the best method of all.

Using the headings

Often the topic you wish to look up will be the heading of a whole article. Suppose you want to read about **fish**. This starts with **F** so you find the letter **F** on the spine of Volume 2 (this volume). Once you have found the first letter of the word, search for the second letter which is picked out in bold type at the top of the page like this: **Fi**sh.

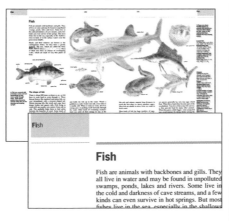

Fish

Fish are animals with backbones and gills. They all live in water and may be found in unpolluted swamps, ponds, lakes and rivers. Some live in the cold and darkness of cave streams, and a few kinds can even survive in hot springs. But most fishes live in the sea, especially in the shallows

People

If you are looking for an article about a person, go straight to Volume 6: the Biography. These articles are in alphabetical order, listed under the surname (family name) as in a telephone directory: **Oakley,** Annie.

Think of another word

If you cannot find what you want under the main headings, think of another word or topic that is very close to what you need. Suppose you want to look up **tragedy** or **comedy**. You know that tragedy and comedy are types of **Drama**. So you look up that article. In this case you will have to search for the words by reading right through.

In ancient times and in the Middle Ages surnames were not common and so you will find many people under their first names: **Akbar**, **Billy** the Kid, **Kongzi**.

Spellings of historical characters vary and you may have to search over a few pages.

Using the index

The most thorough method is to use the index. Comedy is listed in the index. Next to it is the reference: **2** 83, which means there is an article in Volume 2 on page 83 which has something about comedy. Sometimes there may be two or three articles which have something on the subject you want.

Comaneci, Nadia	**6** 267
Combat sports	**5** 64
Comedy	2 83
Comets	**1** 256
Extinction of animals	**2** 153

volume number — page number

So you find Volume 2, page 83 which is the second page of the article on **Drama**.

Suppose you want to read about Ramadan, the Muslim period of fasting. There isn't a main article in the **R**s. The index gives the reference: **2** 108, 166, 171. The first reference is the article on **Eid**, the Muslim festival, which explains Ramadan, the second is for **Fasting** which mentions Ramadan too, and the third is for **Festival**.

Cross references

Almost every article leads on to many more. Look for the red **See also** bar in the margin at the end of an article. This lists other articles which have more information related to what you have read.

This list appears at the end of the article on **Cowboys**.

 See also

American Indians
American West

Biography
Billy the Kid
Buffalo Bill
James, Jesse
Oakley

Contents

Comics

Comics are popular all over the world. Readers of all ages enjoy them for many reasons, but mainly because they are fun to read.

Some of the most famous comics come from the United States. One of the favourite characters of all time is Superman. He has X-ray vision, he can fly, he is enormously strong, and nothing can hurt him except the element Kryptonite. Luckily, he always uses his strength for good and not for evil and, fortunately for the readers, his enemies usually manage to find some Kryptonite from somewhere, or otherwise there would hardly be any Superman stories to tell.

The most popular British comic is the *Beano*. Children (and some grown-ups) enjoy reading about Dennis the Menace, Lord Snooty, and the Bash Street Kids. Dennis is always naughty, but he always gets punished in the end, so we never feel that things are going really wrong.

Flashback

In Victorian times there were popular stories called 'Penny Dreadfuls', but they had few pictures; most of the story was told in words. Real comics had to wait until the end of the 19th century, when new printing methods were invented that made it easier to print pictures. Another reason might have been that the cinema began at the same time, and people quickly became used to stories being told through pictures. Besides, more and more people could read by then, and the comics were so cheap that almost anyone could afford to buy them. ∎

Famous comics
*Comic Cuts
 and Chips* 1890–1953
Rainbow 1914–1950
Eagle 1950–

◀ **A page from the famous comic strip, Tintin, created by the Belgian artist Hergé, whose real name was Georges Remi. His first comic strip was *Tintin in the Land of the Soviets* and was published in 1929.**

 **See also**

Cartoons

Commonwealth of Nations

See also

British empire

Hong Kong is due to be returned to China in 1997.

▼ Self-governing members of the Commonwealth; the date shows when each became independent.

The Commonwealth of Nations is a group of countries scattered all over the world which were members of the British empire in the past. From 1918 to 1947 it was called 'the British Empire and Commonwealth'. The **Commonwealth** meant the countries which governed themselves, like Canada and Australia; the **Empire** meant India and the colonies, which were still governed from Britain.

Since 1947 almost all the colonies have become independent. The numbers of new nations grew very fast. In 1962 there were fifteen independent members of the Commonwealth, and 20 years later there were 47. Only a few very small colonies, mainly islands, remain, including the Falkland Islands and St Helena in the South Atlantic and several islands in the West Indies.

United Kingdom		The Gambia	1965	Kiribati		1979
Canada	1867	Maldives	1965	St Vincent and		
Australia	1901	Singapore	1965	Grenadines		1979
New Zealand	1907	Guyana	1966	Zimbabwe		1980
India	1947	Botswana	1966	Vanuatu		1980
Sri Lanka	1948	Lesotho	1966	Belize		1981
Ghana	1957	Barbados	1966	Antigua and Barbuda	1981
Malaysia	1957	Nauru	1968	St Kitts and Nevis		1983
Cyprus	1960	Mauritius	1968	Brunei		1984
Nigeria	1960	Swaziland	1968	Namibia		1990
Sierra Leone	1961	Tonga	1970			
Tanzania	1961	Bangladesh	1972	**Countries which left the**	
Western Samoa	1962	Bahamas	1973	**Commonwealth**	
Jamaica	1962	Grenada	1974	Burma		1947
Trinidad and Tobago	1962	Papua New Guinea	1975	Irish Republic		1949
Uganda	1962	Seychelles	1976	South Africa		1961
Kenya	1963	Solomon Islands	1978	Pakistan		1972
Malawi	1964	Tuvalu	1978		returned	1989
Malta	1964	Dominica	1978	Fiji		1987
Zambia	1964	St Lucia	1979			

How the Commonwealth is kept together

All the countries accept Queen Elizabeth II as the Head of the Commonwealth. She visits the Commonwealth countries in turn, and meets the leading politicians at their regular conferences.

To help the members to keep in touch an office was set up in London in 1965. The person in charge is called the Secretary-General. The first was a Canadian, Arnold Smith. From 1975 to 1990 Sir Shridath (usually called 'Sonny') Ramphal from Guyana was the Secretary-General. Chief Emeka Anyaoku became Secretary-General in 1990.

Many people meet each other from different parts of the Commonwealth, especially through sport. Some countries play in the cricket test matches and all compete in the Commonwealth Games.

Difficulties

There have been serious problems and quarrels. Britain used to buy much of her food from the Commonwealth, but after she joined the European Community in 1973 she has bought more from western European countries than from Commonwealth countries. New Zealand farmers can no longer sell so much butter and lamb to Britain, and the West Indies sell less sugar.

The most serious quarrels have been caused by the matter of race. The Commonwealth is made up of peoples from different nations and races. It believes that treating black or coloured people unfairly is wrong. South Africa left the Commonwealth in 1961 because other members made it very clear that she was not wanted while the apartheid system treated black people unjustly. There have been times when African and Asian members of the Commonwealth have been angry with British governments for not supporting black people in their demands for justice, and for limiting immigration into Britain. ■

Commonwealth of Independent States (CIS)

See also

Armenia	Turkmenistan
Azerbaijan	Ukraine
Belarus	USSR 1922–
Kazakhstan	1991
Kirgyzstan	Uzbekistan
Moldova	
Russia	
Tajikistan	

The Commonwealth of Independent States was formed in 1991 to include republics of the former USSR both in Asia and in Europe. When the USSR broke up and the republics became independent, many of them thought that it would be a good idea to keep closely in touch with each other. Agreements were reached between members of the Commonwealth of Independent States in areas such as trade, defence and transport. Another important question that the new Commonwealth had to deal with was the problem of the former USSR's nuclear weapons remaining on some of the countries' territories. Not all the former republics of the USSR joined the new Commonwealth. Latvia, Lithuania and Estonia, for example, preferred to develop closer ties with western Europe. ■

Communication

Communication, the passing of messages, goes on around us all the time. Using colour, flowers signal to bees that they are good to visit. Cinnabar moths warn birds that they taste bitter. Noise and movement frighten timid creatures. Load roars warn enemies of danger.

Some animals perform amazing feats of communication. One whale, for example, can probably hear another whale's 'song' as much as 50 km (30 miles) away. Bats and dolphins navigate with sounds too shrill for us to hear. A high-pitched 'silent' dog whistle is easy for a dog to recognize. Minute variations in sound can contain a world of meaning to some insects. A male cicada can click up to 600 times a second to attract a female or warn off another male. The changes in its pattern of clicks are just too fine for a human to detect.

We use gestures as well as words to communicate with other people, to tell them how we feel and what we think. This kind of communication is especially important when we cannot make our speech heard, or when silence is necessary. The hitchhiker's thumbs up sign is used because passing motorists would not hear verbal requests for a lift. Hunters communicate by signs because they do not want to make a noise that would frighten away the prey. A smile communicates pleasure when we see a friend. Sometimes our body says one thing while our words say another. We may say, 'Oh, I don't really mind', but a thumping heart and tense muscles are screaming, 'I hate that idea!' Machines called lie detectors make use of this fact. They measure what our sweat and pulse rate communicate, and it is hard to fake those when we tell lies.

People, though, are special in another way. Language itself is a thing we take for granted. You are using it at this very moment without even thinking about it. It is an immensely rich and subtle form of communication. And since earliest times, humans have recorded what they have seen or felt or thought, in cave paintings, in hieroglyphics, in writing. Others can 'read' it, even after thousands of years. And printing means that many people can share the same information.

Tape and video recordings have extended the ways we can communicate. The postal system, television and radio, the telephone, computer and satellites are all human achievements that have increased the range, speed and complexity of human communication. People can now talk to each other easily, even if they are half a world apart. A fax (facsimile) machine can recreate in London a picture that, moments before, existed only in New York or Tokyo. No other creature we know can achieve anything quite as remarkable as that. ■

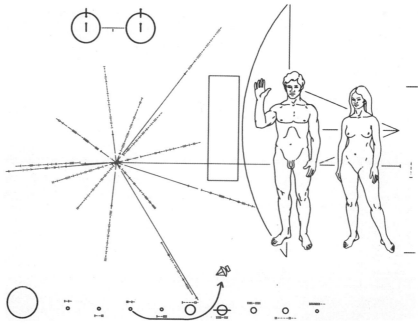

before 3250 BC Cuneiform writing developed in Sumeria.
from 3100 BC Ancient Egyptians used hieroglyphic writing.
before 1500 BC Chinese used pictograms for keeping records.
about 1500 BC Alphabet developed by Canaanites in Syria.

before 8th century AD Block printing used in Korea and China.
11th century AD Movable type used for printing in China.
15th century AD Gutenberg used movable type in Europe.

1837 First practical telegraph in Britain.
1838 Samuel Morse invented Morse Code.
1866 First transatlantic telegraph link between North America and England.
1876 Alexander Graham Bell demonstrated the first telephone.
1877 Thomas Edison built the first phonograph, the forerunner of the modern record player.
1895 The first radio signals transmitted over a mile by Marconi.
1906 Canadian physicist Reginald A. Fessenden was the first person to transmit his voice by radio.
1926 The first public demonstration of television in London.
1928 First transatlantic telephone service.
1960 Radio signals sent into space and reflected back to earth from the Echo 1 satellite.
1970 Electric signals from telephones and TV pictures transformed into pulses of laser light and transmitted via fibre optic cables.

▲ The plaque attached to the Pioneer 10 and 11 spacecraft, showing their origin in case they are ever examined by another intelligent species. The 'dumb-bell' symbol at top left represents a molecule of hydrogen, the most common element in the Universe. 14 lines radiate from our Sun to the relative positions of 14 pulsars – cosmic sources of radio energy. Below the human figures is a plan of the Solar System showing the early stages of the spacecraft's journey from Earth.

Communists

The first Communist Party to take power was the All-Russian Communist Party. Before it changed its name in 1918, it had been called the Russian Social-Democratic Workers' Party.

'The theory of the Communists may be summed up in the single sentence: Abolition of private property.' This quotation, from *The Communist Manifesto* of 1848, explains what communists believe. They want all property, especially land and factories, to be owned by the state on behalf of all the people. Then the goods and services produced can be shared out fairly amongst the people.

Karl Marx and Friedrich Engels, who wrote *The Communist Manifesto*, believed that this would only be achieved by a revolution, when the working class would rise up and take power from the ruling classes. ■

See also

China's history
Cold War
Political parties
Revolutions
Russia's history
USSR 1922–1991

Biography
Marx

Compasses

▲ The needle of a compass is magnetized and will always point north and south. But the north it points to is magnetic north and not true north, so there is always a variation.

Compasses are instruments which show you north and, from that, other directions as well. They are used on ships and aircraft for navigation. Small, portable compasses are used by people who go hill-walking and orienteering.

Most compasses have a small magnetized pointer (called a needle) which is hung, pivoted or floated so that it can turn freely. The Earth's magnetism pulls the needle so that it always points north. A card in the compass shows north, south, east, west and angles in between.

One problem with magnetic compasses is that they point to magnetic north, which is not in quite the same direction as true north. In ships and aircraft, the problem is overcome by using gyroscopic compasses. Lodestone, a magnetic rock, was known in China over 2,000 years ago. By the 1st century AD, sailors were using simple compasses with lodestone needles. A tiny piece of lodestone was fixed to a straw so that it would float in a bowl of water. ■

See also

China's history
Gyroscopes
Navigation

Composers

Composers write songs, symphonies and other musical works. Just as writers use words to make stories, so composers arrange sounds.

How pop composers work

The writers of pop songs often begin with the words (the lyric) and then make up a tune to fit. They write this down, or record it on tape. Then they work with the rest of their group, or with an arranger, to turn it into the finished song. Some pop composers use synthesizers (electronic devices for combining sounds) and computers; with these they build the whole piece from electronic sound.

John Lennon and Paul McCartney of the Beatles were two of the most popular songwriters of all time. Together they wrote the words and music for 24 number one hits, more than any other pop music composer.

Many composers blend live sounds and electronics. They add new ideas to the music layer by layer, like bricks in a wall. Each layer is recorded on a different track, and the tracks are mixed and blended to make the finished song.

Classical music

A few modern classical composers use electronic sounds and work in studios with computers, just as pop composers do. But most classical composers write their music on paper, for other people such as soloists, orchestras and chamber groups to play in live performance.

Mozart is considered to be one of the most prolific of classical composers. He wrote about 1,000 pieces of music before he died at the age of 35.

The composers think up strands of sound, and write them down on music-paper, that is paper already printed with staves (music-lines). They give instructions for every single note that is to be played.

When this work is done, they have a score (master-copy) of the whole piece of music. From this, the composer or a 'copyist' copies out the music for each separate performer of an instrument. This will be the 'part' they play. A composer needs to know all about how music is organized and which instruments or which singing voices are most suitable to carry out the composition. ■

See also

Electronic music
Music
Pop and rock music
Singing and songs

Biography

Beethoven	Lloyd Webber
Bernstein	Mendelssohn
Brahms	Mozart
Britten	Prokofiev
Chopin	Schubert
Debussy	Strauss
Dvorak	Stravinsky
Elgar	Sullivan
Gershwin	Tchaikovsky
Handel	Verdi
Haydn	Vivaldi
Liszt	Wagner

Pop and rock special

Computers

You may have used a computer for playing games. Computers are good for zapping aliens. But they can do many other jobs as well. They can do sums more quickly than a calculator and store more information than a roomful of filing cabinets. They can control machines, fly aircraft and help design cars. The jobs they do depend on the instructions they are given. Today, almost every office and factory uses computers.

Modern computers are electronic. They work using tiny electric currents. They have thousands of circuits inside them. Most of the circuits are packed together on tiny slices of silicon about the size of your fingernail. Each slice has a casing around it and is called an integrated circuit or chip.

Computers handle data (information). The data can be words, numbers, pictures, or a mixture of all three. When a computer is working, it has to store the data it is using. It needs a memory. Chips are used for this as well.

The development of computers

Charles Babbage, a British inventor, is sometimes called the father of the computer. In 1823, he started to build a calculating machine that could do sums and print out the results. The machine used gearwheels to do the calculating. It was so complicated that it was never finished.

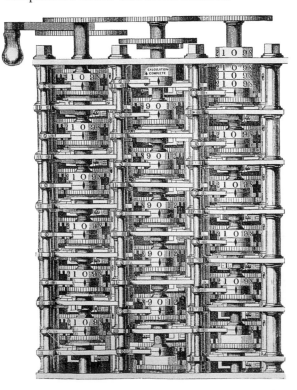

Electronic calculating machines were first made during World War II. They were huge. A British machine, the Colossus, was used to break secret enemy codes. Another, made in America, weighed 30 tonnes. These machines were not really computers because they did not have memories. The first working computer was built at Manchester University, England, in 1948. From this the first commercial computer, the Ferranti Mark One, was developed in 1951. This machine filled a whole room and used as much power as twenty-seven electric fires. The first computers were large, because their memory circuits used ordinary wires and thousands of valves. Valves looked and glowed like light bulbs. Computers used them to store data by switching them on or off in a certain order.

Computers started to get smaller when transistors replaced valves. Transistors were no bigger than a pea and used much less power than valves. When scientists discovered how to pack thousands of transistors on a single chip, computers could be made even smaller.

Nowadays, computers are made in several sizes:

Microcomputers (micros) are the small desktop computers you find in schools and houses. Sometimes they are known as personal computers or PCs. Most can do just one job at a time.

Minicomputers (minis) are larger and more powerful than micros. Some have extra keyboards and screens so that several people can use the computer at once. Each extra keyboard and screen is called a terminal.

Mainframes are the largest computers of all. They have lots of terminals and can do many jobs at once. Most big companies have a mainframe to help them run their business. The computer fills several cabinets and is installed in its own special room.

▲ The first electronic computers weighed tonnes, had smaller memories than modern desk-top micros and used a million times more power.

The first small, cheap home computer, using chips, was made by the Sinclair Company in England in 1980.

◄ Charles Babbage designed this calculating machine in 1823. It was way ahead of its time, but was never completed.

Concentration camps

At various times in history, governments have tried to 'concentrate' troublesome people into camps. For example, when one country conquers or occupies another country, the ordinary people of the occupied country might be herded into camps. In this way they might be controlled, and be less likely to cause problems.

In the Boer War, when Britain fought Dutch-speaking farmers in southern Africa, the British government put many Boer women and children into camps, where many died from disease.

By far the biggest use of concentration camps was by the Nazi government of Germany between 1933 and 1945. The Nazis hated Jewish people. They rounded up Jews in Germany and in the countries they occupied during the war, and sent them to concentration camps. In the camps, Jews had to work hard with little food, and very many of them died. Eventually, some of the German concentration camps became 'death camps' with gas ovens in which Jews were deliberately killed. In Auschwitz, which was in occupied Poland, gas chambers killed and incinerated 12,000 people a day. Four million Jewish men, women and children died in these camps. Others died too: anyone the Nazis thought to be inferior could be sent to the camps. Gypsies were sent, and mentally handicapped people, communists, and homosexuals.

At the end of the war, British, Soviet and American soldiers discovered the camps, filled with dead and dying people. Films of what they found were shown all over the world, and still cause horror when seen today. People still remember the names of many of the camps: Auschwitz, Belsen, Buchenwald, Dachau. These names will stay for ever in the history of the world as a sign of how cruel people can be. ■

More than 20,000 Boer people died in British concentration camps during the Boer War. These were not the first concentration camps, but most historians agree that this was the first time that the actual name was used.

In addition to over 4 million Jews, millions of prisoners of war, political prisoners and ordinary civilians died in the Nazi concentration camps.

Concentration camps and forced labour camps were also used by Soviet communists to imprison their opponents.

See also
Boer War
Holocaust
Nazis
World War II

Concertos

A concerto is a piece of classical music for a solo instrument and orchestra. Often, the composer of a concerto tries to show off the skill and beauty of the soloist's playing. The music is difficult to play and exciting to listen to. Other concertos are more like conversations, where soloists and orchestra share the musical ideas. Most concertos have just one soloist, for example a piano concerto is for piano and orchestra. But there are also concertos for two or more solo instruments and some 'concertos for orchestra', which spotlight every department of the orchestra in turn.

The first concertos were written in the 17th century. They were known as *concerti grossi*. Instead of a soloist, these concertos had a small group of string players, accompanied by an orchestra and harpsichord. ■

Antonio Vivaldi (1678–1741) wrote over 500 concertos. The most famous group of these is 'The Four Seasons', for violin and orchestra.

Composers of some well-known concertos

Piano
Mozart, Beethoven, Schumann, Grieg, Tchaikovsky, Rachmaninov
Violin
Mozart, Beethoven, Mendelssohn, Brahms, Sibelius
Cello
Dvorak, Elgar, Shostakovich
Guitar
Rodrigo

See also
Music
Musical instruments

Concerts

Concerts are musical performances for an audience. Many people give concerts just for the fun of it, or to raise money. There are school concerts, band concerts, choral concerts, and chamber music concerts (called 'recitals'). Biggest of all are pop concerts, when bands and groups perform in front of thousands of people, sometimes filling whole stadiums, squares, city parks or shopping precincts.

Flashback

Until about 250 years ago, most concerts were private. Rich people employed musician-servants, paid to entertain. Then, in 18th-century Europe, musicians began putting on public concerts, for anyone willing to buy a ticket. You could pay a subscription in advance for a whole series of concerts, and the performances were called 'subscription concerts'. ■

In the 19th century, Promenade Concerts were held in pleasure gardens, and people could stand or walk around as they listened to the music.

Today's Promenade Concerts were originally conducted by Sir Henry Wood at Queen's Hall, London. Since World War II they have been held in the Albert Hall.

Concrete

Concrete comes from a Latin word *concretus*, meaning 'grown together'.

Concrete is a tough, hard-wearing building material. It is a mixture of three things: cement, water and aggregate. Aggregate is a gritty or stony material such as sand or gravel. When cement is mixed with water it forms a 'glue' which binds all the materials together. Together, they make a strong artificial rock.

How concrete gets its strength

The strength of concrete depends partly on how much water is added and partly on which kind of aggregate is used. Only a small amount of water is needed to harden the cement. Any extra water has to dry up. It may take a long time to do this, and it may also leave small holes in the concrete which can weaken it. A coarse aggregate such as crushed stone produces a strong concrete but is hard to mix. A fine aggregate such as sand has smooth round particles and is easy to mix. However, it produces a weak form of concrete, usually called mortar. Mortar is smooth, and so it can be used for laying bricks. Most concrete is made from a mixture of sand and stones with the cement. In the right proportions it can produce a very strong concrete.

Cement is a fine, grey powder made by burning lime and clay. It sets into a stonelike mass when mixed with water.

Reinforced concrete

Concrete can withstand great weights, and for this reason it is often used to make floors or roads. But concrete cracks easily when it is bent or stretched. To make concrete beams and pillars stronger, they are reinforced by thin steel rods. Nearly all the concrete used for buildings and large structures is reinforced in this way.

Some uses of concrete

As well as roads, floors, beams and columns, concrete is used to make bridges and bridge supports, dams, airfield runways, railway sleepers, garden ornaments and building blocks of any desired shape and size. Reinforced concrete has even been used to make the hulls of boats. ∎

See also
Bridges
Buildings
Cement

▼ Pouring concrete for a bridge. The concrete hardens round the steel rods, which give it extra strength.

Concussion

Any sharp blow on the head, perhaps from a football or a heavy fall, can cause concussion. When someone is concussed they faint (lose consciousness) for a few seconds. This happens because the blow to the head shakes the brain and throws the nerve cells out of action for a short while. When a concussed person wakes up they may feel dizzy and sick. They may also have double or blurred vision and a bad headache that lasts for several hours. Blows to the head are serious. If you have been concussed you should always see a doctor. ∎

See also
Brains
Heads

Confucians

Confucians follow the teachings of the Chinese sage, Kongzi, who lived in the 5th century BC. Confucius is the Western spelling of his name.

Teachings

Some years after Confucius' death, his teachings were collected into a book called the *Analects*. They teach that the most important thing is to treat others in the same way as you treat yourself. The best kind of life is one full of peace and harmony. A person creates harmony by avoiding any extreme action or wild thoughts. Confucius believed that peace in the world depends on the proper organization of each country; that a peaceful country depends on a peaceful family, and that peaceful family life depends on the harmony inside each individual.

The best kind of person is one who is wise, loves other people, is courageous, unselfish, careful in the way he or she talks about things, respectful to others, especially parents and teachers, studies hard and seriously, is generous and loyal.

Religion or philosophy?

People have always argued about whether Confucians follow a religion or a philosophy of life. For Confucius, Tian (heaven) is a great moral power and the source of everything. But when people asked him about religion, Confucius replied: 'If you cannot serve human beings how can you serve spiritual beings, and if you cannot know life, then how can you know death?'

The teachings of Confucius were developed and handed on by Mengzi (Mencius) in the 4th century BC. Much later in AD 1190 the most important texts were printed and published and so could be read all over China. The three great moral and religious teachings of the Confucians, Buddhists and Taoists have influenced almost all Chinese culture in one way or another. ∎

⊙ See also
China's history
Taoists

Biography
Kongzi

Congo

Congo is a country on the Equator in west-central Africa. Behind the dry coastal plain lie forested mountains, high plateaux and huge swamps. There are many long rivers, including the Congo River, which is also known as the Zaïre River.

Apart from a few pygmies, who hunt in remote parts of the forest, most of the people speak one of several Bantu languages. More than half of these people live in farming villages and grow crops to feed their families. Others cut down trees to sell as timber. But oil from offshore fields is Congo's most valuable product.

From the 15th to the 18th centuries, Congo was a centre of the slave trade. France took over the country in the 1880s and ruled it until it became independent in 1960. ∎

Area
342,000 sq km
(132,000 sq miles)
Capital Brazzaville
Population 1,740,000
Language
French, Lingala, Kongo, Kituba, others
Religion
Christian,Traditional, Muslim
Government Republic
Currency
1 CFA franc =
100 centimes

⊙ See also
Africa
Slave trade

Congress

Congress makes laws in the United States of America. It is similar to Parliament in Britain and other countries. There are two houses of Congress: the Senate and the House of Representatives. Members of both are elected.

The Senate contains 100 members, two for each of the 50 states. The House of Representatives has 435 members. The number for each state varies according to the population of the states. Each member represents about 500,000 people. California has the most representatives (45 in the 1980s), but some states such as Wyoming have only one. Every member of Congress receives a salary, and enough money to pay for a staff and travel.

A bill has to be passed by both Houses of Congress before it becomes law. It is debated in both Houses, and also in committees, which go through it in detail. ∎

Senators are elected by voters from all parts of a state for six-year terms. About one-third of the Senate comes up for election every two years. This means that the Senate is never competely new.

Congressmen and Congresswomen are elected to the House of Representatives for two-year terms. They may be elected either by the voters in one congressional district or throughout the state.

⊙ See also
American Constitution
Parliaments
United States of America

Conifers

male pine cones

pollen grains carried by wind

female pine cone

ripe female cone

scales separated to release seeds

one seed

wing

seed

▲ Male cones grow in clusters and are smaller than female cones. They produce huge numbers of wind-borne pollen grains to fertilize female cones, which contain winged seeds also distributed by the wind.

► Four species of conifer trees.
1 Redwood
2 Cedar
3 Yew
4 Scots pine

⊙ See also
Forests
Timber
Trees
Wood
Woodlands

Conifers are woody plants which bear cones containing seeds. Most are evergreen trees with tough, needle-like leaves able to survive harsh winters and found mainly in cold northern areas such as Canada, Scandinavia and Russia. The best-known is the Christmas tree, also called Norway spruce.

Female cones are made of woody scales arranged in a spiral and each scale holds two or more seeds. First, the female cones are fertilized by pollen carried by wind from male cones. Over the next three seasons the seeds grow and develop wings so that, when the scales of the ripe cone separate from each other, seeds are blown away over long distances by the wind.

Conifers grow faster than deciduous trees, so they are frequently grown for timber. Large forests (such as larch or pine plantations) can be grown on soils too poor for farming, providing a cash crop where nothing else will grow. ■

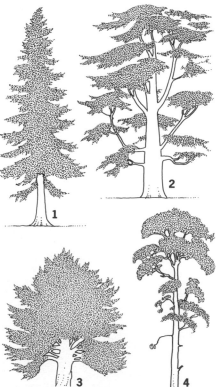

Conquistadores

The first European explorers of South and Central America were Spanish adventurers who are known as the conquistadores, which means 'conquerors'. And conquer is what they did, overrunning the great empires of Mexico and Peru. They were brave but ruthless, greedy men seeking gold and power.

The conquest of Mexico

One of the first conquistadores was Vasco Núñez de Balboa, who stowed away on an expedition to the mainland of America. He became Governor of Darién, on the Isthmus of Panama. He was the first white man to see the Pacific Ocean from America.

Hernán Cortés, the greatest of the conquistadores, was sent to explore Mexico. Cortés founded a colony and made himself governor. With fewer than 500 soldiers he marched inland. The Aztec Indians were scared at the sight of him. They thought he was their god Quetzalcoatl, returned to Earth to haunt them. An outbreak of small-pox killed thousands of Aztecs. Cortés seized the capital, Tenochtitlán, and the land was his.

The conquest of Peru

An even bolder exploit was the conquest of Peru by Francisco Pizarro. He did this with the aid of his half-brother, Gonzalo, a fellow conquistador, Diego de Almagro, and just 180 soldiers. He found the Incas of Peru involved in a civil war. By treachery he took their emperor, Atahualpa, prisoner, extorted a huge ransom and then had him strangled.

Other conquistadores included Hernando de Soto, who travelled up the Mississippi River; Alvar Núñez Cabeza de Vaca, who explored a large part of what is now the southern United States; and Juan Ponce de León, who discovered Florida. ■

Vasco Núñez de Balboa had to stow away on the expedition to America to escape from the people he owed money to when his farming business failed.

After Pizarro kidnapped Atahualpa, the Inca emperor tried to buy his freedom by offering to fill his cell with gold. Even though he did so, Pizarro would not release him.

⊙ See also
Aztecs
Incas
Spanish colonial history

Biography
Atahualpa
Balboa
Cortés
Moctezuma II
Pizarro

Conservation

Conservation means taking good care of all the things around us. It is particularly important for those things that can easily disappear and cannot be replaced. Without careful conservation, many of the things that we enjoy now simply will not be here for the next generation.

Some things are easier to conserve: we can put them in museums or art galleries. Although a painting may need special surroundings to keep it in perfect condition, or an old piece of machinery may need oiling and cleaning from time to time, conservation at this level is fairly easy. It becomes much more difficult when we try to conserve on a bigger scale, or to conserve living things.

Nature

A lot of people are involved with nature conservation, taking care of the plants and animals which share the planet. Until the beginning of the 20th century, people thought we could conserve nature by looking after individual species: by putting wild animals in zoos, or plants in botanical gardens. Now we understand that we need to conserve whole habitats, the places where these plants and animals live.

Polar bears may be able to survive as individual animals in concrete pools in zoos. But to conserve the species properly they each need hundreds of square kilometres of Arctic landscape where they can hunt in seas free from pollution and roam across snowfields that are not disturbed by people. Nearer home, hedgehogs need a whole neighbourhood to live in, with quiet leafy corners for hibernation, and plenty of undergrowth where they can hunt for slugs and worms, without any danger of eating poisonous chemicals.

We can grow primroses in plant pots, but to conserve these wildflowers properly, we need to conserve the woodlands where they grow naturally. Nature reserves are important for providing a safe environment for wildlife, but nature conservation can take place anywhere.

Lots of people are creating new habitats such as ponds and wildflower meadows, in gardens and school grounds. In fact some species thrive best in very special artificial habitats. Many starlings, for instance, spend the cold winter nights roosting on the windowsills of centrally heated office blocks in towns, and then feed all day on the grubs and worms that live in the soil beneath

► The Olympic National Park in the state of Washington, USA, was established by President Franklin D. Roosevelt in 1936. The rainfall here is heavy and the forest is rich with a variety of species including ferns, maples, fir, spruce and cedar.

▼ Conservation notice for the National Park at Gopeshwar, Garhwal Himal, India. The script is in both Hindi and English. National Parks are large protected areas of natural beauty.

► Clearing away debris from the Freshwater Nature Reserve at Thamesmead, south London, England. Wetlands provide habitats for many species of birds and insects as well as fish and amphibians.

▲ Squirrel monkeys have long been exported from South America, though the trade is now restricted by most countries. The monkeys need to be conserved in their natural habitat, the rainforest.

These sources of energy and raw materials can never be replaced. They will run out one day, and so will many of the other minerals we use, some of the metals for instance.

Where a resource is 'non-renewable' the best we can do to conserve it is to use it as carefully as possible, and re-use or recycle the resource after we have used it the first time. Insulating our buildings so they waste less heat energy, recycling plastics, and farming without the use of artificial pesticides and fertilizers are all ways of conserving non-renewable oil so that future generations will still have some.

▼ The black and white half-timbered houses in Eastgate Street, Chester, England were built in a style used in the Tudor period. Such old wooden structures need expert treatment. The stone building with pillars in the classical style is only about 200 years old, but stone needs regular cleaning if it is to be preserved.

▼ The black and white half-timbered houses in Eastgate Street, Chester, England were built in a style used in the Tudor period. Such old wooden structures need expert treatment. The stone building with pillars in the classical style is only about 200 years old, but stone needs regular cleaning if it is to be preserved.

school playing fields, sports pitches and parks. Most of the wildflowers we call weeds can survive only if a farmer or gardener cultivates the soil and accidentally makes a new seed bed for them each year.

Resources

In many poorer countries of the world, people cook their food and heat their homes by burning firewood from local forests. This is causing serious 'deforestation' as the trees are chopped down at a faster rate than they can regrow. In the worst cases this removes the protection the trees provide for the landscape, so the rains beat straight down and the soil is washed away. With proper conservation, which might mean using the firewood more efficiently, planting more new trees and making sure the sheep and goats do not eat them, it is possible to keep replacing the supply of firewood. It is a 'renewable resource'.

In the rich countries, we use a different kind of fuel. We burn oil, or coal or natural gas, often using it to generate electricity. We do not just use it for heating and cooking but to power cars and to manufacture all kinds of other chemicals such as pesticides, fertilizers, paint and plastics.

Buildings

Old buildings are an important part of the landscape, helping us to understand how our ancestors lived. Some old buildings have played an important part in our history. Others have been designed or built by particularly famous people, or are characteristic of a particular style. These kinds of buildings have always been 'conserved', but now the more ordinary buildings are being protected too.

Buildings such as workers' cottages, blacksmiths' shops and village schools are being conserved because they were important for ordinary people in the past. To make sure the character of the place does not get damaged, whole neighbourhoods are being conserved too.

Just as nature conservation has developed from preservation of individual species to protection of habitats, so buildings are now conserved much more as part of their surroundings. ■

◎ See also
Endangered species
Forests
Fuel
Moors and heaths
National Parks
Recycling
Wastelands
Weeds
Wetlands
Zoos

Constellations

Stars in a constellation appear to us on the Earth to be in a group. In reality, most are vast distances away from one another.

Largest
Hydra, the Water-snake

Smallest
The Southern Cross

With brightest stars
Orion and the Great Bear

Dimmest
Mensa, the Table

▶ Some of the constellations visible from northern countries. You would see the sky looking like this from Britain if you stood facing south around midnight in January.

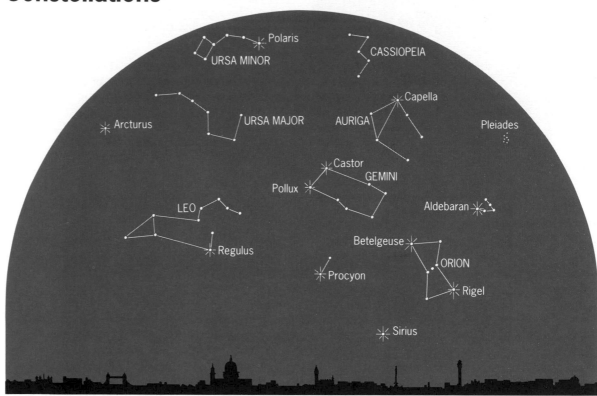

See also
Astronomers
Celestial sphere
Seasons
Stars

▼ Some of the constellations visible from southern countries. You would see the sky looking like this from Australia if you stood facing south-east at midnight in October.

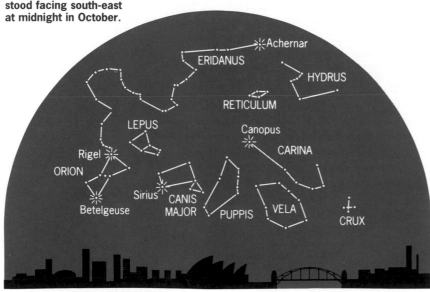

If you look at the stars in the night sky, it is not hard to pick out patterns, such as squares, triangles and crosses, made by the bright ones. For thousands of years, people have been giving names to groups of stars that seem to make patterns. A named group of stars is called a constellation. Some names we use today were given by the Greeks at least 2,000 years ago, and the Arab and Chinese astronomers had their own constellations too. Constellations were probably invented as a way of referring to particular stars.

Many of the old names are of animals, like the Bull and the Swan, and of people from Greek myths, such as Perseus and Andromeda. Among the recently named constellations you will find the Microscope and the Clock.

There are 88 constellations and they cover the whole sky. Astronomers have agreed where the imaginary boundary lines between the constellations are, and the official names they use are in Latin.

Which constellations you can see varies according to the season, the time of night and where you are on the Earth. If you live in the northern hemisphere, some of the easiest constellations to find are in the sky on winter evenings. Orion, the Hunter, has three very bright stars in a row making his belt. Near him you can find Taurus (the Bull) and Gemini (the Twins). On summer evenings, three of the brightest stars are in the Eagle, the Swan and the Lyre. They stand out as a giant triangle and can help you find some of the other constellations. From the southern hemisphere people see different constellations, such as the Southern Cross and the Centaur. ■

Continents

The large masses of land on the Earth's surface are called continents. Most geographers agree that there are seven, but there is sometimes disagreement about where one continent ends and another begins.

Europe is the smallest continent. Some people insist that it is really part of Asia and that the two together should be called Eurasia. There is no clear division between the two. The Ural Mountains and the Ural River are usually taken to be the boundary.

India is so large and has such a distinctive shape that it is called a subcontinent. Oceania is counted as a continent although made up of Australia, New Zealand and other Pacific islands.

Landmasses

Continents cover 29 per cent of the Earth's surface. They all have the same general structure. The heart of a continent is a flat slab or 'shield' of ancient rock. Around this lie regions on which are piled great thicknesses of sedimentary rocks. At the edges are mountains.

Continents are, on average, about 60 km (40 miles) thick. The rocks they are made of are less dense than the rocks underneath. They 'float' on top of the rocks of the Earth's mantle. Continental rocks are much older than the rocks which lie under the oceans. It is not surprising, therefore, that the surface of the continents is much more varied than the ocean floors.

Flashback

All the continents were once joined together in one supercontinent which scientists have named Pangaea. About 200 million years ago Pangaea began to break up and the pieces gradually moved to their present positions. The continents are still moving – very slowly. ■

The explanation of how the continents were formed is found in the article: Plate tectonics.

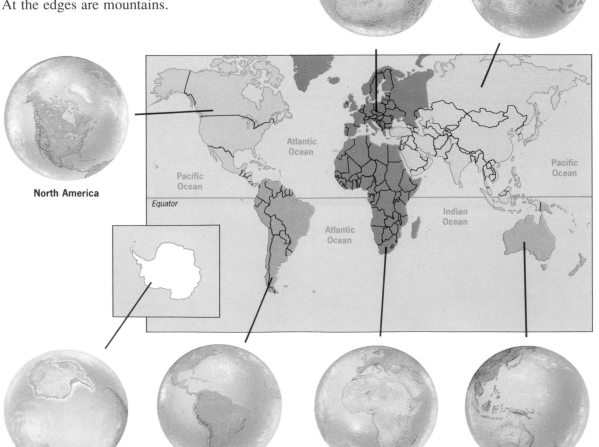

◀ **This map shows the position of the continents. The circular pictures show how each continent appears from space.**

See also
Africa
Antarctica
Asia
Europe
Maps
North America
Oceania
Plate tectonics
South America

Cookers

See also
Cooking
Household equipment
Microwaves

▼ This oven, set into the wall at eye level, has a glass panel and a temperature probe.

▶ A 19th century kitchen range set into a large alcove at Erddig House, Wrexham, Wales. Heat was produced by wood or coal burning in the central grate.

The first gas cookers were manufactured in 1834, but they were not widely available to buy until after 1860.

The first electric oven was manufactured in the USA in 1891.

The first microwave oven was manufactured in the USA in 1947.

Some cookers burn gas. Others use electricity or solid fuel. Gas cookers are particularly easy to use because they heat up instantly and cool down very quickly.

Hobs and ovens

The hob provides a number of areas of heat on which to boil, steam or fry food. On a gas hob the heat source is the flame of the burning gas. On an electric hob the heat is provided by a coiled element which is covered in metal or ceramic glass. Some electric hobs use heat from tungsten halogen lamps instead of elements. One of the newest types of electric hob is the induction hob. This works by creating a magnetic field. Food placed in a metal container in the magnetic field will heat up. With this method only the food gets hot.

The oven is an enclosed method of cooking. In most ovens the temperature at the top of the oven is higher than that at the bottom. Some electric ovens have fans which stir the air to keep the temperature the same throughout the oven. Some cookers have combined microwave and gas or electric ovens.

Microwave ovens and other small cookers

A variety of smaller electric ovens have been developed for specific purposes. Some, such as microwave ovens, are extremely compact and will fit into very small spaces. Microwave ovens can carry out most of the functions of the conventional cooker whilst cooking food more quickly and so saving energy. Heat in a microwave oven is produced when the microwaves enter the food. These cause the food molecules to jump about. The resulting friction between the molecules brings about a rise in temperature, cooking the food from the inside.

Other small cookers, such as electric woks, can be used at table, and some, such as pressure cookers and high energy humidity cookers, speed up the cooking times. Slo-cookers are designed to cook very slowly, and deep fat friers and infra-red grills can be precisely controlled to do a particular job.

Flashback

Until the 18th century most cooking was done over an open fire of wood, coal or peat. Only very large houses or bakeries had ovens. Sometimes people would take their weekend casserole to be cooked in the baker's oven. Then grates began to enclose the domestic fire. Ovens and hobs for pots and pans were placed on either side of the grates and then joined by hot plates over the fires. In the early 19th century the closed range was introduced. These were also used to heat water. They have developed into the modern solid fuel and oil-burning stoves. ■

Cooking

Almost all food can be eaten without any cooking at all. Most people eat raw fruit, and raw vegetables in salads, and the Japanese particularly like raw fish. However, some foods are much softer and easier to chew if they have been cooked. They may also be easier to digest. Thorough cooking also kills harmful bacteria that might cause food poisoning. Cooking often involves combining many different ingredients together. This can make food look and taste much better. Compare the taste of a chocolate cake, for example, with that of its raw ingredients of flour, sugar, fat, cocoa and egg. Different ideas about which foods to cook together have contributed to the very different dishes of the world.

What happens when we cook food?

Cooking causes chemical changes to take place in all food. These changes are irreversible. You cannot unboil an egg or turn that chocolate cake back into its original ingredients. The changes include softening of the cell walls and a tendency for the cells to separate. This can be seen if you look at mashed potato through a strong lens. The contents of the cell are no longer so well protected and some of them may escape. Water, for example, will evaporate during dry roasting, and a roasted joint of meat will shrink as it cooks. Colours and nutrients may be lost if food is boiled. So you should save vegetable water for soups and sauces.

Starch granules in food swell on cooking and become quite jelly-like. This is why flour is used for thickening. The protein in egg sets, and so eggs are used to hold and set dishes like soufflés and sponge cakes.

Different ways of heating

The various methods of cooking use different types of heat. Grilling, barbecuing and toasting depend upon radiant heat produced by burning fuel or heating an element. Heat works on food from the outside in. You can see this if you grill kebabs too close to the heat. They will burn on the outside before the centre is cooked. They also need to be turned so that all sides are exposed to the heat. If, however, meat is roasted in an oven it is surrounded by hot air and does not need to be turned.

In microwave cooking, very short wavelength radio waves are used to heat the food. They penetrate deep into the food, so the heating is more rapid.

Boiling, steaming and stewing use water to conduct heat to the food. Water transfers heat much more quickly than air, but the temperature does not normally exceed 100°C (212°F), the temperature at which water boils. However, in a pressure cooker, water can boil at up to 120°C (250°F) which gives faster cooking. Much higher temperatures are achieved by frying in fat, and so the cooking time will be quicker than cooking in water. ■

The discovery of fire led to the invention of cooking. Prehistoric people roasted pieces of meat and fish on sticks over open fires and used flat stones placed by the fire to bake coarse flat bread. These stones were also used to heat the water in wooden or leather containers to make soup.

The Arawak Indians gave us the name 'barbecue'. They used thin sticks called *barbacoa* to make a mesh on which to cook thin strips of meat.

Some common cookery terms

Baste brush food with melted fat
Beat mix ingredients together vigorously with beater or spoon
Braise brown meat and then simmer in a little liquid in a closed dish
Cream mix ingredients with spoon or mixer till creamy
Dice cut into cubes
Fillet remove bones
Fold add ingredients gently with spoon to mix in without beating or stirring
Marinate soak food in spicy or herbal mixture to improve flavour
Poach simmer food in liquid to cook
Sauté fry gently until golden
Whip beat ingredients rapidly till foamy

boiling
The food is surrounded by water boiling at 100°C. If only a little liquid is used, and kept just below boiling point, this is called **poaching.**

steaming
The food is heated by steam from water boiling beneath it at 100°C. **Pressure cooking** is a type of steaming which uses pressurized steam at up to 120°C.

frying
The food is heated in hot fat at up to 190°C. It may be a coating of fat (as in stir frying), shallow fat, or deep fat.

◄ **Different methods of cooking use different ways of getting the heat to the food.**

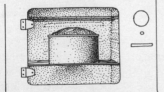

grilling
Radiant heat is used to heat the food, with temperatures reaching 200°C or more. **Toasting** and **barbecuing** work in the same way.

baking
The food is heated in an oven using hot air at up to 250°C. When meat is cooked in this way it is usually called **roasting.**

microwaving
Very short wavelength radio waves penetrate and heat the food.

 See also
Food
Food processing
Heat
Herbs
Microwaves
Spices

Co-operative societies

An earlier experiment in co-operation was made by the Welsh-born reformer Robert Owen in the early 19th century. He organized a model community around his cotton mill at New Lanark in Scotland. Then in 1825 he set up a co-operative village at New Harmony, Indiana, USA. It failed because people working with him did not understand what he was trying to do.

In 1844 the Rochdale Pioneers, a group of 28 weavers, pooled their savings of £1 a head and opened a grocery shop at Toad Lane (t'old lane) in Rochdale, Lancashire. It was no ordinary shop; they shared the profits (after deductions for expenses) among their members in proportion to the amount each member spent. This was the first co-operative society, and the beginning of a worldwide movement.

The idea spread rapidly in Britain, and by 1863 the various co-ops banded together to form their own wholesaling company; this meant they could buy their goods more cheaply. They insisted on good value for money and good quality food, which was not always available when the first co-op was founded. In this way the co-operative societies did a great deal to improve the standard of living of working people.

The British co-operative movement has now branched out into production, farming, fishing and other forms of co-operatives.

Worldwide co-operation

Co-operative societies spread in Europe and the rest of the world. In 1895 the International Co-operative Alliance was founded. It now has its headquarters in Geneva.

One country where the co-operative movement spread most rapidly was Russia. By the time of the revolution in 1917 there were 20,000 co-operative societies. The communist government of the Union of Soviet Socialist Republics (1922–1991) took the co-operative idea further by creating collective farms, which were jointly owned by their workers.

The United States, Canada and many African countries have marketing co-operatives, especially in agriculture. ■

See also
Biography
Owen, Robert

Copper

Copper is a reddish-coloured metal which is a good conductor of heat and electricity. Compared with many metals, copper is quite soft. It is easy to draw it out into wires, and its main use is for electrical wires and cables. Copper is also used for water pipes and sometimes for roofing. A roof made of copper eventually turns green because a substance known as verdigris forms on its surface. Copper can be mixed with many metals to make alloys. Bronze is an alloy of copper and tin, while brass is an alloy of copper and zinc. Most 'copper' coins are in fact made of copper alloys.

Copper metal occurs in nature, but copper is usually made from ores such as cuprite, malachite and copper pyrites. Most of the world's copper comes from the USA, Russia, Zambia, Zaïre and Chile. ■

If copper continues to be used at the same rate as it was used in 1981, then in about 60 years the present known sources of copper will run out.

Copper is found in more than 160 minerals.

See also
Alloys
Metals
Wire

Coracles

These are very small boats which today are only found on the rivers of Wales and Ireland. They are simple to build and are made from two sets of thin wooden strips woven so that they cross each other at right angles. The frame is covered with canvas or flannel and is then covered with tar or pitch to make it waterproof. In prehistoric times the frame was built from thin branches (usually willow) and covered with animal skins. ■

The Assyrians used coracles on the River Euphrates.

Coracles are so easy to build that similar types of boat are found in other parts of the world but are called by different names.

◀ Coracles are still used in Wales for fishing. They are light enough to be carried on the back of one person.

Coral

Corals are small animals related to sea anemones. Each coral animal is called a polyp. Their bodies are filled with fluid and are plastic in shape. The mouth end is ringed with stinging tentacles which are used to catch passing water creatures. The polyp produces a hard limestone skeleton around itself in the shape of a cup. Even after the polyp has died, the hard skeleton remains. Corals often look dead because most polyps only stretch out their tentacles to feed at night. By day they shrink into their cups for protection.

From time to time, the polyps release sperm and eggs into the water. The fertilized eggs hatch into tiny swimming larvae. Some of these may drift on the ocean currents, and help to disperse the corals around the ocean. Many coral polyps are solitary, but some live together in colonies.

Coral reefs

Some coral polyps are formed as buds on existing polyps. These new polyps grow but do not separate completely from their parents and so a colony is built up. Coral reefs are made up of the skeletons of millions of polyps.

Reef-building corals can grow only in clear, clean water no deeper than 50 m (160 ft). Since the last ice age, the sea-level has been rising, so the reefs have been growing up towards the light. Some coral reefs are thousands of feet thick.

Coral reefs are home to many different animals. Sea slugs, starfish, sea urchins and many fish feed on the corals. Other animals, such as crabs and shrimps, live in the crevices in the reef. Other fish, squid and octopus come to feed on them. Sponges, sea squirts and barnacles grow amongst the corals. They filter food from the water. Worms wriggle among the corals, and moray eels and lobsters hide in the coral caves. Larger predators such as reef sharks and barracudas are attracted to the reef from the ocean. ■

◄ Coral reef off Vanuatu.

The Great Barrier Reef, off the east coast of Australia, is so large that it can be seen from the Moon. It is over 2,000 km (1,250 miles) long.

Largest solitary coral
Mushroom coral, about 30 cm long
Distribution
Reef-building corals found in warm, shallow, tropical seas.
Solitary corals found also in dark, cold, deep ocean waters.

Phylum
Cnidaria
Class
Anthozoa
Order
Madreporaria
Number of species
There are 6,000 species of corals and sea anemones.

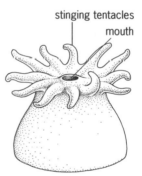

stinging tentacles
mouth

▲ A coral polyp.

See also
Invertebrates
Larvae
Sea anemones

Cork

Cork is a waterproof layer formed on the outside of the young shoots of trees before bark is produced. The cork we use to make bottle stoppers, table mats, lifebelts, sound-proofing and linoleum comes from the cork oak tree which grows in the Mediterranean region. This evergreen tree is cultivated particularly in Spain, Portugal, France, Italy and parts of North Africa.

It has a thick, soft bark, mostly made up of cork. The first crop is taken when the tree is about fifteen years old. This cork is coarse and rough and is mainly used for tanning leather or for making cork boards. From then on, the cork regrows and can be cut from the trunk of the tree about every ten or twenty years. This gives cork of good quality, and the tree will go on cropping cork for about 150 years. ■

See also
Trees

Coronations

► The most important moment at the coronation of Queen Elizabeth II on 2 June 1953. The Archbishop of Canterbury (Geoffrey Fisher) holds the St Edward's Crown before placing it on the head of the new Queen. Looking on are the maids of Honour and the Dukes and Earls of the United Kingdom.

In 1804 Pope Pius VII was invited to Paris to crown the Emperor Napoleon Bonaparte. As the coronation was about to take place, Napoleon took the crown from the Pope and crowned himself.

See also
Jewellery
Kings
Queens
Popes

Coronation means crowning. It is the ceremony in which a monarch (a reigning emperor, empress, king or queen) has a crown placed on the head as a symbol of authority. Most coronations include a religious service, in which the new monarch takes an oath to perform his or her duties. A coronation is also held for the Pope, the head of the Roman Catholic Church.

The most elaborate coronation ceremony today is that for the British monarch. It is more than a thousand years old, and was last held in 1953 for Queen Elizabeth II. The coronation of the Pope is also very elaborate. Many other modern monarchs, such as those of Norway, Spain and Sweden, do not have a coronation. ∎

Cosmetics

This term refers to a whole range of products that people use to beautify themselves. For example, creams and shampoos are used to cleanse the skin and hair; special lotions help to protect the skin from sun or wind; antiperspirants and perfumes are applied to make the body smell nice.

Make-up

Make-up is used to alter the appearance, often by the application of coloured creams or powders to eyes, lips and face. The people who produce and sell make-up promote the idea that people (especially women) have to use it if they want to look beautiful. Fashions come and go, and there are styles for work, leisure and evening.

Actors, clowns, mime artists and people in fancy dress use make-up to make their faces suit the characters they are playing. People who are being photographed under strong lights for film or television use make-up colours so that they do not look 'washed out'. People with scars or discoloured skin use make-up to camouflage defects.

Production

Cosmetics are made from a wide range of waxes and oils with the addition of perfumes and coloured pigments. Powder cosmetics are based on chalk or china clay. They are tested to prove they are safe if used correctly. Many people think it is not right to use animals for these tests, because these may hurt the animals.

Flashback

There is evidence that the ancient Egyptians used cosmetics such as eye colours and perfumes over 6,000 years ago. Since that time they have been used by men and women in cultures all over the world. However, they have sometimes been banned as sinful. The Puritans of New England, for example, thought that their use was immoral. ∎

In 17th century Britain, actors would darken their skin with a thick paste and apply bright-red rouge to their cheeks and lips. Eyes were lined with black and wrinkles drawn onto the face using water paint and a stick.

See also
Circuses
Mime

Today, there are many ranges of make-up which have not been tested on animals, but are safe to use.

During the Italian Renaissance and in Elizabethan times, women made their faces pale by covering them with white lead, applied over the top of old make-up, and used purified mercury to make their skin smooth. Physicians warned that both of these substances were very poisonous and dangerous to use.

Many ancient Egyptian statues and wall-paintings show people with their eyes heavily lined with kohl. They stained their nails, palms and the soles of their feet with red henna, and highlighted veins on their temples with blue. Women lightened their skin with yellow ochre; men darkened it with orange-tinted paint.

Cosmic rays

An Austrian physicist, Victor Hess, discovered cosmic rays. He got a Nobel prize in 1936.

Most cosmic ray particles are protons. The nucleus of a hydrogen atom is made up of a single proton.

All the time, the Earth's atmosphere is being bombarded by tiny atomic particles from space. They travel nearly as fast as the speed of light, which is as fast as anything can go. They were first found by an experiment during a balloon flight in 1912 and were given the name 'cosmic rays'. They have to be studied from balloons or satellites, because they collide with the atoms in the air and only a small fraction ever reach the ground.

Some cosmic rays come from the Sun, but scientists believe that others have travelled huge distances across our Galaxy. They may come from the exploding stars that astronomers call supernovas. ■

See also
Atmosphere
Atoms
Galaxies

Cosmology

▲ Astronomers study photographs, like this one showing clusters of galaxies, to try and learn more about the Universe.

Edwin Hubble (1889–1953) was the American astronomer who discovered that the galaxies are rushing apart and the Universe expanding. Back-tracking from its present size, astronomers can tell that the Universe is at least 15 thousand million years old.

One of the things astronomers try to do is to understand what the Universe is like as a whole. These are some of the questions they want to answer: 'Is the Universe the same everywhere?' 'How did the Universe begin?' 'Will the Universe go on in the same way for ever?' Studying problems like these is called cosmology.

How the Universe began

From photographs taken with the world's largest telescopes, astronomers have found that the Universe seems to be full of galaxies of stars. They can tell how fast a galaxy is moving by the light it gives out. It turns out that all the galaxies are rushing apart and the ones furthest away are going the fastest! This means that the galaxies must once have been much closer together. In fact, the Universe may have started with a 'big bang'.

Flashback

People's ideas about the Universe have gradually changed as they have learnt more astronomy. In the ancient world, people used to explain the Universe with myths and magic. The Greek philosopher Aristotle, who lived in the 4th century BC, thought the Earth was at the centre of the Universe with the Sun, Moon and planets going around it. ■

Something to do

All the galaxies seem to be rushing away from us but it would be just the same if we were in another galaxy. No particular galaxy is in the middle. You can show how this happens with the help of a balloon.

Mark some 'galaxies' on a balloon with a pen. Then blow up the balloon and watch what happens to the galaxies. As the balloon stretches, your galaxies move apart from each other. The balloon's surface is like the Universe. As it swells up it takes the galaxies with it.

Cosmology comes from the Greek word *cosmos* meaning the 'world'.

The earliest civilizations of Mesopotamia thought that the Universe was filled with gods and spirits that were responsible for things that happened in the heavens and on Earth, such as the weather, the seasons and eclipses.

The ancient Egyptians believed that the Sun was a god, born every morning and dying every evening.

See also
Astronomers
Big bang
Galaxies
Stars
Universe

Biography
Aristotle
Copernicus
Galilei

▼ A model of how the galaxies move apart. As the balloon expands, the ink dots move further away from each other.

Costa Rica

Costa Rica is a country in Central America. The coastal areas are tropical and swampy, while the central region is made up of volcanic mountain chains. Coffee and bananas grow on the fertile volcanic soils of the uplands and are exported overseas. The farmers own and work much of the agricultural land. This makes Costa Rica different from most other Central American countries where the land is owned by a few rich landowners. It is also different because it has a stable, democratically elected government. After the last civil war in 1948 the country decided not to have an army any more and since then Costa Rica has remained peaceful. ■

Area
51,100 sq km
(19,730 sq miles)
Capital San José
Population 2,720,000
Language Spanish
Religion Christian
Government
Parliamentary republic
Currency
1 Costa Rican colón = 100
céntimos

Costume

▼ All through the centuries in Europe one style of dress has slowly changed into another.

In the western world the style of dress has changed a lot since ancient times. People want to wear the latest fashion, and those who can afford it all wear the same fashionable length of skirt or cut of trousers; one colour is fashionable one season and another the next.

A knowledge of costume tells us about how people used to live and what they looked like. Film and theatre designers need to know about the history of costume so that they can design the correct clothes for their characters. ■

In eastern countries people have tended to wear the same style of clothes for long periods. The way a sari is draped has not changed for centuries, though the type of fabric does change.

Celtic

Roman

Norman 1060s–1100s

Medieval 1390s–1430s

Late Medieval 1460s–1480s

Tudor 1530s

Elizabethan 1580s–1600s

Stuart 1630s

Georgian 1750s

Regency 1815–1820

Victorian 1870s

Edwardian 1900s

1920s

1960s

Cotton

Cotton is a fabric which is clean, cool and comfortable to wear. Because cotton can absorb moisture and let it out, the skin can breathe, and so you do not feel hot and sticky as with many man-made fabrics. It is not affected by static electricity in the atmosphere and therefore stays clean much longer than other materials. Cotton is easily dyed and printed and can be treated to become crease resistant, flame retardant or water repellent. All this means that cotton has many other uses as well as for clothes. It is made into towelling, cheesecloth, curtaining, furniture fabric and heavy-duty industrial fabrics.

The cotton plant

Cotton fibres vary in length from less than 2 cm (¾ in) to 4 cm (1½ in) or more. Short and medium-length fibres account for about 90 per cent of world production. The finest cotton fabrics are made from long fibres. In all cases the fibres are first spun into a single thread and then spun together. Two or more threads are woven into cloth.

Cotton is planted fresh each year in tropical and subtropical areas. The plant produces seed pods (bolls) which contain about 30 seeds, each covered with soft, downy hairs. As the bolls ripen they grow and then burst open to reveal a fluffy mass of fibres. When the fluffy mass is separated from the seeds it is known as cotton lint, which is what is used to make fabrics. The cotton seeds are not thrown away. The fat is extracted to produce an edible oil, and the seeds are then processed into cattle cake and fertilizer.

Growing and picking

Machinery is used on the largest cotton plantations for almost all jobs from sowing to picking. On the smaller plantations in poorer countries, the cotton worker uses teams of oxen or buffalo and picks the cotton by hand. Hand picking is better in some ways than machine harvesting. The cotton pickers select and pick only really ripe bolls. However, a worker can pick only 110 kg (240 lb) of seed cotton a day. A machine can pick that amount in an hour.

Where cotton is grown

More than 75 countries grow cotton on a commercial basis. The largest producers are the USA, China and Uzbekistan. Then come India and Pakistan. Cotton is also grown in Egypt, Mexico, Colombia, Brazil, Syria and Guatemala.

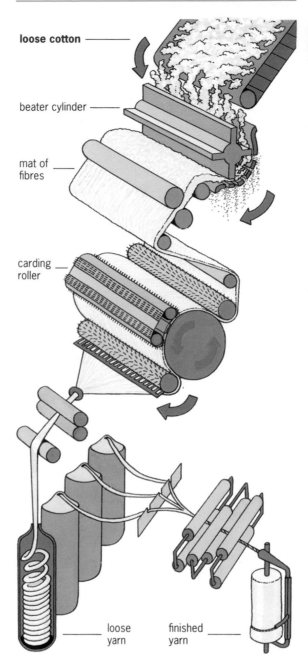

loose cotton

beater cylinder

mat of fibres

carding roller

loose yarn

finished yarn

◄ Cotton fibres are only a few centimetres long. They are combed and twisted together to make a much longer yarn.

Flashback

Cotton was grown in places as far apart as Mexico, North India and China. The Arabs introduced cotton fabric to Europe but at first it was not very important compared to wool and silk. In the 17th century, fine cotton fabrics from India became fashionable, and in the early 18th century cheaper fabrics began to be made in England from cotton grown in Virginia. The Industrial Revolution gave a real boost to manufacture when the flying shuttle, spinning jenny and power loom were invented. American cotton was shipped to Liverpool, and Lancashire became the centre of British cotton production. ■

Remains of cotton seeds and clothes have been found which date back to 3000 BC.

⊙ See also
Dyes
Fabrics
Materials
Spinning
Textiles
Weaving

Countries

A country can also be called a nation or a state.

The official name of a country is not always the familiar name. The country of Burma changed its name to Myanmar in 1989.

See also
Colonies
Government
Monarchies
Nations
Republics
States

A country is a territory (land) with its own people and its own laws. It can either be self-governing or a colony ruled by another country. If a country has a head of state who is born to the position, like a king or queen, it is a monarchy; if not, it is a republic. The United Kingdom is a monarchy. France, Germany, Italy and the USA are republics but all have democratically elected governments. Some countries are ruled by their monarchs, not by an elected government and there are republics ruled by a dictator or by a group of military officers. ■

Country and western music

In the early 1960s, half of all the records made in America were recorded in Nashville.

The performers of country and western music often wear stetsons and elaborate cowboy outfits glittering with imitation diamonds (called rhinestones). The singers use a nasal tone of voice with a southern American twang to it, and they are backed by guitars, banjos and fiddles.

There are many different country and western styles. 'Singing cowboys', such as Gene Autry and Roy Rogers, were once popular. They sang about branding, cowboys and life on the range. Bluegrass bands play fast, exciting instrumental music on banjos and fiddles. Ballad singers including Johnny Cash, Dolly Parton and Waylon Jennings sing songs that are stories, about travelling, loneliness, hard work, prison or disappointed love. Nashville in America is one of the main centres of country and western music, and the Grand Ole Opry, the best-known country programme in America, is broadcast from Nashville.

Country and western music originated in the southern United States from a tradition of English ballads, which had been brought to America by British immigrants during the 19th century. Many country and western songs tell a story, and often revolve around the important moral or religious values of southern life at this time. The term 'country and western' was first used in the 1950s to describe songs with a rural or southern sound.

Country and western music was originally called 'hillbilly' music, after the 'hillbillies' or poor farmers of the southern states of America

who first played it. Hank Williams, one of the most popular country singers of the 1950s, said this about the music:

'Hillbilly singers sing more sincere than most entertainers because the hillbilly was raised rougher than most entertainers. You got to know hard work. You got to have smelled a lot of mule manure before you can sing like a hillbilly.' ■

See also
Folk music
Pop and rock music
Singing and songs

Country code

The country code is twelve 'rules' for enjoying the countryside and helping other people to enjoy it, too. The code was worked out by the Countryside Commission in Britain, with the help of many other organizations which care for the countryside. ■

1 Enjoy the countryside and respect its life and work.

2 Guard against all risk of fire.

3 Fasten all gates.

4 Keep your dogs under close control.

5 Keep to public paths across farmland.

6 Use gates and stiles to cross fences, hedges and walls.

7 Leave livestock, crops and machinery alone.

8 Take your litter home.

9 Help to keep all water clean.

10 Protect wildlife, plants and trees.

11 Take special care on country roads.

12 Make no unnecessary noise.

In 1949 the National Parks Commission was set up to preserve nature and make it available for recreation and study in National Parks. It was replaced in 1968 by the Countryside Commission, which has wider powers covering the whole countryside, and can give grants to help conservation and the development of suitable recreational and leisure facilities.

See also
Conservation
National Parks

Cowboys

Cowboys tend cattle on the wide grazing lands of North America. Today they are more often called cowhands. The United States has about 114 million beef and dairy cattle, and most of them are raised on ranches (large farms) in the western states. There are cowhands in South America too, where they are called *gauchos*.

The work of cowhands

Today there are about 20,000 cowhands in North America. Some of them still ride the range (grazing-land) on horseback, like the cowboys of Western films. Most use pick-up trucks, aeroplanes and helicopters, linked with one another and the ranch house by two-way radios.

Even with all this modern technology ranchers still depend on mounted cowhands for much of the work, riding over difficult country. A typical cow-handling crew consists of half a dozen men in the cold winter months, double that number in the busy, dusty summer season. Because cattle graze in open country, the cowhands have to brand (burn a mark onto) the young calves to show which ranch they belong to. From time to time they round up the cattle to count them or sell them.

The cowboy in history

Cattle-raising for beef became big business in about 1870. Then the range was open to all, and cattle from many ranches grazed together. During the next 20 years there were about 40,000 cowboys riding the range, tending the cattle, and driving them for weeks over long trails to rail depots for shipment to the east.

As well as the hard work, riding in all weathers and looking after the cattle, cowboys in those days faced danger from rival ranches, and from rustlers (cattle thieves). The West was a rough, tough place, where some American Indians were still trying to defend their lands, and cowboys carried guns.

Then as now the cowboy's chief tool was the

lasso (rope), which he used to catch cattle and horses. Above all he had to be a superb horseman. Each cowboy had a string of half a dozen horses, never riding the same one two days running. Out on the range he often had to sleep rough in a makeshift camp.

▼ 'Stampede by Lightning' is the title of this painting by Frederic Remington (1861–1909). He travelled widely in the American and Canadian West during the 1880s.

The gauchos

Gauchos, the cowboys of South America, worked on the pampas, the grassy plains of Argentina and Uruguay. Most of them were of mixed Spanish and Indian descent, wearing baggy trousers held up by silver-studded belts. As well as lassos they used the *bola*, a cord with a heavy ball at each end, which they threw to entangle and bring down cattle. Today there are few gauchos left, and the pampas, like the range of North America, is broken up by fences.

A living legend

Books and films have turned cowboys into a legend. They were not as glamorous as they are in films, and the great days of the cowboy were over by the end of the 19th century. But their way of singing lingers on in 'Western music', and their skills are displayed in rodeos (displays of cowboy skills) and 'Wild West' shows. ■

Cowhands, now as in the past, have their own language for their work. For example, they call food *chuck*; a cowhand's hat is a *stetson* (originally the name of a brand of hat); a cowhand's working horses are a *string*; and a new hand who does not know the work is called a *tenderfoot*.

See also
American Indians
American West

Biography
Billy the Kid
Buffalo Bill
James, Jesse
Oakley

Crabs

The crab has a body which is wider than it is long. The head and the middle part are joined together to form a single, heavily armoured unit. The abdomen is small, and tucked up below the main part of the body. All crabs have ten legs, the front pair of which usually end in large claws. The crab uses these

► Brightly coloured male fiddler crabs have one claw so large that they cannot use it for feeding. It is used to display to females and fight other males.

to defend itself and to tear up its food. Crabs usually walk sideways, as they can move more quickly this way. Some crabs, such as the ghost crabs of the tropics, are particularly fast.

Most crabs spend all of their lives in the sea, although some, like the shore crab, can stand short periods out of the water at low tide. The few kinds that live in fresh water have to return to the sea to breed. Hermit crabs spend a lot of time out of water. These are not true crabs as they have long abdomens, like lobsters', but not armoured. They protect themselves by tucking their soft abdomens into the shells of dead sea snails. ■

Distribution
Mainly on seashores and in shallow seas throughout the world. A few are found in deep water and a few live almost entirely on land.
Largest crab
Japanese spider crab, leg-span measures over 2·6 m
Smallest species
Includes the pea crabs, which are about the size of a pea when adult
Lifespan
Varies, but small shore crabs probably live for at least 3 years. A shore crab is known to have moulted its shell 17 times in 3 years.

Phylum
Arthropoda
Class
Crustacea
Order
Decapoda
Number of species
Over 4,500 true crabs

See also
Crustaceans
Lobsters

Crafts

A craftsman or a craftswoman is someone who can use their hands in a particularly skilful way to make useful and beautiful things. In the Middle Ages men who earned their living by following a particular craft (for example, goldsmiths, weavers, leather workers, stonemasons) formed guilds. Before a person could become a full member he had to produce a 'masterpiece'. This was an example of his best work and was judged by people who were already 'masters of the craft'.

Today we can use the term crafts-

man or craftswoman to describe people who do all kinds of skilled work like spraying paint onto a car, making furniture or making a dress.

An artist is a person who has very special gifts. The artist has the skills of the craft worker but is able to use these skills in new and creative ways. For example, a craftsman makes pots; an artist may also make pots, but decorates and shapes them in a style that has not been used before. A craftswoman may be skilled with her needles; an artist will be able to design the picture on the tapestry as well as work it in thread. ■

See also
Basket making
Embroidery
Guilds
Lace
Macramé
Pottery
Sewing
Spinning
Tie and dye
Weaving

Cranes

Cranes are used to help us lift and move heavy objects. Your hand is a sort of crane, when you use it to lift and move things. It can grip a load, lift it, and put it where you choose.

jib

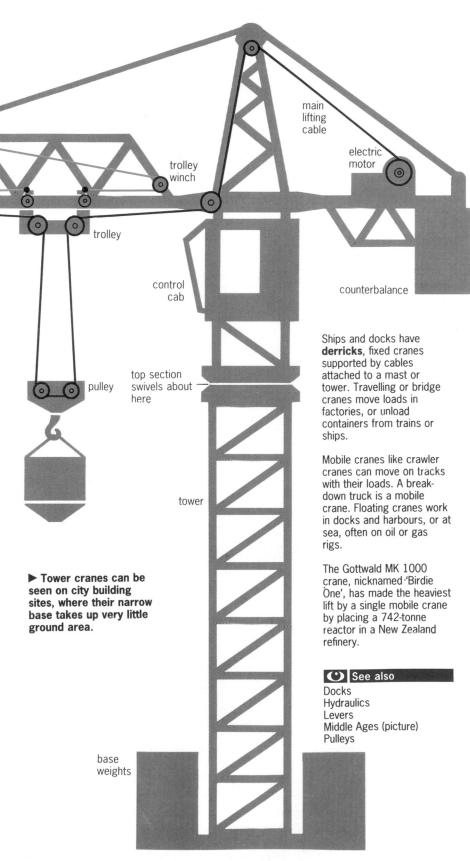

main lifting cable

electric motor

trolley winch

trolley

control cab

counterbalance

top section swivels about here

pulley

tower

base weights

▶ **Tower cranes can be seen on city building sites, where their narrow base takes up very little ground area.**

How cranes work

Cranes usually make use of wires, ropes or cables running through grooved wheels called sheaves. Pulling down is easier than lifting up, so a simple pulley (a rope over a wheel) enables you to lift a heavy weight by pulling downwards. With more wheels in the system, lifting can be made even easier. The longer the pull, the lighter the load appears. The weight is then shared between three or more ropes, so that the weight seems to be three or more times lighter. But you then have to pull the rope three or more times further to raise the load by the same amount.

The arm of the crane (the jib or boom) is a long lever. The hook is gradually wound in by cables running round a drum. To balance the weight of the load, especially when the crane is turning round, a block of iron or concrete is attached to the other end of the jib or boom.

Most cranes have an open structure; the jib and tower are a metal framework. This makes them both light and strong, without flat surfaces to catch the wind. The framework is made of triangles, which are strong and resist bending. Legs called 'outriggers' may spread the crane's weight over a large area to keep the crane stable.

Some cranes have electromagnets instead of hooks. These are magnets, powered by electricity, that can be switched on and off. Magnetic loads, like scrap cars, can be lifted or put down at the touch of a switch.

Flashback

The Romans raised loads using a treadmill turned by slaves walking to turn the crane's cable drum. In the Middle Ages, cranes were common in European ports, and builders used cranes to build the cathedrals. The application of the steam-engine during the Industrial Revolution made cranes more efficient, by replacing muscle power. ■

Ships and docks have **derricks**, fixed cranes supported by cables attached to a mast or tower. Travelling or bridge cranes move loads in factories, or unload containers from trains or ships.

Mobile cranes like crawler cranes can move on tracks with their loads. A breakdown truck is a mobile crane. Floating cranes work in docks and harbours, or at sea, often on oil or gas rigs.

The Gottwald MK 1000 crane, nicknamed 'Birdie One', has made the heaviest lift by a single mobile crane by placing a 742-tonne reactor in a New Zealand refinery.

◑ **See also**
Docks
Hydraulics
Levers
Middle Ages (picture)
Pulleys

Creation myths

Adam and Eve
The creation story, at the beginning of the Old Testament of the Bible, tells how God took six days to make the world and everything in it, including Adam, the first man, and Eve, the first woman.

Creation myths are stories about how the world and the human race began. Nowadays scientists suggest answers to such questions as 'How was the Earth formed?' or 'Why is it light in the day and dark at night?' But in the days before science, people made up stories, or myths, instead. All over the world, the questions are the same. But the stories come from different climates, different religions, different kinds of people.

How human beings appeared (Greece)

At the dawn of time, there were no beings in the universe but gods and titans. One of the titans, Prometheus, sat alone in the empty world, moulding clay between his fingers. Just for fun he made a tiny clay model of a god. He called the goddess Athene to come and look, and she breathed life into the naked brown doll. It began running about, piping and squeaking, and Prometheus and Athene smiled to see it. Prometheus moulded more and more dolls from clay, and Athene gave them life. The doll-people tumbled at Prometheus' feet, helpless as kittens. The human race was born.

See also
Myths and legends
Norse myths
Pandora

How the Sun and Moon began (Australia)

In the Dream Time, at the beginning of creation, there was no light. Birds and insects flew blindly about; animals blundered in the darkness; human beings felt their way with sticks. Then two men, Jurumi and Mudati, met by chance in a clearing and sat down to talk. Their walking-sticks rubbed accidentally together, and a spark jumped out, landed in a pile of dry leaves and set them on fire.

Jurumi and Mudati were terrified. They thought the fire was a living creature, roaring for food. They fed it with grass, bark and branches. It took them months to learn its ways, to tame it and control it. The world's other creatures kept well clear, watching the fire and the humans with wary eyes. Jurumi and Mudati used fire to rule all other created things. They used it to rule darkness, too. Soon after it was discovered, they gave blazing torches to two old women, goddesses who had existed since time began. The goddesses soared into the sky, and light from their torches filled the world. One woman's torch burned gold-yellow, and she called it Sun; the other's was as silver as the sea, and she called it Moon.

How the world began (Japan)

When the universe began, there was no world. The gods lived high in space. There were fourteen of them, and each owned a corner of the universe. Down below, there was nothing but mud, thick and lifeless.

One day, two more gods were born. They were twins: Isanami and Isanagi. While they were babies, the other gods welcomed them, playing with them and smiling at them in their cradles. But when Isanami and Isanagi grew up the other gods shouted, 'Go away! There's no room here. Go down to the mud. Make that your home!'

Isanami and Isanagi flew down through space, and hovered over the mud-sea. They held a long-handled spear. Its tip was made of stars, sharp as diamonds. They put the tip of the spear into the mud-sea, and began to stir. The mud thickened, and stuck to the spear-point. When Isanami and Isanagi pulled up the spear, lumps of mud splashed back into the sea. The small mud-lumps made islands; the big lumps made continents. Grass grew, and trees, flowers and bushes covered the new land. So the world began, and the other gods looked down and envied Isanami's and Isanagi's beautiful new home. ∎

Cricket

Cricket is an eleven-a-side game played with bat and ball. The players on the batting team try to hit the ball to score runs. One run is scored each time the two batsmen run from one wicket to the other. If they hit the ball across the boundary of the field, they score four runs, or six if it crosses the boundary without bouncing.

The other team tries to get the batsmen out. The bowler, who must bowl the ball with a straight arm, can hit the wicket to get a batsman out 'bowled'. If the batsman's leg (or any other part of his body) stops the ball hitting the wicket, he can be out 'leg before wicket' (LBW). Fielders can catch batsmen out if the ball is hit in the air, and can run out batsmen if they hit the wicket with the ball before the batsman reaches it. Batsmen can also be out 'stumped', when the wicket-keeper takes the ball and breaks the wicket with the batsman out of his ground, and 'hit wicket' if they break it themselves.

The batting team's innings ends when ten batsmen are out or when they declare their innings closed. Then the other team bats and tries to score more runs to win the game.

Competitions

Cricket matches last anything from an afternoon to five days for Test Matches. Tests are played between the main cricket countries, England, Australia, West Indies, New Zealand, India, Pakistan and Sri Lanka. Each country also has its own competitions, with games lasting one, two, three or four days.

◀ Bats dating from the 18th century onward. In 1771 the width of the bat was limited to 4¼ inches and in 1835 the maximum length was set at 38 inches. Note how the shape and weight of bats have changed over the years.

People have played cricket in England for many centuries, but the game we know today began in the 18th century. The first great club was Hambledon, a village in Hampshire, who were good enough to take on and beat 'All England' in those days. The Marylebone Cricket Club (MCC), formed in 1787, drew up the laws of cricket in 1788 and revised them in 1835. Overarm bowling was allowed in 1864, the same year W. G. Grace began to play. He scored 170 and 56 not out two days before his sixteenth birthday, and went on to become one of the greatest cricketers of all time. ■

1864 County Championship begins in England

1877 First Test, Australia v England

1882 Australia's first Test win in England leads to an 'obituary notice' for English cricket in the *Sporting Times* and the start of the 'Ashes' Test matches between England and Australia

1938 Highest Test score by team: 903–7 dec., England v Australia

1956 Most wickets by bowler in Test match: 19 by J. C. Laker, England v Australia

1958 Highest Test score by a player: 365 by G. St A. Sobers, West Indies v Pakistan

A batsman makes a 'duck' if he gets out without scoring a run. A 'golden duck' is when you are out first ball!

See also

Biography
Sports special

▼ The wickets, close fielders and umpires. Law 3: 'Two umpires shall be appointed, one for each end, to control the game as required by the Laws with absolute impartiality.' The wicket-keeper wears leg guards and gloves. Close fielders are poised for catches.

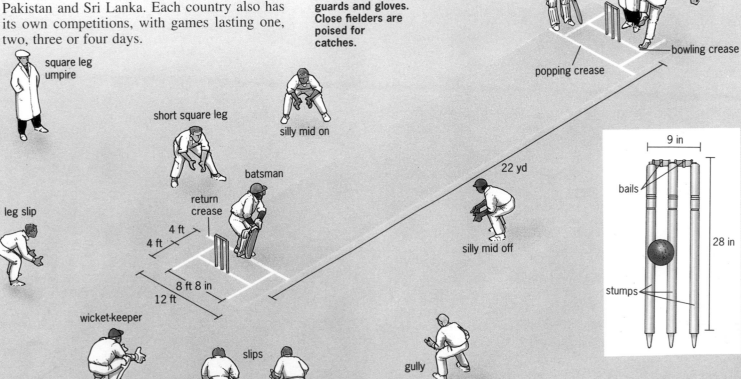

Crickets

Crickets are related to grasshoppers. Their large back legs enable them to leap many times the length of their own bodies. They are generally active at night, some digging tunnels to rest in while it is light. Most kinds eat leaves, but some bush crickets feed on other insects.

Like grasshoppers, crickets 'sing'. They do this by dragging comb-like teeth on one wing across a thickened area on another. The front of the body acts as a sound chamber to make the song louder. Some tropical crickets sing so loudly they can be heard 1½ km (1 mile) away. Crickets' ears are on their front knees. ■

Phylum Arthropoda
Class Insecta
Order Orthoptera
Family Gryllidae
Number of species
More than 5,000 bush crickets and 2,000 true crickets

◀ Bush crickets are also known as katydids. This lichen katydid is found in Costa Rica and is protected from enemies by its convincing camouflage.

◉ See also
Grasshoppers
Insects
Locusts

Crimean War

▲ Queen Victoria created a special medal for great courage: the Victoria Cross.

The Crimean War was a quarrel about power. Britain, France and Turkey fought Russia over who was to be most powerful in the eastern Mediterranean.

Britain and France decided to attack the Crimea in south Russia. They wanted to capture Sebastopol, Russia's important port on the Black Sea. Neither side had fought a war for 40 years, and there was chaos.

The British army travelled in dirty, badly organized ships. Many soldiers died of cholera before they even reached the Crimea. Nearly 500 men and horses died needlessly in the 'Charge of the Light Brigade' because a mistaken order sent them charging down a narrow valley into a death-trap of Russian guns. When winter came, there were not enough tents, so soldiers had no shelter. The British wounded had no proper care, and suffered terribly. But some officers lived in luxury. Lord Cardigan, commander of the Light Brigade, brought his own comfortable yacht with him. The British and French finally captured Sebastopol, mainly because the Russians were also very disorganized.

The reporter William Howard Russell sent news by telegraph to *The Times* newspaper. When people heard the truth, things began to change. Florence Nightingale set up proper hospitals for the wounded. People began to realize that officers should have a proper training, and ordinary soldiers needed better conditions. But the war settled nothing between the countries who fought each other. ■

1854
Crimea invaded
Battle of Alma
Battle of Balaclava (Charge of the Light Brigade)
Battle of Inkerman
Florence Nightingale arrived
1855
Sebastopol captured
1856
War ended

◉ See also
Victorian Britain

Biography
Nightingale
Seacole
Victoria

RUSSIA
Dnieper

0 kilometres 100
(62 miles)

Sea of Azov

Black Sea
Crimea
Eupatoria
Alma
Sebastopol Inkerman
Balaclava

✕ Battle
→ Route of Allied forces (British, French, Turkish)

◀ Photographs of battles were taken for the first time. People were very impressed because they knew they were seeing a real picture of war. This is a gun emplacement.

Children and crime
(English Law)

Below the age of 10, a child cannot be found guilty of a criminal offence.

Between the ages of 10 and 14, children can be convicted of crimes if it can be shown that they knew what they were doing was wrong.

From 14 years onwards, children are assumed to know as much about crime and the laws of the land as adults. They are, though, usually tried in special juvenile courts.

At 17 years of age, a child becomes an adult in the eyes of the law.

Some acts are regarded as crimes in one country and not in another. In countries which have Islamic (Muslim) laws, drinking alcohol and adultery are seen as crimes. This is not so in most countries of the world.

See also
Detectives
Law
Mafia
Police

Crimes

All states have rules which govern how the people of that state behave to each other, to each other's property, and towards the state itself. These rules are the law of the land. Some breaches of the law come under the civil law. Others come under the criminal law and these are crimes.

Many crimes have been regarded as crimes for centuries and in countries all over the world. Murder and other forms of unlawful killing are crimes. So are assault and other forms of violence towards a person, including rape and other sexual offences. Theft, robbery, burglary, criminal damage to property, fraud and forgery are all crimes. If violence is threatened in the course of a theft, the charge will be robbery. If someone breaks into a place to steal, the crime is burglary. In some cases omitting to do something may be a crime. Wilful neglect of a child so as to cause suffering is a crime. Failure to pay for a television licence is a crime in the United Kingdom. ∎

Croatia

Area
56,538 sq km
(21,829 sq miles)
Capital
Zagreb
Population
4,685,000
Language
Serbo-Croat
Religion
Christian
Government
Parliamentary republic
Currency
1 Croatian dinar = 100 paras

See also
Bosnia
Serbia
Yugoslavia

Biography
Tito

Croatia is a country in southern Europe with a long coastline on the Adriatic Sea, known as the 'Dalmatian Coast'. The dramatic limestone scenery of this coastline and its Mediterranean climate, made it popular with tourists until the war in the 1990s.

Zagreb, the capital, is on the site of a Roman town. The old part of the city is dominated by the filigree spires of a Catholic cathedral, which was begun over 1,000 years ago.

For most of this century Croatia was part of Yugoslavia, until 1991 when it became independent during a civil war with Serbia. Much of its farmland was destroyed in the war or fell under Serbian control. ∎

Crocodiles

Crocodiles are water-living, hunting reptiles. They belong to an ancient group of animals which has changed little since the days of the dinosaurs. They may seem harmless as they bask beside warm rivers or lakes or float, log-like, in the water, with only their nostrils and eyes above the surface. But they are far from harmless. When swimming, the thrust of their flattened, oar-like tails drives them fast towards their prey.

Young crocodiles feed on insects, but for most of their lives fish is their main food. Their jaws are set with sharp pointed teeth, ideal for holding such slippery prey. Big, old crocodiles can tackle larger creatures and may even be a danger to humans and livestock.

Crocodiles are gentle mothers. After mating, a female makes a nest of mud and plant debris near the water's edge. Here she lays her eggs and stays on guard near by until they are ready to hatch. When they are ready the babies croak from inside their eggs and the mother helps them to escape. She gathers them into her huge mouth and carries them to the water. Here she continues to guard them, for they have many enemies, including their own father!

Large crocodiles have few natural enemies, being protected by a thick, leathery skin armoured with small plates of bone. But the skin of young crocodiles makes valuable leather, and many have been killed for this. Nowadays, some crocodiles are farmed for their leather and meat, but most species are endangered and need careful conservation. ∎

▲ Young crocodiles use a hard, horny knob on the tip of their jaw to cut their way from the egg. At first they grow fast. As they get older they grow more slowly, but they never stop growing completely.

Distribution
Rivers, lakes and the edge of the sea in warm parts of the world
Size
Some Nile and salt-water crocodiles may grow to over 6·5 m in length.
Weight
Up to 1·5 tonnes
Number of eggs
25–95
Lifespan
Over 100 years

Subphylum
Vertebrata
Class
Reptilia
Order
Crocodilia
Number of species
13 species of true crocodiles

See also
Alligators
Endangered species
Reptiles

Crusades

Crusade comes from the Latin word *crux*, which means 'cross'. This was because the first crusaders had sewn Christian crosses onto their clothes.

Crusades were medieval wars. They were waged by the knights of Europe against non-Christian peoples. There were crusades against the Moors in Spain and the heathens of northern Europe. But the best-known crusades were against the Muslims of the Middle East, between 1096 and 1291. The crusaders wanted to help the Christian Emperor of Constantinople in his wars with the Muslim Turks. They wanted to seize the holy city of Jerusalem too, and protect Christian pilgrims who went there. But perhaps they were keenest of all to win lands, fame and fortune far from home.

An attractive idea

Pope Urban II was eager to launch the First Crusade. 'Let wars between you cease,' he told Europe's knights in a speech at Clermont, France, in 1095. 'Go on this journey so that all your sins can be wiped out. And you will be sure of undying glory in the kingdom of heaven.' This idea appealed to many knights. But it also appealed to thousands of ordinary, unarmed men

See also
Byzantine empire
Chivalry
Knights
Saracens

Biography
Louis IX
Richard I
Saladin

and women. In 1096 they marched right into Asia Minor, and were massacred by a Muslim army. The crusading knights who followed them fared much better. They defeated the Muslims in battle, successfully besieged Nicaea and Antioch, and in 1099 they captured Jerusalem. By 1100 there was a Christian king of Jerusalem. Christian princes were ruling over Antioch, Edessa and Tripoli too. Now they had to hold onto their new lands.

Crusaders in difficulties

They built marvellously strong castles. Special new 'orders' of knights, like the Templars and Hospitallers, made a splendid standing army. Yet the Christians were always outnumbered by the Muslims, and more crusaders from Europe were desperately needed. They came in the Second Crusade of 1147–1149, led by the rulers of France and Germany. But they achieved very little, and the Muslims continued to close in. At last in 1187, the Muslim Sultan Saladin of Egypt recaptured Jerusalem. A Third Crusade was launched at once, led by the Emperor, the French king, and Richard I of England. But the Emperor was drowned on the way. Then the other two leaders quarrelled. Jerusalem stayed in Muslim hands.

The Fourth Crusade

In 1204, a Fourth Crusade was directed at Egypt. But the crusaders headed instead for Constantinople. Forgetting their holy mission, they seized this Christian city, ransacked it, and made it the centre of a new empire of their own. It lasted only until 1261. And in 1291 the final Christian stronghold, the city of Acre, fell to the Muslims.

The children's crusade

But the strangest and saddest crusade had taken place in 1212. It was a crusade of thousands of European children. They believed that God was going to let them walk through the Mediterranean Sea to the Holy Land, so that they could take Jerusalem. But many children died on the march to the sea, and then the waters would not part. In the end, seven shiploads of children left Europe. Two of the ships were wrecked. The passengers on the other five were sold into slavery. ■

◄ Crusading knights moving in on Jerusalem in 1099. The city was holy to the Muslims as well as to the Christians. That was why there was such a long and bitter struggle to control it.

Crustaceans

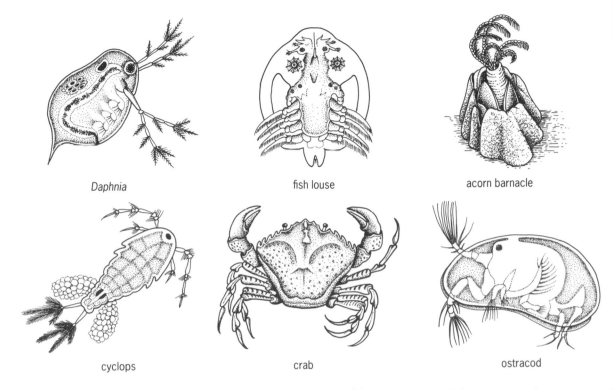

Daphnia

fish louse

acorn barnacle

◀ **The main kinds of crustacean.**

cyclops

crab

ostracod

Phylum
Arthropoda
Class
Crustacea
Number of species
About 31,400

▼ **An Atlantic prawn. This is a deep sea species and, like many crustaceans of the dark depths of the oceans, is red in colour.**

The word 'crustacea' means 'crusty ones'. This is a suitable name for a group of animals which all have a jointed crust or shell to support and protect them. Sometimes this is very thick, for the horny material (chitin) of which it is formed may be strengthened with a substance like chalk. Crabs and lobsters, for instance, are very effectively armoured in this way.

Almost all crustaceans live in water. Those which live on land, like woodlice, are not as well waterproofed as their distant relatives the insects and spiders, so they can exist only in damp places, where they are in no danger of drying out.

It is not always easy to decide if an animal is a crustacean, for they vary very much in size and shape. One way of telling with the larger species is to count their legs. All of them have at least five pairs of legs or pincers. Also, almost every kind of crustacean goes through a stage, early in its life, when it is a nauplius. Generally this is a microscopically tiny larva which swims in the water. In some cases, the nauplius stage occurs in the egg, so the young already look like their parents when they hatch.

Crustaceans are very important animals. In the sea, and in some lakes, they may be the most numerous form of animal life. The small species

feed on minute plants. They are then eaten by bigger crustaceans which are food for fish, birds or even whales. A blue whale can eat more than two tonnes of the shrimp-like crustacean, krill, in a single meal. The number of tiny crustaceans that the krill themselves have eaten is also enormous. A few kinds of crustaceans are important as food for human beings, particularly some of the crabs, prawns, lobsters and their relatives. ■

👁 **See also**
Crabs
Krill
Larvae
Lobsters
Plankton
Prawns
Woodlice

Crystals

▲ Quartz crystals occur in many rocks, including granite and quartzite.

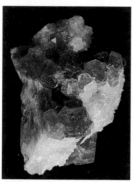

▲ Fluorite is mined in Cumbria, UK and is used to produce an acid which is important in the pottery and plastics industries.

Crystals come in many shapes and sizes. Diamonds are probably the most beautiful crystals of all. Their clear, flat faces seem to sparkle in the light. Other gems, such as emeralds and rubies, have colours which make them especially attractive. However, not all crystals are as rare or valuable as these. We sprinkle tiny crystals of sugar and salt on our food. And there are even more crystals all around us. Many solids, including metals and plastics, are made of millions of microscopic crystals which stick together to form larger blocks of material.

Heat from deep inside the Earth formed many of the crystals found in rocks. The heat melted minerals in the rocks. Later, when the minerals cooled, they solidified to form crystals. Others were formed when water on the ground evaporated, leaving behind minerals which had been dissolved in the water.

Atoms in crystals

If you look at some crystals of salt through a magnifying glass, you will see that all salt crystals are the same basic shape: a cube. Like all substances, salt is made up of tiny particles called atoms. In a crystal, the atoms are arranged layer upon layer in regular rows, rather like eggs in a crate. Atoms of the same substance always arrange themselves in the same way. Scientists can work out how they are arranged by looking at the shape of a crystal and the angles of its faces.

More complicated substances like plastics or drugs, or even viruses have their atoms joined together to form molecules which can be made up of a small number of atoms or tens of thousands. But the molecules are all the same and they can arrange themselves regularly in a crystal. ■

Something to do

Try 'growing' your own salt crystals. Add two teaspoonfuls of salt to half a cupful of warm water and stir until the salt has dissolved. Pour the liquid (called salt solution) into a saucer and leave on a windowsill for a day or so. As the water slowly evaporates, salt crystals will form in the saucer. For bigger crystals, keep the saucer topped up with salt solution.

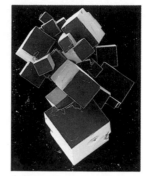

▲ If you 'grow' your own salt crystals they will look like this if magnified 200 times. A turquoise tint has been added so they are easier to see.

See also
Atoms
Diamonds
Electronics
Gems
Ice
Minerals
Salt
Silicon

Cuba

Area
110,861 sq km
(42,804 sq miles)
Capital
La Habana (Havana)
Population
10,356,400
Language Spanish
Religion Christian
Government Republic
Currency
1 Cuban peso = 100 centavos

Cuba is a tropical island state in the Caribbean Sea. It is as big as all the other Caribbean islands put together and its population of over 10 million makes up one-third of the total population of the West Indies.

Most of the land is flat, but the Sierra Maestra in the south rises to over 2,000 m (6,500 ft). The climate is warm. Annual rainfall averages about 1,200 mm (47 in). Cuba is one of the world's main producers of sugar. Most of the agricultural land is owned by the state, which has been ruled by a Marxist government since 1959. Tobacco is also grown, and Cuba is famous for its fine cigars.

Flashback

Spain ruled over Cuba for almost 400 years until 1898, when it achieved independence as a result of the Spanish-American War. This century Cuba has been governed by a series of dictators until Fidel Castro led a revolution in 1959. Soon afterwards Cuba became a communist state. ■

See also
Caribbean
Caribbean history
Spanish colonial history
Sugar
Tobacco

Biography
Castro

▼ Children on their way to school in Havana, the capital city of Cuba.

Cub Scouts

Cub Scouts are younger members of the Scout movement. To join, they have to make a promise and receive the Scout World Badge. Cub Scouts can go camping and learn first aid and many scouting skills.

There are more than 250,000 Cubs in the United Kingdom, aged 8 to 11 years old. Younger boys can join the Beaver Scouts at the age of 6. Throughout the world there are millions more Cub Scouts in more than 150 countries.

Flashback

When the Scout Movement started in 1908, younger boys wanted to join. In 1914 Sir Robert Baden-Powell, known as B-P, wrote the Wolf Cub Handbook. B-P was friendly with Rudyard Kipling, author of *The Jungle Book*, and he used these stories for the junior Scouts. He called them Wolf Cubs and they met in Packs. The leader was Akela, named after the Great Grey Lone Wolf of Kipling's story. These names are still used today. The Wolf Cubs have officially changed their name to Cub Scouts in Britain. ∎

◀ **Group of Cub Scouts involved in an experiment.**

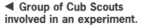 **See also**
Brownies
Guides
Scouts

Biography
Baden-Powell
Kipling

Cuckoos

The call of the European cuckoo has given the bird its name. There are many different species of cuckoo found all over the world and they vary in size and appearance. Most are forest birds, although the greater road runner lives in desert scrub. Generally those which do not breed in the tropics migrate to warmer areas for the winter.

Cuckoos eat mainly insects, and some, including the European cuckoo, commonly feed on hairy and nasty-tasting caterpillars which are disliked by other birds.

Nearly half the world's cuckoos are like the European cuckoo and are 'brood parasites', which means they lay their eggs in other birds' nests and leave the 'foster parents' to rear their young. Some cuckoos lay an egg which looks like one of their foster parents' eggs.

◀ **Recently hatched cuckoo rids the nest of all other eggs. This cuckoo is in a reed warbler's nest.**

Subphylum
Vertebrata
Class
Aves
Order
Cuculiformes
Number of species
130
Size
15–90 cm

Young European cuckoos hatch ahead of the foster parents' eggs and then the naked and blind chick pushes all the other eggs out of the nest, one by one, so that it alone can have all the food brought by both parents. ∎

 See also
Birds

Curling

Traditionally, the game was played outdoors in countries with cold winters. Now it is usually played on indoor ice rinks.

The earliest curling stone still in existence has the date 1511 cut into it, and is held in Stirling, Scotland.

This is a game like bowls, but it is played on ice with granite stones weighing 18–19 kg (40–42 lb) each. The stones are slid along a playing area called a 'rink'. There are usually two teams of four, each with two stones, and each side aims to get the most stones close to the 'tee', which is at the centre of a target area marked on the ice.

As the stone slides along the rink, the player's team-mates sweep in front of it with brooms, according to directions called out by their captain or 'skip'. Sweeping affects the direction and distance of the sliding stone. ■

Customs and excise

Two special kinds of taxes are known as customs duties and excise duties. Governments use them to raise money and control trade. Customs duties are charged on imports: that is, goods coming into a country. Ordinary travellers are allowed to import a small amount of goods duty free.

Excise duties are charged on goods and services inside a country, such as the special British taxes on alcohol and tobacco. Value Added Tax (VAT) is a kind of excise duty that is charged on most goods and services in many countries, especially the member countries of the European Community. ■

Customs duties, or import taxes, are also known as tariffs. When a group of countries joins together to reduce or abolish customs duties on their imports and exports, it is called a 'customs union'. The European Community is a customs union.

In Britain the Customs Department began in 1671. The Excise Department joined it in 1909 to form HM Customs and Excise.

See also
Smugglers
Taxes
Trade

Cycling

The first ever cycle race, held over 1,200 metres, took place in Paris in 1868. The Tour de France started in 1903. Although it is still the most famous long race, there are others like the Giro d'Italia in Italy and the Vuelta a España in Spain.

▼ A group of cyclists in the 1987 Tour de France are battling their way up the hills of La Plagne-Morzine. The leader of the race is awarded a yellow jersey to wear on the next day's stage.

The best-known kind of cycle racing is road racing, in which massed groups of colourfully dressed riders battle it out over long distances on public roads. A road race may be a short evening event for local club riders, or a long and famous race like the Tour de France.

Time trials are races in which riders set off separately at intervals of a minute. Riders are timed, and have to wait until all have finished to see who has won. This kind of racing is very popular in Britain, where road racing was banned for many years and is still very difficult to organize on the crowded roads.

Track racing is done on a steeply banked oval track. Many different kinds of races are held, such as the 'pursuit', in which riders set off at opposite sides of the track and try to catch each other.

Cyclo-cross is cross-country racing. A typical course will force the riders to dismount and carry their bikes for part of the way.

Mountain bikes are rugged machines with fat tyres and straight handle-bars. Cross-country races for these machines are becoming more popular.

Other games involving bikes are cycle speedway and bicycle polo. ■

▲ Three of the French team in the track racing world championships. Their special bikes have solid carbon fibre wheels to reduce air resistance and make them go faster.

Some very fit cyclists compete in the Triathlon. They have to swim 4 km, then cycle 200 km and finally run a marathon. The most famous triathlon event is called the 'Iron Man of Hawaii'.

See also
Bicycles
Marathon

Biography
Sports special

Cyclones and anticyclones

Cyclones and anticyclones affect the weather. A cyclone is an area of low air pressure, which means the air is rising. In an anticyclone the air pressure is high because the air is sinking.

Both cyclones and anticyclones often move, but cyclones usually move faster than anticyclones.

If you look at the weather maps for three or four days in a row you will often be able to see the track of a cyclone moving across the country.

▲ This satellite photograph of a tropical cyclone was taken over the northern Pacific Ocean. You can see the swirling mass of clouds.

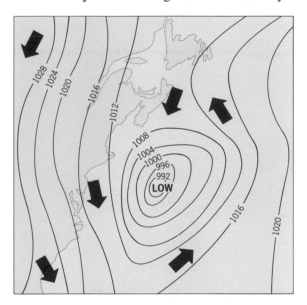

▲ In a cyclone the air pressure changes causing strong winds and stormy weather.

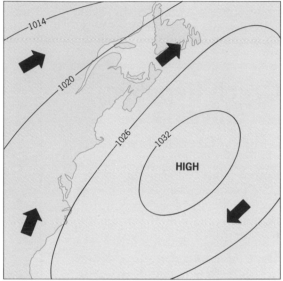

▲ In an anticyclone high air pressure remains stable over a wide area.

—— isobars (lines joining places with equal air pressure) Numbers show air pressure in millibars.

 arrows show wind direction

Cyclones

Cyclones have different names in different parts of the world. In Britain they are usually called 'depressions'. In tropical and subtropical areas a cyclone with very strong winds is called a hurricane or typhoon. The weather in most cyclones is cloudy, rainy and windy. A tropical cyclone seen from a satellite is a great swirling mass of clouds.

Cyclones form over the sea, and the violent winds can do great damage as they roar across the oceans and islands. When a cyclone moves over large land areas it gradually fades out. Hurricanes are given names by forecasters who track their progress and give warnings to people in their paths. A hurricane has wind speeds of 34 metres per second (75 mph) or more. But it is difficult to know exactly what speed the winds reach because the wind speed recorders are often blown away.

Anticyclones

A very large anticyclone stays over the vast area of Russia known as Siberia every winter. It is called the Siberian anticyclone. If you look at a weather map of northern Asia, you will see the Siberian anticyclone hardly changes its position from October to March. The weather in Siberia in winter is always bitterly cold. The temperature often reaches –30°C (–22°F). Other parts of the world also have anticyclones in some regions in certain seasons. The weather map over the Sahara Desert often shows an anticyclone in the winter months.

Anticyclones sometimes stay over western Europe for a week. When this happens in the summer the weather is hot and sunny. There are few clouds in the sky and no rain, although there may be fog in the mornings. But in some parts of the anticyclone there may be summer thunderstorms when the air is hot and humid. ■

 See also
Depressions
Hurricanes
Weather

Cyprus

See also
Mediterranean
Ottoman empire

Cyprus is an island at the eastern end of the Mediterranean Sea. The capital, Nicosia, is in the centre of a lowland area between two mountain ranges. From the city walls, you can see the hazy slopes of the Kyrenia range to the north. To the south are the Troödos mountains which rise up to Mount Olympus 1,951 m (6,400 ft) high.

Cyprus sizzles in the summer heat, but winters are cooler with some rain. Tourists come to the south coast beaches all through the year.

Britain took the island from the Ottoman Turks in 1878. When it became an independent country in 1960, the government was shared by the Greek and Turkish Cypriots. The shared government did not work, and United Nations soldiers came to keep peace.

When the government changed in 1974, Turkey took over the north where most Turkish-Cypriots lived. The Greeks in the area fled south. The island was divided by a barrier between the Greek south and Turkish north, running through the middle of Nicosia. ■

Area
9,251 sq km
(3,572 sq miles)
Capital
Nicosia
Population
691,700
Greek-Cypriot 81%, Turkish-Cypriot 19%
Language
Greek, Turkish, English
Religion
Christian, Muslim
Government
Parliamentary republic
Currency
1 Cyprus pound = 100 cents

Czech Republic
and **Slovakia**
(formerly **Czechoslovakia**)

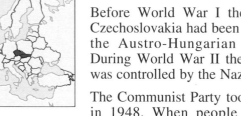

Czech Republic

Area
78,664 sq km
(30,372 sq miles)
Capital Prague
Population 10,302,000
Language Czech
Religion Christian
Government
Federal republic
Currency
1 koruna = 100 halers

Before World War I the former Czechoslovakia had been a part of the Austro-Hungarian empire. During World War II the country was controlled by the Nazis.

The Communist Party took power in 1948. When people tried to introduce more democracy in 1968 Czechoslovakia was invaded by the USSR. Twenty years later the calls for freedom became so strong that in 1989 the Communist Party lost power. Democratic elections were held in 1990. Two years later, the Slovaks voted to set up a separate state, and two separate republics were created on 1 January 1993.

Czech Republic

There are two regions in the Czech Republic, Bohemia and Moravia. These contain several important industries. Skoda cars and trucks are made in Plzen where Pilsner beer is brewed. There are also many farms in the south producing sugar beet, wheat, maize, flax and hops.

Slovakia

Slovakia in the east is a mountainous country which contains many natural resources such as coal, gas and iron ore. There is also a growing timber and paper industry in its forests. However some of its industries were subsidized by the communists and now that those subsidies have ended, the industries have declined. ■

Slovakia

Area
49,035 sq km
(18,932 sq miles)
Capital Bratislava
Population 5,274,335
Language Slovak
Religion Christian
Government
Parliamentary republic
Currency
1 koruna = 100 halers

◀ Wenceslas Square in Prague, which is named after the patron saint of the Czechs.

See also
Communists
Europe
World War II

Biography
Dvorak

Dams

A dam is a barrier built across a stream, river or estuary. It is used to prevent flooding, to generate electricity by hydroelectric power or to hold water for drinking or irrigating land. The dam blocks the water flow and the water collects behind the dam to form a reservoir. Modern dams are mainly of two kinds, embankment dams and masonry dams. Masonry dams are usually built of concrete.

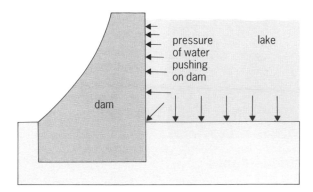

▲ **A gravity dam is one kind of masonry dam. The base of the dam,** **where the water pressure is greatest, is made of concrete.**

Embankment dams

These dams are wide banks of earth or rock. They are usually built across broad rivers. In cross-section, an embankment dam looks like a triangle with a wide base. The base is much wider than the top because the pressure of the water is always greatest at the bottom of a dam.

The advantage of embankment dams is that the materials that make them up are usually cheap and easy to obtain. Embankment dams can also withstand movements of their foundations, because they are made of loose material. The danger with these dams is that water gradually seeps through them. Eventually it can weaken the dam and wash it away.

Engineers try to deal with this problem either by lining the dam with a waterproof layer, such as clay, or by providing outlets to allow some of the water to drain away. ■

The Aswân Dam in Egypt, which spans the River Nile, is one of the world's largest embankment dams. It is 105 m high. The reservoir behind it, known as Lake Nasser, is over 300 km (190 miles) long.

▲ **The Hoover Dam, Colorado River, USA, is over 220 m high and 379 m long. The reservoir behind it, known as Lake Mead, is 185 km (115 miles) long, and 180 m** **deep. It has a hydro-electric power-station at its base which supplies most of the electricity for the states of Arizona, Nevada and southern California.**

See also
Concrete
Hydroelectric power
Irrigation
Nile
Rivers
Water supplies

Dance

Dance can often express thoughts and feelings far better than words can. You could say that dance speaks to our eyes as music speaks to our ears. But it can be very confusing because there are so many different kinds of dancing. Dance which is for celebration or ceremonies is called folk dance and is usually part of a long tradition of local customs. Social dance is fun and informal, like ballroom dance, disco and break dance. These styles have no particular message, except for bringing people together.

All types of dance have special steps and movements which must be learnt and these skills are called technique. When a dance technique is mixed with music, costume and scenery to tell a story or create a mood it is called performance dance. It happens on TV, film, in theatres, arts centres and open spaces. It tries both to communicate ideas and feelings and to entertain. Shaping technique and ideas into dance performances is called choreography. Most choreography is easy to understand, but with some dance you need to know how to 'read' the messages.

◀ *Gahu* is a circle dance from northern Ghana, performed here by dancers from a company of master drummers and dancers called *Adzido*, which in the Ewe language of Ghana means Oak Tree. This company performs traditional African dances for audiences to enjoy.

▼ In the 2nd century BC an Indian named Bharata wrote an important document on dance called the *Natya Shastra*. The three syllables of Bha-ra-ta are short for *bhava* (expression), *raga* (melody) and *tala* (rhythm). Put together they form Bharata Natyam, shown here by solo performer Sitakumari.

▶ Abstract contemporary dance has no story. By noticing the shapes the dancers make in relation to the other dancers, the space around them and the type of movements they make, the audience uses its imagination to help it understand the dance.

Indian dance

This is closely linked with the Hindu religion and storytelling and was first performed in temples. Each region has a different style: Kathakali, Bharata Natyam, Mohiniattam, Kuchipudi, Kathak, Orissi and Manipuri. Costume, makeup and music are all very important. The main musical instruments are cymbals, the sitar, and drums such as the tabla and mridangam.

Contemporary dance

Unlike in ballet, dancers can point their feet and flex them, dance barefoot and use the floor for rolling and falling. They can twist and contract their whole bodies. The major styles are named after the teachers and choreographers who developed them; Martha Graham and Merce Cunningham have companies in the USA. British companies include Rambert Dance and the London Contemporary Dance. Both have schools which train dancers.

African dance

In each part of Africa people have different styles of dance. Combined with music, song and decorated costume, dance in Africa is part of everyday life. It celebrates weddings, naming and initiation (coming of age) ceremonies. African dancers use techniques of clapping and rhythmic stamping and also isolated and repeated movements of the shoulders, hips and rib cage.

These movements developed into jazz dance when slaves transported from Africa took their dances to America. In the Caribbean, dances have developed from a combination of African and European folk dance.

◄ American dancer Fred Astaire, seen here with partner Ginger Rogers in the film 'Top Hat', was one of the most graceful tap dancers. He died in 1987 after a long career in film musicals which inspired many other dancers.

Tap dancing

This began in the USA, as a mixture of clog dancing, Irish step dancing and African dance. Black people danced it first. Using lace-up shoes with metal heel and toe taps, the dancers strike out complicated rhythms, usually to jazz music.

Social dance

Ballroom, disco and square dance are all types of dancing for pleasure to popular music. Ballroom dancing includes modern sequence dances such as the tango, waltz and quickstep. Latin American dance includes the Paso Doble, Jive and Cha-Cha. Old Time dancing has dances such as the Veleta and the Boston Two-step which date from Victorian times. Formation dancing, where several couples dance in patterns together, is also very popular. There are classes, examinations and competitions open to all ages.

◄ Spectacular costumes, often hand-made, are an appealing part of ballroom dancing. Competition winners like these often become professional, being paid to give demonstrations of their skill.

▼ Break dancing needs youth, energy and skill. It started as a style of street dance in New York in the 1970s and has developed its own style of music, language, clothes and shoes. This movement is called the hand-spin and can be dangerous.

Exercise and some steps

▶ These drawings show a dance exercise devised by Merce Cunningham. The exercise is performed smoothly to develop a supple spine and strong legs.

▶ The jazz walk combines fast side stepping with hip swings.

▶ The tap shuffle consists of a sharp forward tap followed by a back tap. To this can be added a hop, making a shuffle hop.

▼ By placing three pairs of dancers behind each other, the choreographer of this dance has used perspective to create a feeling of depth. The dancers at the back of the stage can be seen through the shapes made by the joined arms and legs of the two main dancers at the front.

Choreography

Choreography comes from two Greek words, *choreia* meaning 'dance' and *graphia* meaning 'writing'. Choreography means writing dances. The idea for a dance can come from a story, a painting or a piece of music.

The choreographer works with the dancers, teaching them steps and movements which will express his or her ideas. He or she will make patterns from the movements, perhaps choosing a group of steps, called a motif, to use regularly through the dance. This helps the audience to make sense of the patterns and shapes that they see. The choreographer works closely with the designer and the composer to make sure their ideas are in harmony.

Dances can be written down. This is called choreology or dance notation. There are two different methods, named after the people who invented them: Benesh and Laban notation. ■

 See also

African music
Ballet
Drums
Folk dance
Indian music
Initiation ceremonies
 (photograph)
Jazz
Musicals

Biography
Graham, Martha
Film special (Astaire and
 Rogers, Gene Kelly)

Dark Ages

The term Dark Ages has been used by archaeologists and historians to refer to the period in Europe after the end of Roman civilization. The word 'dark' was chosen because there are few written records of the people who moved into the old Roman empire, people the Romans would have called 'barbarians'. This period was also thought of as 'dark' because there seemed little archaeological evidence left to discover. As we discover more, the term Dark Ages is used less and less.

People looking for new lands

In 5th-century Europe, people on the edges of the old Roman empire were looking for new lands. Some wanted to conquer new territory but most wanted more room to settle in. Tribes from Scandinavia and the Low Countries moved into what had once been Roman Britain.

Huns, Franks, Goths and Vandals

In the rest of Europe there were also great movements of people. The Huns moved from Russia into northern Italy and even further west. The Franks moved into France. The Goths pushed south into Greece, then Italy, sacking Rome in AD 410 . The Vandals came from Hungary and swept through to North Africa by 429. The last Roman emperor in the West, called Romulus Augustulus, only reigned from 475 to 476. Odovacar, who led his armies in Italy, took over and declared himself king. The 'barbarians' now controlled the Western empire.

New kingdoms and new kings

The security of life under Roman rule had broken down. In many places it was replaced by a number of small kingdoms. This often happened where there was a powerful chieftain. As this is a period where there are few written records, a number of stories arose about these chieftains. ■

For England we have no records between 410, when Roman troops left, and 597 when Saint Augustine came to Canterbury. After that there is Bede's history and some brief chronicles, but no details till the time of King Alfred.
For France and Italy, where the invaders became Christian at once, there are some records, but not many till the time of Charlemagne.

Irish monks were among the best scholars in western Europe in the Dark Ages.

The most famous stories from this period are about King Arthur and his knights.

See also
Anglo-Saxons
Archaeologists
Arthur and his knights
Roman ancient history
Roman Britain

Biography
Arthur
Attila

Darts

This is an indoor game played by throwing darts, which are really miniature spears, at a target called a dartboard. There are various versions of the game, and various kinds of dartboard, but the game which is played by professionals on TV, and which is most popular in pubs and clubs, uses a 'clock' board which was invented in England in 1896. This is designed so that if you aim for a high score and just miss, you will probably hit a very low score. The clock board has a double ring and a treble ring: if you hit the '20' segment of the board in the treble ring, you score 60.

In the most common darts game you start with a number of points, usually 301 or 501. You throw three darts at each turn and you subtract your score until you reach zero. The first player to reach zero is the winner. There are two catches. The first is that you have to get out exactly: if you only need 75 then you must not score 76. The second is that you must throw a double or a bull's-eye to get out. ■

▲ The popular 'clock' style dartboard. A dart in the centre of the board, the 'bull's-eye', scores 50 points. One in the ring around the bull's-eye scores 25. The board's outer ring doubles the score of any dart which lands within it. The narrow inner ring trebles a dart's score.

Day and night

In the Christian world the day begins at midnight; for Jews the day begins at sunset.

▶ **Half of the Earth is in sunlight (daytime) and half is in shadow (nighttime). As the Earth spins, Chicago moves from the shadow of night (top), through dawn (middle) into daytime sunlight (bottom). In San Francisco, sunrise comes later.**

In medieval monasteries the day was split up into 'canonical' hours, such as matins and vespers, the periods of the day allotted to certain prayers.

◑ **See also**
Celestial sphere
Equinoxes
Midnight Sun
Seasons
Time

Day begins when the Sun rises in the east and night comes when the Sun sets in the west. The Sun seems to move across the sky because we watch it from the Earth, which spins around once every 24 hours. The Sun is shining all the time, but we can only see it if our part of the world is facing towards the Sun.

When you see the Sun rise, it is already up at places further east. As the Earth turns, places further and further west have dawn in turn. This is why there are time differences between countries. For example, the time in New York is five hours earlier than it is in London.

The length of day and night changes with the seasons. At places near the Arctic and Antarctic, the Sun never sets in the middle of summer and never rises in the middle of winter, so day and night can last for weeks. ■

Something to do

You can show how different places get day and night in turn with a globe of the Earth and a torch for the Sun. In a dark room, shine the torch at the globe so that one half is lit up. Then turn the globe slowly eastwards.

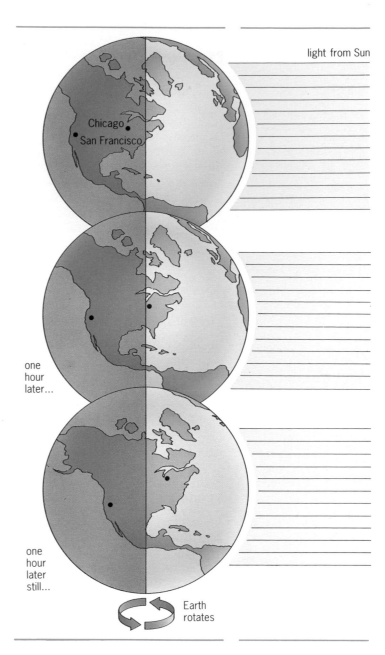

light from Sun

Chicago
San Francisco

one hour later...

one hour later still...

Earth rotates

Days of the week

Sunday
Latin: *Solis dies*
(day of the Sun)
Monday
Latin: *Lunae dies*
(day of the Moon)
French: *Lundi*
Tuesday
Latin: *Martis dies*
(day of Mars)
French: *Mardi*

◑ **See also**
Norse myths

People have organized days into blocks of seven, called weeks, for a very long time. The Jewish people made each seventh day, the Sabbath, a special day of rest. The Babylonians also had a seven-day week. Astrologers brought it into the Roman empire and named the days after the Sun, Moon and planets. After Emperor Constantine made Christianity the official religion of the Roman empire in the 4th century AD, these names began to be generally used. Sunday was made an official holiday in AD 326.

The names of the planets were also names of Roman gods: Mars, god of war; Mercury, the messenger god; Jupiter, the thunderer; the goddess Venus. The Anglo-Saxons used their own versions of the names of the Norse gods instead: Tiw's day (Tyr, god of war); Woden's day (Odin, the chief Norse god); Thunder's day (Thor), and Frige's day (the goddess Frigg). Saturday kept the name of the Roman god Saturn, and Sunday and Monday were called after the Sun and Moon. ■

Wednesday
Latin: *Mercurii dies*
(day of Mercury)
French: *Mercredi*
Thursday
Latin: *Jovis dies*
(day of Jupiter)
French: *Jeudi*
Friday
Latin: *Veneris dies*
(day of Venus)
French: *Vendredi*
Saturday
Latin: *Saturni dies*
(day of Saturn)
French: *Samedi*

Deafness

Some people are totally deaf, while others, who are partly deaf, can hear some sounds. We hear when sounds travel down the ear passage to the eardrum, then through the middle ear to part of the inner ear called the cochlea. This changes sounds into nerve impulses which go along a nerve to the brain, where hearing occurs.

Some people are deaf because sound is blocked on its way to the cochlea. Some causes are wax in the ear passage, a heavy cold with catarrh, and damage to the eardrum or cochlea. Ear wax is removed by washing the ear canal. Other causes may need surgery.

Deafness also occurs when the nerve from the cochlea to the brain, or the brain itself, is damaged.

Some children inherit a defect which causes deafness. Children can also be born deaf if their mother has German measles while pregnant.

A hearing aid can help partly deaf people by increasing the loudness of sounds. Many deaf people learn to understand speech by lip-reading, and some communicate by sign language. ■

See also
Ears
Sign language

Death

Average age of death in UK in 1984,
72 (men)
77 (women)
Average age of death in UK in 1900,
48 (men)
52 (women)

Death is the natural end of life. All living things die. When a person dies, the heart stops beating, breathing stops, and soon afterwards all activity in the brain stops. Death causes great sadness to relations and friends. We mourn the loss of the person who has died. Sometimes we may feel angry that someone has died and left us, or guilty that we were not always as kind as we could have been. In time we can remember without too much sadness. All religions have customs and rituals about death which help family and friends to pay their last respects. ■

See also
Funerals

Decimals

If you are measuring a length or a temperature, you will not always end up with an exact number of centimetres or degrees. Decimals, also known as decimal fractions, like 4·6 or 15·25, allow you to write numbers which are not necessarily whole numbers. Numbers to the right of the decimal point are read singly: 15·25 is read as 'fifteen point two five' and not as 'fifteen point twenty-five'.

Decimals use the idea of place value in just the same way as whole numbers do. Each place is ten times smaller than the one to its immediate left. The 6 in 4·6 stands for six tenths, and the 5 in 16·25 stands for five hundredths. It is a compact way of writing 'sixteen and two tenths and five hundredths', or what is the same thing, 'sixteen and twenty-five hundredths'.

A decimal can be thought of as the sum of two numbers. There is a whole number part to the left of the decimal point and a fraction less than one to the right of the decimal point. Some numbers are difficult to write as decimals. The square root of two is the number which we multiply by itself to get two. A calculator gives an approximate value of 1·414213562, but however many places of decimals we use it will still not be enough to give the value exactly. ■

The word decimal comes from the Latin word *decem* meaning 'ten'.

Many countries have a decimal money system. A British penny is one hundredth of a pound and an American cent is one hundredth of a dollar.

Some common fractions like ½ and ¼ are represented easily as decimal fractions:

½ = ⁵⁄₁₀ = 0·5,
¼ = ²⁵⁄₁₀₀ = 0·25,

but fractions like ⅓ go on for ever:

⅓ = 0·3333333333...

We write this as 0·$\dot{3}$

Unlike ⅓, the value of root two does not have a repeating pattern.

Something to do

Look out for decimals around you, on TV, in shops or in newspapers. What are they being used to measure?

Decimals can be added, subtracted, multiplied and divided just as whole numbers can. A calculator is useful for this. Explore what happens when you add two numbers bigger than a half but less than one, such as 0·75 and 0·6. What happens when you multiply them together?

See also
Arithmetic
Fractions
Numbers
Percentages

Deer

one year   three years   five years

Distribution
Mainly in cool woodlands, almost all in the northern hemisphere
Largest
Elk (called the moose in North America), height at the shoulder up to 2·3 m, weight up to 800 kg
Smallest
Pudu, height at shoulder 38 cm, weight as little as 7 kg. This is one of the few South American deer.
Number of young
1 or 2 per year
Lifespan
Varies with the species, moose and red deer are known to have survived for over 26 years.

Subphylum Vertebrata
Class Mammalia
Order Artiodactyla (cloven-hoofed animals)
Family Cervidae
Number of species 38

► Herd of fallow deer.

See also
Cattle
Domestication
Horns and antlers
Reindeer

Deer are cloven-hoofed animals that feed on plants and chew the cud as cows do. Most live in herds in cool woodlands, though some prefer swampy places. They use their hearing, smell and sight to detect enemies.

The males of most species of deer have branched, bony growths called antlers, growing from the top of their heads. The size of the antlers shows a male's age and position in the herd. In the breeding season they are used for spreading scent produced by glands on their faces. This attracts females and warns away other males. They are also used in fighting for females. Fighting males lock antlers and push, until the weaker deer breaks away and runs. The winner does not follow him far. He remains to protect and mate with the females, who seem quite uninterested in the noisy battles which take place around them.

Most deer produce only one calf (or fawn) at a time. It is able to stand almost as soon as it is born, but cannot, at first, follow its mother. She leaves it hidden in the undergrowth, where it is well camouflaged by its spotted coat. The mother does not go far from her baby and returns to feed it in the morning and evening. After a few weeks it is strong enough to join the herd.

Deer are eaten by many kinds of flesh eaters, but human beings are their most serious enemies. A few kinds of deer, such as the red deer, are now being farmed. ■

Democracy

See also
Congress
Elections
Government
Greek ancient history
Parliaments

Democracy means 'the rule of the people'. The ancient Greeks were the first people to have a democracy. The earliest democracy was in Athens, about 2,500 years ago. It was a meeting of all the free men of the city, who took decisions by vote. Women did not have the vote.

Today countries are too big for such meetings to be held. Instead, the people elect representatives to a parliament or a congress. The representatives then make decisions on the people's behalf. In this way the people have their say, by choosing representatives who will vote the way they want them to.

In a democracy everybody over a certain age can vote, and so take part in elections to government, whatever their race, religion or sex. Decisions are taken, and laws are passed, by a majority vote. In some countries, certain decisions must be taken by a minimum proportion of those voting, perhaps two-thirds. In other cases a majority of just one vote is enough. ■

Denmark

Denmark is a Scandinavian country in northern Europe. Greenland and the Faeroe Islands also belong to Denmark.

Denmark's mild climate and flat countryside are perfect for farming. Fields are neat and farmhouses are often half-timbered, whitewashed, and have thatched roofs. Denmark's main exports are butter, condensed milk, ham, bacon and beer.

Area
43,075 sq km
(16,631 sq miles)
Capital
Copenhagen
Population
5,124,794
Language
Danish
Religion
Christian
Government
Parliamentary monarchy
Currency
1 Danish krone = 100 øre

▶ Denmark is famous as the home of Lego, the construction toy. This is Legoland, a theme park at Billund, about 30 km from Esbjerg.

The Danes eat a lot of fish. The Danish fishing fleet lands millions of tonnes of cod, herring and shellfish each year. Fresh, warm Danish pastries, often with a soft vanilla or marzipan filling, are especially good with morning coffee. *Pølser*, grilled or fried sausages similar to hot dogs, are typical Danish street food.

Flashback

Denmark was a strong monarchy in the Middle Ages, controlling Sweden, Norway, Iceland and parts of Germany. In 1849 there was a new constitution and the monarch from then on ruled with elected representatives of the people. Denmark was neutral in World War I. It was occupied by Germany in World War II. ■

The Vikings came from Denmark and other parts of Scandinavia.

See also
Europe
Greenland
Vikings

Biography
Andersen (writer)
Bohr (scientist)
Brahe (scientist)

Dentists

Dentists show their patients how to look after their teeth and gums from an early age. But much of their work is with teeth that are diseased. They cut out the decayed parts of teeth and replace them with a filling. Sometimes they take out a whole tooth and put a false tooth in its place.

Dentists have to train for at least six years before they are allowed to start work. Some dentists work in hospitals or schools, but most have their own surgery.

Flashback

Skulls of early humans often contain crudely repaired teeth, and ancient false teeth have been discovered. In England in 1400 Henry IV appointed Matthew Flint as 'tooth-drawer in our City of London' and paid him sixpence a day to treat anyone needing attention. Having a tooth pulled was dangerous and agonizing. Sometimes it was done as a punishment, and was one of the executioner's jobs.

Until the 19th century, dentists had a very bad reputation. Then dental schools and hospitals were set up. In 1878 the British government passed a law to make sure dentists were properly trained. ■

A wood panel from an Egyptian tomb, 3000 BC, shows Hesi-Re, physician and dentist or 'toothist'.

The modern dental drill was invented in America in 1872; based on a sewing machine, powered by a treadle worked by the dentist's foot. The most recent drills, powered by compressed air or water, revolve at up to half a million times a minute.

The patron saint of dentistry is St Apollonia. She was tortured in AD 249 in Alexandria by having her teeth pulled out one at a time, because of her beliefs in Christian teachings.

See also
Teeth

Depressions

Depressions are areas in the world's atmosphere where the air pressure at the Earth's surface is low. This means that the air is rising. A depression is a type of cyclone. In Britain the weather is constantly affected by depressions. These depressions form over the Atlantic Ocean and move eastwards across Britain and western Europe.

Cold and warm air

In the northern hemisphere, cold air from the Arctic meets warm air from the tropics over the Atlantic Ocean. These two masses of air meet in a series of swirls because the Earth is spinning. Each swirl is a depression. Cold air moves around each side of a parcel of warm air, gradually squeezing it upwards from behind. Depressions move towards the east. The line where two different masses of air meet is called a 'front'. A depression has two fronts. The first is the forward edge of warm air pushing against cold air. This is the 'warm front'. Following it is the edge of cold air pushing against warm air. This is the 'cold front'.

Depressions over Europe

The warm and cold fronts are where most of the clouds form in a depression.

A depression may take a couple of days to pass over the British Isles. Since it is made up of two blocks of cold air, like a sandwich around a warm sector, the temperature on the ground changes as the depression passes over. As the warm front passes over, the temperature rises by one or two degrees Celsius and there is often low stratus cloud covering most of the sky, and a little rain. Behind the warm sector comes the second mass of cold air. This arrives at the cold front.

The cold front is pushing the warm air upwards. As the warm air rises, large clouds are formed, and there is heavy rain. Behind the cold front there are often big clouds that look like blobs of cotton wool. As the depression continues, the cold front usually moves faster than the warm front. Thus the cold front catches up the warm front and pushes the warm sector up above the ground. The two different masses of air start to mix and the front is called an occluded front.

Mediterranean depressions

Depressions also move through the region of the Mediterranean Sea. Most of these depressions form at the western end of the Mediterranean. But they also move eastwards. Some travel into the Middle East and

Warm air meets cold air
The boundary between a mass of warm air and a mass of cold air is called a **front**. This is what a front would look like if the Earth stood still. But because the Earth is spinning, the air is always mixing where warm and cold air meet. This happens in a series of swirls, called depressions.

Warm and cold fronts
A wedge of warm air is trapped in the cold air. The warm air gradually rises over the cooler air because it is lighter. The warm front is marked on weather maps by a line with half moons on it. The cold front is shown by a line with triangles. The air rises fastest at these points and the result is usually bad weather.

Bad weather
You can tell when a depression is coming by the clouds. First comes cirrus, then altocumulus, followed by stratus. Last of all, at the cold front, comes cumulonimbus, the big anvil-shaped rain clouds. Eventually the cold front catches up and the warm wedge of air is squeezed upwards.

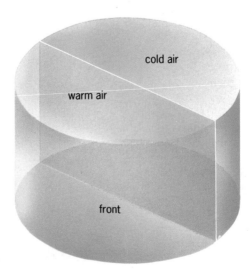

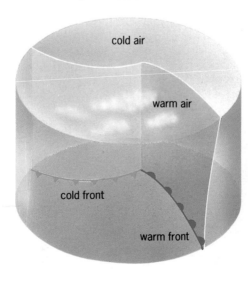

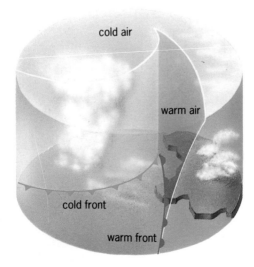

occasionally even as far as northern India. Most of these depressions occur in the spring or winter and bring rainfall to the Mediterranean region.

Strong winds blow at the fronts of depressions. When depressions pass over deserts in any part of the world, these strong winds can blow sand and dust from the earth. A wall of dust is raised and moves with the depression. It is hot and dirty and when the wall arrives everything goes dark as the air is filled with dust. ■

◄ This dust storm in South Australia has been blown by the strong winds at the front of a depression. A few minutes after this photograph was taken the photographer could not see his hand in front of his face because of the dust.

👁 See also
Clouds
Cyclones and anticyclones
Hurricanes
Weather

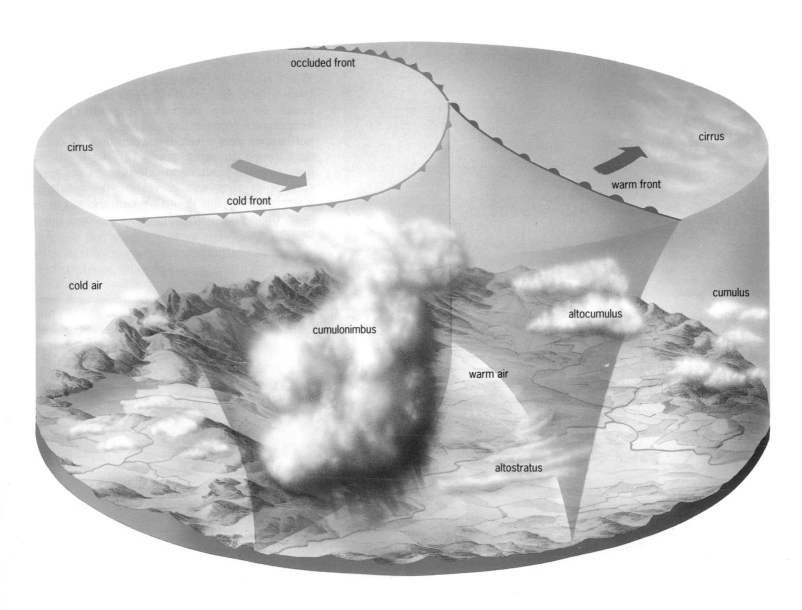

Designers

Designers are creative problem solvers who set out to meet needs which they or others have identified. This can mean designing a saleable gadget or article. Some of these products are designed to do a particular task, such as carrying small children. Fashion designers work out ideas for new clothes. Graphic designers produce posters, advertisements and page layouts for books. On a larger scale, interior designers try to improve the appearance and environment inside a building. Other designers tackle gardens, parks and even new towns. Some designers are involved in planning events or finding a better system or way of doing something, such as feeding lots of people at the same time. Whatever the problem, the designer has to solve it by making the best use of all the available resources, including materials, space and time. A well-designed solution will look good as well as work well.

▼ The first designer to use tubular steel for furniture was the Hungarian-born American Marcel Breuer, who worked in both Berlin and America in the 1930s. The idea came to him while riding his tubular-framed bicycle.

► Levi Strauss, an American immigrant tailor from Bavaria, designed the 501 denim jeans in 1850. Originally they were designed as work clothing, but since the 1960s Levi jeans have become fashionable for young and old.

► The Coca-Cola bottle was designed in 1955 by Raymond Loewy. Even though most coke is now sold in cans or plastic bottles, the company still uses the original bottle in advertisements because it is so popular and creates a particular image.

► In the late 1950s the British designer Alec Issigonis saw the need for a small car that performed well. He designed the Mini, which proved very popular and was still selling well in 1988.

The problem

There are many different ways to go about designing, but it usually starts from a need. Sometimes this need is identified by the designer who can write his or her own design brief, listing all the information that is known about the problem. In many cases the designer will work to a brief that other people have written.

Owen Finlay Maclaren was a retired aeroplane designer. In 1965 he saw the need for a lightweight, convenient pushchair for parents who wanted to take their children on buses or in a car.

Thinking and researching

Good designers are creative thinkers. Owen Maclaren had to decide how to tackle his problem. He thought about existing pushchairs and tried to think of different solutions. The idea of designing a pushchair that would fold up, like an umbrella, into a small space occurred to him.

He then had to think about how he could design one that would work. He did some research to find out about the materials he could use and how they could be joined. Some were too heavy or too expensive and others too difficult to use. The pushchair had to be safe and easy to use, and look good.

Developing ideas and planning

The first ideas which designers have usually need developing. Owen had to investigate the best way of constructing a frame that would fold easily. He made models to try out his ideas. Attaching the seat and wheels to the frame was one of the problems he had to solve. Careful drawings helped Owen clarify his ideas and provided the information about size, materials and construction that were needed to make the first 'Maclaren Buggy'.

Realization

The stage of turning the idea on paper into a real article is called realization. Designers often pass their drawings for new articles to other people to construct.

Owen made the prototype (first) buggy himself in his own workshops. He used the metal aluminium because it was very light. The new folding pushchair weighed only 2·7 kg (6 lb). Would it be convenient for parents and comfortable for toddlers?

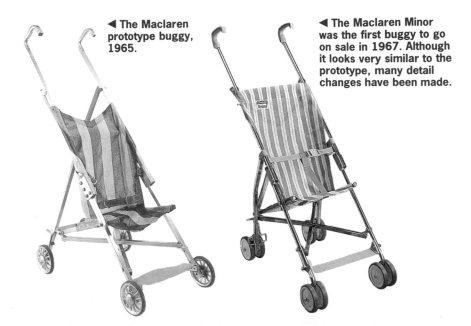

◄ The Maclaren prototype buggy, 1965.

◄ The Maclaren Minor was the first buggy to go on sale in 1967. Although it looks very similar to the prototype, many detail changes have been made.

Testing and evaluation

Once the prototype has been made, it is thoroughly tested to see if it works well or needs improving. The buggy was tested to see if it was safe. It was tried out by parents to see if they found it easy to use. Owen used his own observations and their comments to make some modifications. In February 1967 the first Maclaren Buggy went on sale. It proved a very successful design and many millions have been sold in over 50 countries. ■

▲ The latest buggy to be made by Maclaren shows that the designers have continued to develop the initial design of the prototype.

Detectives

When a crime has been committed, uniformed police are soon on the scene. They may be joined by other police officers in ordinary clothes, who belong to a section with just one duty: criminal investigation. The job of these detectives is to identify the people who committed the crime and bring them to trial.

This can be a very difficult job to do. For one thing, it is not enough to discover who has committed the crime. Detectives must provide evidence to the court which will convince the jury, beyond reasonable doubt, that the accused person did carry out the crime.

When looking for evidence, detectives may search for physical clues, such as fingerprints, bloodstains, weapons and the tools used. More often, though, they will collect evidence by interviewing people who might have some information about the crime. The most valuable evidence is often given by witnesses who actually saw the crime take place.

Modern aids for detectives

Detectives have many scientific aids in tracking down people who commit crimes. One of the most useful is the computer. The mass of information collected by detectives can be very difficult to sort out if it is all on paper. If, however, it is fed into a computer, it can be analysed electronically in a fraction of the time it would take a human brain to do it. For instance, police computers are often used to trace drivers from the licence plates of motor cars.

Detectives can also call on fingerprint experts, who can match prints found at the scene of a crime with those in police records.

Photographers can record the scene of a crime so that detectives can study it again and again. In the police laboratories, forensic scientists can match substances such as samples of blood, fragments of cloth or the dust in somebody's clothes. Many criminals have been found guilty with evidence such as this.

Questioning

Finally, when people are suspected of a crime, detectives can question them, often leading them to confess or betray themselves. There are rules about how such questioning is carried out, and it will always be recorded in writing or on tape or video. ■

In Britain the registration number of every motor vehicle with its owner's name and address is on the police computer.

The most important weapon against crime that detectives have is their network of information. This includes computerized sources, witnesses and informants, and all other evidence.

See also
Crimes
Fingerprints
Gangs and gangsters
Law
Police

Detergents

We need detergents because water, on its own, is not very good at wetting things and cleaning them. A detergent helps water to wet things more thoroughly and remove any dirt on them. Detergents are made from chemicals obtained from oil. They work in a similar way to soap, but do not form a scum.

How detergents are made

Most detergents are made by mixing alkyl-benzene, a chemical produced from crude oil, with sulphuric acid. The acid is then removed, leaving the detergent. Other substances are added to detergents to make them clean better. Chemicals called phosphates are added to soften the water. Enzymes may be put in the detergents to dissolve the stains on clothes made by blood, sweat, food and drinks. A substance is added to make the clothes look whiter, together with a foaming agent. The foaming agent produces a lather. It makes the water look soapy, but does not actually help with the cleaning.

Detergents and pollution

Early detergents were not easily broken down by the bacteria in sewage treatment works. As a result, these substances entered rivers. Rivers often became covered with foam. This foam prevented oxygen from getting to the water, so that fish and other water animals died. The detergents also washed the natural oils from water birds' feathers, and many of them became waterlogged and drowned.

More recently, scientists have developed detergents which are broken down by the bacteria at sewage works, but even these detergents are not perfect. They contain phosphates which, when they enter rivers and lakes, make water plants grow rapidly. When these plants die and decay, they take oxygen from the water. Without this oxygen, fish and other water animals cannot breathe, and so they die.

Detergents have been used to treat beaches polluted by oil. But too much detergent can cause as much damage to marine life as the oil itself. ■

The first detergents were developed by Fritz Gunther, a German scientist during World War I. Detergents for household use were available in the USA in the 1930s. They became common in America and Europe in the 1950s.

See also
Enzymes
Pollution
Soap

Developing countries

The developing countries include Bangladesh, Bolivia, Cuba, Ethiopia, Indonesia, Nigeria, Pakistan, Sri Lanka, Zambia and over a hundred more. China and India are both counted as developing countries.

Contrast between developed and developing world in the 1980s

Annual income per head of population

USA	$11,695
UK	$7,550
Haiti	$290
Burkina	$190
Bangladesh	$117

Literacy

USA	99%
UK	99%
Bangladesh	23·8%
Haiti	15%
Burkina	5%

Life expectancy

	Male	Female
USA	70	77
UK	71	77
Haiti	52	53
Bangladesh	47	48
Burkina	43	45

This is a term used to describe the countries of the world which are not rich and which are in the process of improving agriculture, building more factories and making better roads. They are also trying to improve the standard of living for people by building more and better schools, hospitals, clinics, and other services. These countries are also sometimes called the Third World.

There are huge differences between the individual nations but they do share some things in common. Many of them are in or near the tropics. Most were once ruled as colonies by European countries and became independent less than 50 years ago. Their European rulers encouraged farmers to grow tropical crops such as tea, coffee, cocoa, sugar cane, cotton and rubber which Europeans wanted. These crops were exported to factories in the ruling country. So were any useful minerals that were found.

When the colonies became independent, they could earn money by exporting raw materials, but they did not have many factories. In order to develop industry, many of these countries, especially those in South America and Africa, borrowed huge sums of money from the richer nations. Now they find it hard to pay off their debts.

Some Third World countries have managed to develop industries of their own. These are sometimes known as 'newly industrializing countries'. They are mainly in south-east Asia and South America.

Yet other developing countries are still very poor. Most of their people are farmers and there is very little industry. These are sometimes called the 'less developed countries'. Most of them are in Africa and southern Asia. These countries are given special help by the United Nations. ■

See also
Third World

Devil

The Devil is the name given to the most powerful evil being that exists. Religious people believe that he is not as powerful as God, and many people today think that he is a symbol for wickedness, not a real being. Other names for him are Baalzebub, Satan or even 'old Nick'.

The origin of the idea of the Devil among Jews and Christians seems to be the belief that some angels rebelled against God and were thrown out of heaven. These were called demons or devils and the leader of them is the Devil. He and his hosts of demons have been fighting with God ever since. Hell is the place where demons and the Devil live. In the Middle Ages Christian artists painted vivid pictures of the wicked being tortured in hell after their death.

One of the most famous stories about the Devil is how he tried to tempt Jesus to use his special powers in wrong ways. But Jesus resisted his temptations.

Muslims use the Arabic name *Iblis* for the Devil. He has a similar place in Islam to that of the Devil in Christianity. ■

The name 'devil' comes from the Greek word *diabolos*, meaning 'slanderer'. This is where the word 'diabolical' comes from.

See also
God
Hell

Dew

You can see dew early in the morning as tiny droplets of water on grass and on the threads of spider webs.

Dew comes from moisture in the air that has been cooled to form water droplets. If you boil a kettle, steam disappears into the air; the air is cooled when it touches a cold window and the water vapour turns into liquid water droplets called condensation.

In the garden, air just above the ground has a lot of moisture in it. This is water from the soil and from plants themselves. At night, water vapour condenses on the cold grass to form dew. ■

If the temperature drops below zero and dew freezes, it is known as hoarfrost.

See also
Cold
Fog
Frost
Rain
Weather

Diabetes

About one person in every 100 in the UK has diabetes.

Diabetes is a disease in which the body is unable to control the levels of sugar in the blood or tissues. This problem starts because not enough of a hormone called insulin is being made in the pancreas, a small gland tucked behind the stomach. If diabetes is untreated it can be very dangerous.

Uncontrolled changes in sugar levels can cause great tiredness and then unconsciousness. But, with proper treatment, a person with diabetes can lead a normal life.

Treatment might be simply a change in diet. More often it consists of drugs in the form of pills that boost insulin manufacture in the body, or the injecting of extra insulin.

If extra insulin has to be given, it must be injected, and diabetics soon learn to inject themselves with this life-saving hormone once or twice a day.

Nowadays microbes (bacteria) can be changed so that they make large amounts of human insulin. This is an example of genetic engineering. In the past doctors had to use pig or cow insulin. ■

⊙ **See also**
Blindness
Genetics
Hormones

Diamonds

The weight of diamonds is measured in carats. 1 carat is equivalent to 0 2 g. The largest diamond ever found weighed 3,105 carats, or 621 g.

Diamonds are valuable gemstones. Natural or 'rough' diamonds look like small pebbles of cloudy glass. The finest stones are either colourless or blue-white. It is only after they are cut and polished that diamonds take on their brilliant sparkle.

Diamond is the hardest known natural substance. One diamond can be cut only by another diamond.

Diamonds are crystals of pure carbon. They occur in all shapes and sizes. They were formed under great heat and pressure, often in the cores of ancient volcanoes at great depths. They are found in igneous rocks and gravels in areas as far apart as South Africa, Australia, Brazil, India and Siberia. South Africa and Russia are the largest producers.

Diamonds can also be made out of graphite, the substance in pencil 'lead'. The graphite is squeezed in giant presses at a very high temperature. However, the diamonds produced are minute.

These synthetic diamonds and small natural diamonds are useful for making dentists' drills, glass cutters and the teeth of diamond saws used for cutting rocks. ■

▲ **A diamond cut into the shape of a pear.**

⊙ **See also**
Carbon
Crystals
Gems
Minerals

Dictators

Dictators are rulers who have complete power over the countries they govern. Many dictators seize power by force. For example, Francisco Franco, who ruled Spain for 36 years until his death in 1975, took office following a civil war. He used the title of *el Caudillo* (the leader).

Most dictators have the title of president, but they are not democratic heads of state elected by their people like, for example, the president of the USA.

The best-known dictators of modern times were Adolf Hitler, who ruled Germany from 1933 to 1945, and Joseph Stalin, who ruled the USSR for 29 years from 1924 until his death in 1953. Both men used secret police to control their political opponents, and had many of them put to death. Hitler's ally, Benito Mussolini, was dictator of Italy from 1922 to 1943.

Several African and Latin American nations, such as Uganda and Haiti, have been ruled by dictators during the 20th century.

In ancient Rome the Senate used to appoint one man as a temporary dictator in time of war or other emergency. In 44 BC Julius Caesar was appointed dictator for life, but he was assassinated almost at once. ■

In Latin American countries, dictatorship is often called *personalismo* or *caudillismo*. *Personalismo* means that people glorify the leader of the country, like General Santa Anna in Mexico in the 19th century or Juan Perón in Argentina in the 20th century. Many South American *caudillos* have ruled as dictators just as Franco did in Spain.

⊙ **See also**
German history
Russia's history
Spain's history

Biography
Caesar
Franco
Hitler
Mussolini
Stalin

Diets

The type of food which you eat most of the time is called your diet. Your diet should provide all the things that your body needs for growth, repair and health. Sometimes people change their diet for health reasons. This may be to lose weight, to control a disease, to prepare for sporting events, or because they are pregnant.

Healthy eating

A healthy diet is one that provides the right nutrients in the right amounts. A diet that includes plenty of cereals, fruit and vegetables provides a good balance of nutrients. A diet that is mostly made up of chips, sweets and salty snacks is much less healthy, because it is unbalanced. It contains too much fat, sugar and salt, and not enough protein and vitamins.

People's diets vary from country to country, and this can affect their health. The people of Japan and China are often healthier than those in many Western countries. This is because their diet is well balanced. It contains a lot of vegetables and cereals, especially rice, but little sugar and hardly any milk or cream. Many people in Europe, North America and Australia eat lots of meat, eggs, cream, cakes, sweets and biscuits. This kind of diet is unbalanced. People who eat this kind of diet are more likely to be overweight, and to have heart disease, high blood pressure and tooth decay. Such people may spend more money on their food, but they may be less healthy than people in poorer countries who have a simpler diet.

Slimming diets

Clever advertisements and magazine articles are full of diets which are supposed to make you slim. In fact no food has any special slimming properties. The only sensible way to get, and stay, slim, is to eat less fattening food (fats, oils and sugars), and take more exercise. This will help remove excess fat from the body and make you feel stronger as well.

Special diets

Pregnant women should eat more high protein foods (eggs, fish and meat) than they usually do, because these are needed for their baby's growth. Athletes also need proteins to develop their muscles, and starchy foods such as bread or pasta for energy.

Some people cannot eat certain foods because they cause allergies such as skin rashes. Others must avoid foods they cannot digest. People with coeliac disease, for instance, cannot digest gluten in wheat and so avoid all things made from wheat flour. ■

See also

Allergies
Cereals
Fats
Food
Malnutrition
Nutrition
Obesity
Proteins

Special diets

Low animal fat (low cholesterol) diets for people suffering from heart disease.
Low sugar diets for diabetics.
Low salt diets for people with high blood pressure.
High fibre diets for people with constipation and digestive upsets.

Hospitals employ dietitians to plan special meals for people who have digestive diseases such as ulcers, or who are recovering from an operation.

Eat less of these

Fats and oils give you a lot of energy, so it is easy to eat more than you need. They make you fat and cause heart disease.

Sweet foods give you energy but nothing else. They rot your teeth and make you fat.

Factory processed foods have some goodness removed, and salt, sugar, colouring, preservatives and other chemicals added.

Eat more of these

Low fat proteins build you up without making you fat.

Vegetables and cereals give energy, vitamins, minerals and fibre. They fill you up without making you fat.

Fruit gives energy, vitamins and minerals to keep you healthy.

Digestive systems

The digestive system of an animal breaks its food down into liquid. The gut is a long tube that stretches from the mouth to the anus.

You chew food to break it into small pieces which are easy to swallow. Your front teeth bite off a chunk. Then your tongue pushes it to your back grinding teeth. These break up food and mix it with saliva. Saliva is produced by the salivary glands. It softens the food and begins to digest it. When the food is well chewed you swallow it.

The chewed food then passes down the gullet (oesophagus) to the stomach. It is pushed through the gut by muscular squeezing called peristalsis. In the stomach it is churned up and mixed with acid and digestive juices called enzymes. The acid and digestive enzymes kill any bacteria in the food and help to break it down into smaller substances which will dissolve in water. This enables the food to pass easily through the gut wall into the blood.

Partly digested food is passed from the stomach to the small intestine. Here digestion is continued by more digestive enzymes produced by the wall of the intestine and a gland called the pancreas. Digestion is helped by bile from the gall-bladder in the liver. Bile acts as a detergent, changing oily food into tiny droplets which are easier to digest.

The small intestine is lined with a carpet of tiny, finger-shaped bumps called villi. These give the intestine a huge surface area. Through it digested (liquid) food, along with vitamins, minerals and water, is taken into the blood. The blood system carries it first to the liver, and then to all parts of the body, to provide energy and materials for growth and repair.

The parts of food which cannot be digested, such as fibre from vegetables and fruit, pass into the large intestine. The large intestine is made up of the colon, rectum and anus. The undigested food remains in the colon for between 12 and 36 hours. Water and salt are removed from it during this time. It passes into the rectum and out of the anus as faeces. ■

Your small intestine is over 6 m long and, because of its villi, has an inside surface area of 10 sq m. There are about 40 villi in each square millimetre of small intestine.

◉ See also
Blood
Enzymes
Glands
Human body
Livers
Mouths
Stomachs
Teeth

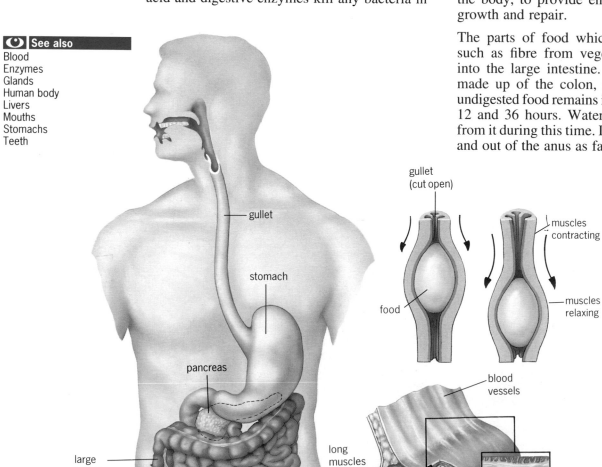

gullet

stomach

pancreas

large intestine

appendix

rectum

small intestine

gullet (cut open)

muscles contracting

food

muscles relaxing

◀ Food is moved along the gullet to the stomach by circular muscles. These muscles squeeze together (contract) behind the food, and relax in front of the food so that it is pushed along. The food moves forwards at about 20 cm a second.

blood vessels

long muscles

circular muscles

villi

◀ A carpet of villi 1 mm high lines the small intestine. These give the intestine a huge surface area for absorbing digested food.

Dinosaurs

Dinosaurs were among the most varied and amazing kinds of animals that have ever lived on Earth. They were a type of reptile, related to the crocodiles and also the birds. Some, like *Compsognathus*, were as small as a chicken. Others, like *Apatosaurus*, were larger than ten elephants. These are just two different species. Over a thousand species of dinosaurs are known to have existed.

The first dinosaurs lived about 225 million years ago. The last ones lived about 65 million years ago. So we know that dinosaurs flourished on Earth for about 160 million years.

Strange giant bones

Dinosaurs are known from their fossils, the remains of their bones preserved in the rocks. The first fossil of a dinosaur that was recorded came from a stone quarry near Oxford. The end of a giant thigh-bone was brought to Robert Plot, the Professor of Chemistry at Oxford University, in 1677. Plot had no idea that it came from a giant extinct reptile. He thought it might have come from an elephant, or from a giant human being. More giant bones were found here and there in the next century, but no one had any idea what they were.

In the 1820s more bones were found near Oxford and the Professor of Geology studied them. These bones included a jaw with long, sharp teeth, each the size of a steak knife. He realized that these came from a giant extinct reptile, and he gave it a name: *Megalosaurus*, meaning 'giant lizard'. This was the first dinosaur to be named.

The second species of dinosaur given a name was *Iguanodon* (iguana tooth). The name was invented by Gideon Mantell, who thought it was a giant lizard, since the fossil teeth were like those of a modern iguana lizard, only dozens of times bigger.

More fossils were found and the English scientist Sir Richard Owen showed that they belonged to a group of large reptiles that had lived a very long time ago, and which were quite unlike any of the living reptiles: lizards, snakes, turtles and crocodiles. He invented the name dinosaurs, from Greek words meaning 'terrible lizards'.

Bone hunters

In America, in the late 19th century, teams of bone collectors went to the western states of Wyoming, Montana, Colorado, and Utah, and

sent huge crates of bones back to the museums and universities of the east coast. Often whole freight trains would be loaded with hundreds of tonnes of these dinosaur bones.

Nowadays large teams of dinosaur collectors visit parts of Australia, China, Africa, central Asia, Europe and America. Fossils of dinosaurs are still being found all over the world.

Putting flesh on the fossils

How do the scientists who study dinosaurs know what they were like when they were alive? After all, most of the evidence we have about dinosaurs is their fossilized bones and a few footprints. Yet in museums and books there are full-colour paintings of just what the dinosaurs are supposed to have looked like. How accurate are these reconstructions?

▲ Uncovering dinosaur bones in the Uintak Bad Lands of Utah, North America in the early 20th century.

Subphylum
Vertebrata
Class
Reptilia
Order
Dinosauria
Number of species
More than 1,000

Largest number of dinosaurs found together
Over 100 skeletons of *Coelophysis* in a Late Triassic rock deposit found in 1947 in New Mexico, USA.

◄ Sometimes fossil dinosaur footprints are found in the rock. These provide evidence of how fast dinosaurs could move and whether they lived in herds.

► From dinosaur bones we can build up a picture of what the dinosaur may have looked like.

► First the skeleton of the dinosaur is made up from the bones that have been found. Almost always some of the bones are missing, so they have to be made up with plaster or fibreglass as best can be. The skeleton then tells us the general size and shape of the dinosaur, and how it stood.

► Next, the size and the positions of the main muscles of the body are guessed at, as well as the likely outline of the belly. In this way, the overall shape that the body would have been can be worked out.

► Finally the scientist must guess what the scales and the skin were like when the animal was alive. He or she can also imagine what colour it was, and perhaps what kind of expression it had on its face.

Biggest dinosaur egg
Hypselosaurus egg from the Late Cretaceous of France: 30 cm long; 2 litre capacity.

Reconstructions

The first job of the scientist is to make sure that the bones are collected properly. There may be other fossils in the rocks, such as leaves, insects or shells, that give clues about the climate and the plants of the dinosaurs' world. Rocks can also give a great deal of information about the climate, and about whether the bones are preserved in an ancient river or lake, for example.

The bones are carefully mapped in the place where they are found, so that they can be put back together again in the laboratory. Each bone then has to be wrapped in sackcloth soaked in plaster in order to protect it. Back in the museum laboratory, the plaster cast is cut away, and the bones are carefully cleaned up. The rock in which the bones are often embedded has to be carefully removed, with chisels and needles. The bones can then be fixed together with a metal frame for display in a museum as a complete skeleton.

If scientists discover that the dinosaur is a new kind that has never been found before, they will study the bones carefully in order to find out how the animal lived, and what other kinds of dinosaur it is related to. They can guess where the big muscles were and so work out the shape of the body as it was. The bones also show how the dinosaur walked and ran, and the teeth show what it ate. Fossil footprints of some dinosaurs have also been found and these can also give clues as to how the dinosaurs moved.

The main thing that is not based on known facts is the colour. We cannot tell whether dinosaurs were green, grey and brown, like modern reptiles, or whether they were purple with orange spots. We can only suppose that they blended in with the landscape.

Main groups of dinosaurs

So far more than a thousand species of dinosaurs have been discovered and given names. But some of these are known from only a few bits of bones, so we have not much idea of what they were like.

The first dinosaurs were fairly small two-legged creatures which fed on insects and lizards. They had long tails, and short arms which could be used to grasp things. Sometime in the Triassic period of Earth's history, about 200 million years ago, the dinosaurs evolved into two main branches. These can be told apart by the way their hip-bones are arranged. Those with lizard-like hips are called Saurischia; and those with bird-like hips, Ornithischia.

The lizard-hipped Saurischia split into two lines in the Late Triassic period. The first of these, the Theropoda (beast feet), walked on two legs and ate meat. The chicken-sized *Compsognathus* and the fearsome 15 m (50 ft) long *Tyrannosaurus* belonged to this group. The other lizard-hipped line, the Sauropodomorpha (reptile feet), were plant eaters. Some of the

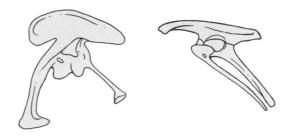

species in this group, such as *Diplodocus* and *Apatosaurus*, had enormously long necks. We suppose this enabled them to stretch up for leaves and twigs on tree-tops.

The bird-hipped dinosaurs, the Ornithischia, were plant eaters. Their fossils are first found in rocks of the Early Jurassic period. One type, the Ornithopoda (bird feet), included animals that walked on two legs. *Iguanodon* was one of these. The other bird-hipped dinosaurs were all armoured, with great bony plates on their backs, like *Stegosaurus*; spiny backs, like *Scolosaurus*; or horned heads, like *Pentaceratops*.

◀ Dinosaurs can be divided into two main groups with different shaped hips. The saurischians had hips like lizards. The ornithischians had hips more like birds.

Long dinosaur
Diplodocus 27 m

Tall dinosaur
Brachiosaurus 12 m

Small dinosaur
Compsognathus 75–91 cm; 3 kg

Large dinosaur
Ultrasaurus
Length 20 m
Weight 130 tonnes

Other species of dinosaurs are being discovered and probably even larger species existed.

◀ This is a family tree to show how the dinosaurs evolved over millions of years.

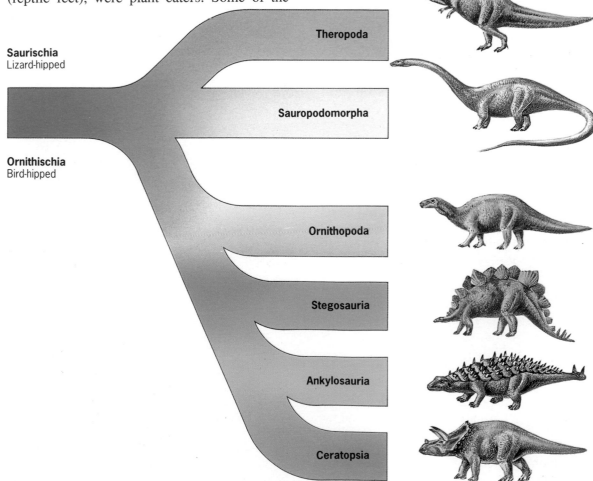

Saurischia
Lizard-hipped

Ornithischia
Bird-hipped

Theropoda

Sauropodomorpha

Ornithopoda

Stegosauria

Ankylosauria

Ceratopsia

have been feeding all day, because they were so large, up to 100 tonnes in weight, and because of the relatively small size of their heads. Some of the ornithopods were able to eat very tough plants like reeds and ferns. This is shown by their unusual teeth, which were arranged in many rows. Some of them had as many as 2,000 teeth in operation at any time! The theropods were all meat eaters. The small theropods must have fed on lizards and other small animals, but the larger ones must have preyed on the plant-eating dinosaurs.

The end of the dinosaurs

No one knows why the dinosaurs disappeared. As far as we can tell, the dinosaurs lived right to

Warm-blooded or cold?

▲ Reconstruction of reptiles in their natural habitat in the late Triassic period, about 220 million years ago. Numbers 2 and 3 are dinosaurs.

1 *Kuehneosaurus*
2 *Plateosaurus*
3 *Coelophysis*

► Some of the dinosaurs and plants which lived 150 million years ago (Jurassic period) in America.

1 *Diplodocus*
2 *Stegosaurus*
3 *Camarasaurus*
4 *Allosaurus*
5 *Compsognathus*

Scientists do not know whether dinosaurs were warm-blooded or cold-blooded. A cold-blooded animal like a lizard needs heat from the Sun to keep warm. It does not always have cold blood and it does need to warm up to become active. Warm-blooded animals, such as birds and human beings, burn up food to keep their bodies at the same warm temperature all the time. Since the climate was warm, the dinosaurs would have had no problem in keeping warm during the day. The big dinosaurs could stay warm through the night because it would take a long time for their massive bodies to lose heat. Smaller dinosaurs may have warmed themselves by exercise. Scientists are still arguing about these questions.

Dinosaur diets

Most dinosaurs fed on plants. Some of the giant sauropodomorphs probably ate the leaves of the tops of trees, using their long necks. They must the end of the Cretaceous period, 65 million years ago, and then disappeared quite suddenly. Up to this time, there had been no more than a small dwindling in the numbers of kinds of dinosaurs. The main problem that faces scientists is to know exactly how long the disappearance of the dinosaurs took. It could have happened in one day, or it might have taken as much as a million years. It is not yet possible to tell more accurately than this.

Many other kinds of plants and animals disappeared at about the same time. In the sea, the ammonites and belemnites disappeared, as well as the last of the great sea reptiles: the long-necked plesiosaurs, and the mosasaurs.

So what did happen?

There are two main theories now which explain the disappearance of the dinosaurs. One is that climates were changing and becoming cooler everywhere. The dinosaurs and many other animals and plants were not able to adapt enough to the new colder conditions. After a time, they just died off.

The other theory is that the Earth was hit by a giant meteorite. This exploded on the surface of the Earth and sent up a huge cloud of dust which spread around the Earth and blacked out the Sun. This caused the Earth to freeze up for a while. Plants and animals died off everywhere, and only those which could withstand the cold were able to survive and then recolonize the Earth a year or so later. No one can decide which of these theories is correct. ■

▲ These dinosaurs (and the pterodactyl) lived on land that is now Canada about 75 million years ago in the late Cretaceous period.

1 *Pterodactylus*
2 *Tyrannosaurus*
3 *Parasaurolophus*
4 *Struthiomimus*

See also

Earth
Evolution of living things
Extinct animals
Fossils
Geological time
Prehistoric animals

Diseases

A disease, or illness, happens when all or part of the body is not working correctly. This may be caused by something which goes wrong inside the body, by germs and other parasites, by diet or by other outside causes.

Germs and disease

Germs are very simple microscopic creatures which cause disease. They include viruses, bacteria and fungi.

Viruses cause colds, flu, chickenpox, mumps and other diseases in humans, foot and mouth disease in cattle, and mosaic disease, which destroys the leaves of many crop plants.

Bacteria cause food poisoning, whooping cough and tuberculosis in humans, tetanus (lockjaw) in humans and cattle, and canker in fruit trees.

Fungi cause athlete's foot and ringworm in humans, foot rot in cattle, and many serious plant diseases such as mildew and blight.

The spread of germs

Colds, flu and tuberculosis are spread by coughs and sneezes, which can hurl germ-laden droplets of moisture up to 4 m (13 ft). Many germs are spread when infected animals or humans touch healthy ones. Germs can be left behind on such things as cups, towels and combs, and spread to other people using them. Food and drink are easily contaminated with germs from dirty hands, flies, and pets. Mosquitoes and fleas can spread germs when they bite skin to suck blood.

Diet and disease

A diet containing vitamins and minerals is essential for health. Vitamin D and calcium are needed for strong bones and teeth, and vitamin C is needed for healthy skin and gums, and to heal wounds. Heart disease can be caused by eating too much fat, tooth decay by too much sugar, and too much salt can cause high blood pressure.

Developmental diseases

Sometimes, as a baby grows inside its mother, parts of it are not formed correctly. The heart, for instance, may grow with a hole between its right and left sides so blood does not flow properly.

Inherited diseases

These are passed from parents to their young. The offspring are born with them and cannot be cured, but treatment can often lessen the harmful effects. Examples are haemophilia, in which the blood clots very slowly, and sickle cell disease in which some red blood cells are sickle-shaped and cannot carry oxygen.

Mental diseases

These are problems of the mind. They show themselves as unusual or dangerous behaviour, or by great unhappiness (depression). They can harm a person just as seriously as other diseases.

Preventing disease

Preventing disease is as important as curing disease. Infection is reduced by a healthy way of life, including: keeping yourself clean, caring for your teeth, eating a healthy diet, controlling your weight, not smoking or taking drugs or drinking too much alcohol, and by taking regular exercise. Immunization against germs, especially in babies, is also very important. ∎

The most common infectious disease is the common cold. More than 900,000 working days are lost as a result of this disease in Great Britain alone each year.

In Western countries more people die from diseases of the heart and blood vessels than any other disease. They are caused by eating too much fat, sugar and salt and not exercising enough.

▲ Sickle cell anaemia is an inherited disease. The red blood cells, which are normally circular, become elongated. This picture shows normal cells and sickle cells.

▶ Every time you sneeze droplets of water and mucus fly out. If you have a cold or flu these droplets contain germs which can affect those around you, so you must always sneeze into a handkerchief.

▶ This tree is diseased. It is being killed by chestnut blight.

Divers

Divers may go beneath the surface of the sea for a number of reasons: to assist in building docks, repairing oil rigs, salvaging ships, or perhaps just to explore the sea-bed.

The simplest form of diving is to fill your lungs with air by taking a deep breath and then dive as deep as you can. Unassisted diving like this allows you to stay below for no more than about 2 minutes and to reach a depth of about 10 m (30 ft).

To stay down longer or go deeper you must be supplied with oxygen or air, which, of course, contains oxygen. The ordinary diver's suit is made of rubber and has a metal helmet with a glass window in it. A pump on the surface forces air down a pipe connected to the diver's suit and allows fresh air to be breathed.

▶ Pressurized diving bell with emergency tanks and umbilical cord, on a ship in the North Sea.

After a long, deep dive a diver may be kept in a decompression chamber for hours and even days.

The stale air which the diver breathes out escapes from the suit and bubbles up to the surface. With a suit like this, a diver can go down to about 60 m (200 ft). With an aqualung, a diver uses a mask to breathe oxygen directly from bottles carried on the back. There is no need for an air line to the surface, so the diver can swim around much more easily.

The deeper divers go the greater the pressure of water, and the more the nitrogen in the air they breathe dissolves in the blood. When this happens divers must come up very slowly or the nitrogen will form bubbles in the blood rather like the bubbles you see when you take the top off a lemonade bottle. This effect is very painful and is called 'the bends'. It is very dangerous, and if divers come up too quickly it will kill them.

Flashback

The type of diving suit with metal helmet and air line was designed by Siebe in 1830 and is still in use. In World War II many navies used 'frogmen' who carried their own air in bottles on their backs and wore flippers on their feet. When divers today have to go to a great depth they breathe a mixture of oxygen and a special gas called helium which has the strange effect of making their voices sound squeaky. ■

▲ Scuba diver equipped with camera and flash unit, in the Red Sea, Israel.

SCUBA divers are divers who carry their own air supply with them in aqualungs. **S**elf **C**ontained **U**nderwater **B**reathing **A**pparatus.

Scuba divers have reached depths of over 130 m.

People have dived over 80 m just holding their breath, but deep diving like this is extremely dangerous.

See also
Air
Breathing
Pressure
Swimming

Divorce

Divorce is the ending of a marriage according to the law. Some religions do not allow divorce but regard people as married for ever. The laws about divorce vary from one country to another, and sometimes from state to state within a country. This is true in the United States of America.

The people seeking divorce have to agree about sharing fairly all the things that belonged to them as a married couple. In Britain the law court

sometimes makes an order telling the couple what they must do if they cannot agree. The court insists that proper arrangements are made for any children of the marriage, and wants to know what the children's wishes are about whom they will live with. A special court officer often meets the children to talk it over with them. If at all possible, arrangements are made so that the parent who is not living with the children can still have access (see them regularly). ■

In the West the number of people getting divorced has increased rapidly. In Great Britain about 1 in 3 marriages end in divorce. Britain and Denmark have the highest divorce rates in Europe.

See also
Marriage

Diwali

► An Indian girl holds one of the *divas* (lamps) used to celebrate the festival of Diwali. The *divas* were originally clay bowls filled with oil or *ghee* (clarified butter) and a cotton wick. Nowadays small candles or electric lights are also used to decorate houses, temples and gurdwaras.

Diwali (or Deepavali) means a row or garland of lights. It is the name given to an autumn festival which is celebrated for different reasons by Hindus and Sikhs.

The most famous Diwali story is from the *Ramayana*, an Indian poem. Rama, the rightful ruler of Ayodhya, goes into exile for fourteen years. His faithful wife, Sita, and one of his brothers go with him into the forest. Sita is kidnapped by the wicked demon Ravana. Hanuman, the monkey-god, helps Rama to rescue her and they kill Ravana. After fourteen years, Rama returns to his kingdom and the people welcome him by lining the streets with *divas*.

Hindus make offerings to Lakshmi, the goddess of wealth, who is believed to visit clean, brightly lit homes at Diwali. They decorate their doorsteps with *rangoli* patterns, entertain their friends, give each other presents and send Diwali cards.

Sikhs also decorate their homes and exchange gifts. They remember the story of Guru Hargobind, who refused to be freed from captivity without 52 Hindu fellow prisoners. He was told that all those who could hold onto his cloak could leave; so he wore a cloak with tassels and they all left together. ■

See also
Festivals
Hindus
Ramayana
Sikhs

Djibouti

Djibouti is a small state on the east coast of Africa at the southern entrance to the Red Sea, an area known as the Horn of Africa. The country is a member of the League of Arab States. The people of Djibouti are mainly of Somali and Ethiopian origin. Most of those who live in the foothills outside the capital city (also called Djibouti) are extremely poor and make a meagre living from grazing animals.

Djibouti city is a hot and humid port. Between 1883 and 1977, France controlled the country. ■

Area
23,200 sq km
(8,960 sq miles)
Capital
Djibouti
Population
470,000
Language
Arabic, French, Somali, Afar
Religion Muslim
Government
Republic
Currency
1 Djibouti franc = 100 centimes

See also
Africa
Arabs
Middle East

DNA

DNA (DeoxyriboNucleic Acid) is a chemical substance found in every cell in every part of your body and it is responsible for what you look like and for making your body work properly.

DNA looks like a twisted ladder with each rung consisting of a pair of chemicals. It is a very long ladder, made of thousands of shorter ladders joined together. These shorter ladders, each with about 200 rungs, are called genes. Each gene carries a coded message that allows one type of protein to be made. The different proteins then determine every detail of your appearance: colour of hair and eyes; shape of nose and ears. The genes also contain the instructions needed to keep a cell working, whether it is in your liver, brain or blood.

Every cell in your body contains the same DNA but it is not found in a cell as one long twisted ladder. The DNA comes as 46 different ladders. Each of these DNA ladders is called a chromosome. 23 of these chromosomes are from your mother and 23 are from your father, which is why you may look like your parents. ■

▲ Tiny pieces of six different chemicals join together to form DNA. The shape is a double helix (spiral), too small to be seen with a normal microscope.

See also
Genetics
Proteins
Reproduction

Biography
Crick and Watson
Franklin, Rosalind

Docks

A dock is an enclosed area of water where ships are loaded and unloaded. Ships enter and leave through a lock. This means that the water in the dock can be kept at a constant level, even though the sea-level outside is changing with the tides. ■

See also
Locks
Ships

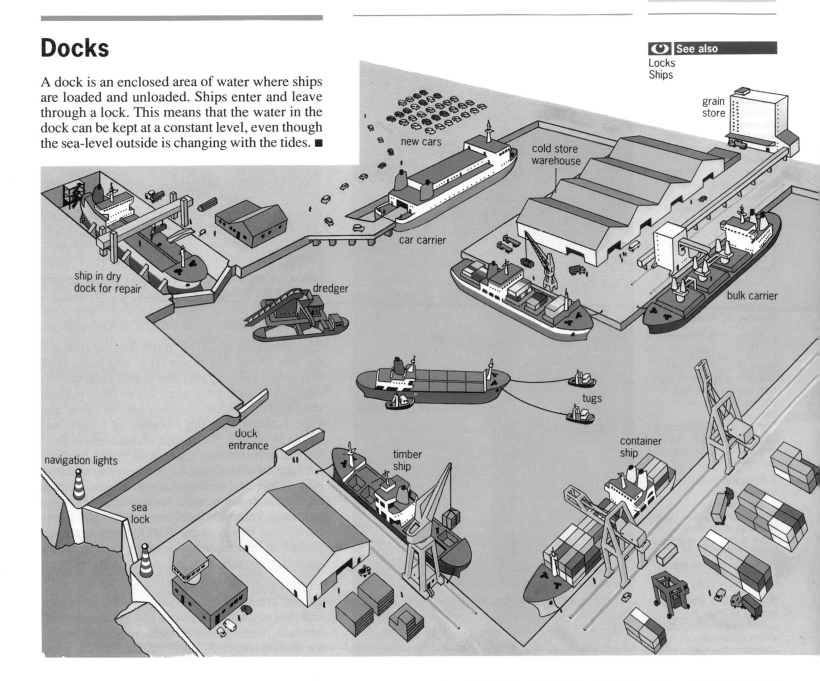

new cars

grain store

cold store warehouse

car carrier

ship in dry dock for repair

dredger

bulk carrier

tugs

navigation lights

dock entrance

container ship

sea lock

timber ship

Doctors

People with the title of Doctor are usually doctors of medicine, who have been trained to prevent and cure illness.

The training varies from country to country, but normally students study medical sciences for two or three years, then practise dealing with patients for another two or three years. The medical schools are usually part of a university. Most countries keep a register of doctors who are qualified, and have laws making it illegal for people not on the register to work as doctors. Laws forcing all doctors to be trained were not

passed until 1858 in Britain, and 1909 in the USA.

There are two main types of medical doctor: the family doctor or general practitioner, and the specialist. People who are ill usually go first to a general practitioner (GP) in a local health centre or consulting room. The GP diagnoses any problem, and decides whether to treat the patient or to send the patient to a specialist for treatment.

Specialist doctors usually work in hospitals. Some specialize in surgery, some in looking after children or old people, and others in treating particular diseases. In a big hospital there might be 50 to 100 specialist doctors. ■

University and college teachers often have the title Doctor. This means they have a degree, called Doctor of Philosophy. This can be in any subject, but must involve some original research.

See also
Clinics
Hospitals
Medicine
Surgeons
Biography
Garrett Anderson
Hippocrates

Dolls

Dolls are toys which are shaped in human form. Throughout history they have been given to children for them to play with and also to help them learn about their world. Egyptian graves from thousands of years BC have been found to contain dolls made from wood and clay.

These days dolls are usually made from moulded plastic and vinyl. They often have moving limbs, and modern technology has produced dolls which can move on their own and say simple sentences. Some of the best-selling dolls like Sindy and Barbie dolls, have many clothes and accessories for children to collect. In the same way, Action Man dolls are sold with lots of items of uniform and weapons. Very often a successful film or television programme will lead to dolls being made of the main characters.

Flashback

Doll-makers have been in business for many hundreds of years. Nuremberg in Germany became a centre for Dochenmacher (doll makers) in the 15th century, and for the next four centuries Germany remained the main country for doll and toy making. Any dolls from that time which still exist are extremely valuable collectors' items. In 1987, Sotheby's, the London auctioneers, sold a 17th-century doll for £67,100 to someone who was starting a doll museum.

Sometimes dolls have been used for religious purposes. In ancient Greece and Rome, girls dedicated their childhood dolls to the goddesses Venus and Diana when they reached the age when they could be married. And in the Middle Ages, Christians in Europe began to use dolls to make models of the nativity scene to teach children about the birth of Jesus. In North America, too, Hopi Indians use kachina dolls to teach their children about their religious customs. The Hopi children, though, are also allowed to play with these dolls for fun. And throughout the world this remains the main reason why children want dolls. ∎

See also
Toys

◀ Laetitia Powell dressed this doll in 1792, in fashionable visiting dress. Laetitia dressed many dolls and labelled them with the date and the type of outfit they were wearing. The doll's head is a later replacement.

◀ This doll was dressed to look like a pedlar in the 1850s. You would know a pedlar by her red cloak, black bonnet and the tray of small wares which she travelled around the country selling.

▶ A doll that was popular with young children in the 1980s.

◀ On the fifth day of the fifth month of the year, Japanese families celebrate the boys' festival. The girls' festival is on the third day of the third month. This warrior, in full dress, is brought out for the boys to see on 5 May.

Dolphins

▲ Spinner dolphins are very acrobatic and they get their name from the way they jump high out of the water and spin round in the air, apparently just for fun.

Largest
Killer whale, up to 10 m long
Smallest
Tucuxi, which may measure little more than 1 m and weighs about 36 kg. There are several other species about 1·5 m long.
Number of young
1 every other year. All baby dolphins are very large, some are half the length of their mother at birth and most are about ⅔ of her length. Most species suckle for about a year.

Subphylum Vertebrata
Class Mammalia
Order Cetacea
Family
Delphinidae (true dolphins)
Number of species 40

Some species of dolphins are very rare, but most are not endangered.

See also
Feet and hands
Porpoises
Whales

Dolphins are small whales, which in most cases have a long snout, crammed with up to 200 small pointed teeth, ideal for catching fishes. Most are creatures of the open sea, though some come into inshore waters.

Four species of dolphins are known as river dolphins, as they live in fresh water in South America, China and India. The Amazon and La Plata dolphins have more of a neck than other whales and are thought to be 'living fossils', because of their similarities with ancient fossil whales.

The true dolphins are slender, streamlined creatures, some of which are capable of swimming at speeds of up to 55 km/h (34 mph). Most of them have a large, curved fin in the middle of the back which helps to stabilize them. The largest of the dolphins is the killer whale, in which the fin can be up to 2 m (over 6 ft) in length.

Dolphins are thought to be among the most intelligent of animals. They seem to be friendly towards humans, and are sometimes kept and trained to do tricks, to help underwater engineers or to take part in submarine warfare. In a few cases dolphins are hunted by humans. In others, they get caught accidentally in fishing nets. ∎

Domesday Book

At Christmas, 1085, King William I of England held a council in Gloucester, where 'he had much thought and very deep discussion. . . about this country – how it was occupied and with what sort of people'. Twenty years after the Norman conquest, William decided that he needed to know who owned the land, who lived there, how much it was worth, and what taxes he could expect. He divided the country into seven districts. Probably the important barons in each district collected most of the information. By the end of 1086 the huge survey seems to have been complete. It was all written down by a clerk in Winchester in two big books which still exist, 900 years later.

Domesday Book is written in Latin, but it is not difficult to pick out some of the words and abbreviations used by the monks who wrote it down.
Place-names are written in red with a line through them. A shortened word has a line or a squiggle along the top:

plough *car*

holds *ht*

T.R.E. means 'in the time of King Edward'.

⁊ marks the beginning of a paragraph.

Roman numerals are used.

People did not seem to like the Domesday survey much at the time. An English monk wrote that it was shameful that there was not even one ox or cow or pig left out (though he probably exaggerated). Domesday Book may have got its name because 'doom' means God's judgement, and people felt they were being judged when they had to answer so many questions about what they owned. Domesday tells us that about 250 people controlled all the land in England in 1086. Only two of them were English. The population may have been about 2·5 million.

Domesday Book is very unusual; no other medieval king in Europe did anything like it. Today, it gives us an enormous amount of evidence about Norman England and how the feudal system worked. ∎

▲ This extract is about Bradford which was then a small village. The end of the second line and beginning of the third say: 'Ilbert holds it. It is waste. In the time of King Edward it was worth £4.'

No national survey was made in Britain again until a government census was made in 1801. Since then the government has made a census (count of the population) every ten years.

See also
Feudal system
Normans
Population: human

Biography
William I

Domestication

Most of our pets and the animals that surround us are domestic animals. That is to say that they are tame and that they breed easily in captivity. Many wild animals can be tamed, but usually they are nervous except with people that they know well, and often they do not breed in captivity.

All domestic animals were bred from wild species but, although related wild animals may still exist, many of our domestic animals no longer exist in the wild. Most of these wild ancestors were first caught and kept by people in prehistoric times, who found that the animals could be useful in many ways.

Selective breeding

One of the first animals to be tamed by prehistoric people was the wolf, the ancestor to all domestic dogs. People found that tamed wolves could help them in hunting the bison, wild horses and deer which were their food. Among the cubs born to the tame wolves, some were very different from their parents, either in size or colour, or in some other way. People

tended to keep these oddities, and breed from them. This is called selective breeding and it resulted in many different breeds being formed. Almost all domestic animals look different from their wild ancestors because of selective breeding.

Later, other kinds of animals were tamed and kept. Most of these were animals which lived in herds feeding on plants, such as cattle, horses, sheep, goats and camels. They were kept for meat, milk, fur and hides and they were often used as beasts of burden, to carry or pull loads.

Very few birds have been domesticated but chickens, pigeons, ducks, geese and turkeys are domestic species.

Many kinds of domestic animals were bred to suit particular local conditions. Now Rare Breeds Societies have been formed to save these ancient varieties from extinction, for they may have genetic qualities which would be useful to animal breeders in the future.

Hunted to extinction

Once an animal had been fully tamed, human beings regarded its remaining wild relatives as a threat. For instance, a tame cow might join a herd of wild cattle roaming nearby and the farmer might never get her back again. The same sort of thing could happen with any domestic animal. As a result of this, the wild relatives of almost all domestic animals were hunted, often to extinction.

The aurochs, which was the ancestor of today's cows, became extinct in about 1627. Arabian camels are extinct in the wild and, apart from a few in zoos, there are hardly any wild horses or donkeys. But in some parts of the world, domestic animals have escaped into the wild. Camels and horses have both run wild in Australia and North America. Domestic animals that have become wild are called feral animals.

Taming species today

Nowadays, when many kinds of wild animal are becoming very rare, attempts are being made to domesticate new species. African antelopes, especially the eland, have been tamed in parts of Africa and in Russia. Red deer are being kept as domestic animals in some parts of the world. Some small creatures, including budgerigars, golden hamsters and gerbils, have recently been domesticated as pets. ∎

▶ **Some of the main species of domestic animals and the ways in which people find them useful.**

animal	uses
cat	keeps houses, farms and other buildings free of mice and rats; as a pet
camel **llama** **yak**	transport, skin, meat and milk; dried dung used as fuel
chicken **duck** **goose**	eggs, meat and feathers
cow	meat, milk, leather, horn and transport; dried dung may be used as fuel
dog	hunting, herding, guarding, warmth, transport, fur, meat and as a pet
goat	meat, milk, wool and skin
horse	transport, meat and skin
pig	meat and skin
rabbit	meat, fur and as a pet
sheep	wool, meat, skin and milk
water buffalo	transport, meat and milk

Dominican Republic

Area
48,442 sq km
(18,703 sq miles)
Capital
Santo Domingo
Population
6,766,000
Language
Spanish
Religion
Christian
Government
Republic
Currency
1 Dominican Republic peso
= 100 centavos

The Dominican Republic is a Caribbean country that occupies the eastern two-thirds of the island of Hispaniola. The capital is Santo Domingo, the oldest colonial city in the western hemisphere. It was founded by Bartholomew Columbus, the brother of Christopher, in 1496 and has many fine historic buildings.

The four mountain ranges in the western part of the country rise to Pico Duarte, which at 3,175 m (10,416 ft) is the highest point in the Caribbean. Fertile plains cover most of the rest of the country. The climate is hot throughout the year.

Most people are descended from Spanish settlers and African slaves. Many are farmers, and they grow sugar, coffee, cocoa and tobacco. The government also tries to encourage more tourists to enjoy the many fine beaches.

Flashback

Santo Domingo was ruled by Spain from the time of Columbus until 1795. Since then it has been occupied by France, Haiti, Spain and the United States of America. But the country has been independent for most of the time since 1844. ■

See also
Caribbean
Caribbean history
Spanish colonial history

Dormice

Dormice are small, plump, furry-tailed rodents. They have long whiskers and large eyes, which are often made to look even bigger by a ring of dark fur. They are good climbers and usually live in woodlands or rocky places.

Dormouse means 'sleep mouse', for most dormice hibernate, in a deep sleep which may last for more than six months in a cold winter. Dormice snooze during the day, coming out of their nests at night to feed on seeds, nuts and fruit as well as insects and spiders. One species, the edible or fat dormouse, was kept by the Romans for food. ■

Distribution
Europe, Africa and Asia
Size
Up to 34 cm including tail (edible dormouse).
The only British dormouse, the hazel dormouse, may be as little as 11·5 cm overall.
Number of young
About 3–4 (sometimes two litters in the same season)
Lifespan
3–6 years in the wild

Subphylum Vertebrata
Class Mammalia
Order Rodentia
Family Gliridae
Number of species
About 8

◄ The garden dormouse uses its feet to cling tightly to branches as it climbs in search of food. Its bushy tail cannot grip but helps to keep balance.

See also
Hibernation
Rodents

Down's syndrome

Babies born with a condition known as Down's syndrome grow up with some mental handicap which can be quite severe. Also they all have a similar appearance. Usually they are short, with widely spaced eyes with a fold of skin at the inner corner, a flattish nose and a high forehead. People born with Down's syndrome cannot be cured.

People with this condition need a lot of support from their families and friends because of their mental handicap. But they can make friends, and love and need people as much as others do. In fact they often have very happy, affectionate personalities. A few are able to look after themselves and earn their own living.

Down's syndrome is caused by an accident in cell-division when the eggs develop inside the mother. The result is that Down's babies always have 47 chromosomes in each of their cells instead of the normal number of 46. This tiny difference causes all the features of Down's. ■

In the United Kingdom about one in 1,000 babies are born with Down's syndrome.

See also
Cells
Genetics
Mental handicap

Dracula

The British author, Bram Stoker, made Count Dracula the demon villain in his book *Dracula*. In this story, the count was a vampire, one of the 'undead'. Vampires first appeared in European legends; they were particularly popular in Hungary at the beginning of the 18th century. Vampires are even more popular today, and star in many films.

Vampires are supposed to be the tormented spirits of evil people. At night, and only at night, they rise from their coffins, usually as bats, and go off for a drink. Unfortunately, what they like to drink is human blood. Their victims also become vampires. During daylight they must lie in their coffins. Mysteriously, they cast no shadow and have no reflection.

The stories tell us that you can be protected against vampires by a crucifix or garlic. Getting rid of Dracula for good is easy, but rather messy. You simply hammer a stake through his heart. This does not seem to be a very reliable method, for in spite of this treatment, he keeps coming back in yet more films. ■

Vampire bats
There are in South America two species of blood-sucking bat that have been called vampire bats. These bats feed from the blood of cattle and other warm-blooded creatures. They feed at night and it is probable that the cattle do not feel their bites except as a mild irritation. However, there is nothing supernatural about these bats.

Traditional weapons against vampires
Garlic
A silver bullet
A crucifix
A wooden stake

Dragonflies

▲ **Libellulid dragonfly of Florida, shown at rest spreading its beautiful gauzy wings.**

Dragonflies swoop and speed over streams and ponds. They are the fastest flying of all insects, and some may reach a speed of 57 km/h (35 mph). They have four wings, which are used independently so you can hear them rattle as they fly. This does not stop them from being very agile in flight, as they can even fly backwards.

Dragonflies are hunters, catching and eating other insects. These are held in a sort of shopping basket made of the dragonfly's forward-pointing, spiny legs.

Mating

When you see dragonflies by water, you may notice that they fly up and down a piece of the bank. This is because the males patrol a territory which they defend against others of their own kind. If a female comes along, the male grabs her by the back of the neck. She then loops her body round until she makes contact with the second segment of his abdomen, where he has stored sperm for mating. They mate on the wing and afterwards often stay together while the female lays her eggs.

Life of the nymph

The nymphs (larvae) that hatch from the eggs do not look like their gauzy-winged parents. They live and grow in the water, feeding on all sorts of small creatures, up to the size of tadpoles. Food is caught by the mask, a sort of hooked arm which the nymph shoots out from its face. The nymph may spend two or three years in the water before it is ready, one summer day, to climb up the stem of a water plant and shed its skin for the last time to become an adult dragonfly. ■

Largest dragonfly
Wingspan about 35 cm. Some fossil dragonflies were much bigger, the largest had a wingspan of nearly 1 m.

Phylum
Arthropoda
Class
Insecta
Order
Odonata
Number of species
About 5,000

A dragonfly's eyes take up most of the space on its head, for these insects have very good sight. They can see food up to 40 m away. Their sense of smell is poor, and their antennae are tiny and threadlike.

The change from nymph to adult is called metamorphosis.

See also
Insects
Metamorphosis
Ponds

Dragons

People have been telling one another stories about dragons for a very long time. Dragons are mythical creatures: a mixture of bird and snake, good and evil. The dragon in the Bible (*Revelation*, chapter 12) was so greedy that it needed seven heads to eat all the people it wanted to. For Christians, the dragon stood for evil, Satan. The Archangel Michael defeated the dragon, proving that good overcomes evil. The ancient Egyptians had a similar myth. Their dragon, Apophis, spread chaos and darkness over the Earth each night, and was overcome by the Sun-god, Ra, each morning.

The red and the white dragon

The Romans brought the sign of the dragon with them when they occupied Britain. In the 20th century the Welsh officially took the red dragon as their national emblem.

Quite a different dragon is the one that Saint George is reputed to have slain. This was white, with bat-like wings, and was terrorizing many people including the daughter of the King of Lydia somewhere in the Middle East. By killing it, George overcame evil with good once more. He became the champion of Christendom and, in time, the patron saint of England.

An evil dragon

One of the most famous dragons of all time is the Nidhögg, the Dread Biter, that threatens to destroy the universe itself. He is found in the early Norse legends, where he continuously gnaws the roots of the giant tree, Yggdrasil, the Mighty Ash. People of the time thought that the tree was the universe. They believed that the Earth is in the middle part of the tree. Above it are the leaves, which from far away look like sky. In their branches an eagle and a serpent are locked in the terrible fight between light and darkness. The roots of the tree are deep in the underworld. Its trunk passes straight through the waters, the Earth, and the world of men. One day the Nidhögg, which represents the forces of evil, will be defeated, the tree will recover, and a safer universe will be made for gods and people.

Some good dragons

In the Far East the dragon is seen as a force for good. The Chinese dragon, *Long*, is king-like: he lives in rivers, lakes, and oceans, and roams the skies. For over 2,000 years the Chinese people have performed special dances to him, asking him to send them rain to feed the Earth and to bring them good fortune. In ancient Chinese stories a dragon guards the heavenly house of the gods, while another dragon became the emblem of the emperors. Some hills in China look, from the distance, like sleeping dragons. It may happen that, when modern engineers from the cities come to the farmers and tell them that a new road must be made that will cut the hill in two, the farmers protest. They try to persuade the officials to make the road somewhere else, because by disturbing the dragon they will wake him from his sleep in anger. ∎

Dragons are found on:
The shield of an ancient Greek king
The standards of Roman armies
The prows of Viking ships
The flag of Wales
The throne of the Chinese emperor

See also
Beowulf

Biography
George, Saint

◀ This painting of Saint George and the dragon is by the Italian artist, Uccello, who lived from 1397 to 1475 during the Renaissance. He followed tradition in giving the dragon bat-like wings but he did not paint the dragon white.

▼ Some Chinese living overseas, including these people in Singapore, celebrate New Year's Day with a dragon dance. According to legend the dragon wards off evil spirits and so brings good fortune.

Drama

Drama is the performance of a story which then becomes known as a play, and the people who pretend to be different characters in it are called actors.

Acting

▼ Peter Terson's play *Zigger Zagger* is about the effects of football hooliganism on a young man who becomes caught up in it. It is being performed here by the National Youth Theatre, in Britain, which helps young people to gain experience of acting.

Almost everyone, at some time in their life, pretends to be someone else. Children play at being soldiers or nurses or mothers and fathers. This is an early form of acting. However, to become a professional actor time has to be spent studying exactly how other people do things. It is important to make the audience think, by using the right movement, facial expression and speech, that the actor really is the person he or she is pretending to be in a play. Otherwise no one will believe the story.

Drama today

As well as going to the theatre or the cinema, millions of people, all over the world, watch soap operas, situation comedies and various other types of drama on television, or listen to plays on the radio. A play can make us laugh or cry, become excited or frightened as the story is acted out. By clever use of words and acting, the playwright and the actors involve us, the audience, in some way. That is one of the reasons why drama will always be popular. But apart from just entertaining us, many plays help us to understand more about the world in which we live and the problems and feelings that are common to all of us.

Some do this by showing ordinary people in 'real life' stories and settings, or by portraying famous characters in historical events, and others by dealing with important modern issues in ways that make us think more deeply than we might have done.

The beginnings

It is possible that early drama dealt with the origins of the universe, food, life, death, and religion. Perhaps by painting their faces or wearing masks and acting like gods or spirits, people could appear to bring the gods to life, or drive away evil spirits. Perhaps, if hunters acted a successful catch before setting out, they could make it come true. Prehistoric people may have acted out all sorts of rituals, but they were never written down, so little is known of them.

As civilizations developed, plays were written down and learned, and could be performed over and over again with different groups of actors.

▶ These 'Frog-men' from the central highlands of Papua New Guinea are wearing clay masks to act out a drama which may be similar to dramas performed by people in prehistoric times.

There is an illustration of a Greek theatre in the article on Theatres.

▶ Greek plays are still acted today, sometimes in the very same theatres in which they were originally performed. This performance of the tragedy of Agamemnon and his son Orestes was acted at the National Theatre in London in 1981. The actors and chorus wear masks, just as they did in ancient Greek theatres.

The Greeks

About 2,500 years ago, the Greeks began to develop a powerful kind of drama. Their plays told of the sufferings endured by famous characters as they struggled to please their rather strict gods. They nearly all had unhappy endings. This type of play is called a tragedy. One tragedy, *Agamemnon*, by Aeschylus, tells the story of the warrior hero's return from the Trojan War and his murder by his wife and her lover. In the next play, his son Orestes kills them, only to be punished in turn by the gods.

Later on, the Greeks wrote comedies which were amusing and made the audience laugh. The plays by Aristophanes had jokes about what was going on in the city at the time and poked fun at the politicians and their ideas. The Greeks went on to write more lighthearted comedies about everyday topics such as couples falling in love and all the obstacles they had to overcome. A comedy is a play that not only makes the audience laugh, but also has a happy ending.

Greek drama was very different from the plays written today. All the actors were men and they all wore masks. A large group of them, called 'the chorus', were responsible for telling much of the story. This 'chorus' spoke and moved together, and sometimes sang and danced.

Drama in the market place

In Europe in the Middle Ages, the main subject for drama was Bible stories. People gathered in the market places to watch performances of the story of Adam and Eve, or Noah and the Flood. These were called mystery plays. Parts would be taken by ordinary people, just as in community plays today.

◄ One of Shakespeare's most famous plays is *Romeo and Juliet*. In this 1989 production by the Royal Shakespeare Company, Juliet is shown on her balcony while Romeo clings to the rope below.

Shakespeare and Elizabethan theatre

At the time of Queen Elizabeth I of England in the 16th century, people began to use drama as a way of telling all kinds of stories, not just biblical ones. In London, special theatres were built and people paid to see professional actors perform newly written plays. One of the greatest playwrights was William Shakespeare.

Melodrama

In the 19th century melodramas became very popular. These were vivid, exciting stories with a lot of music and fighting in them, and the audience cheered the hero and booed the villain. Almost every melodrama ended with good overcoming bad. The scripts of these plays were printed, together with drawings of the characters and scenes, to be cut out and used in toy theatres by Victorian children. They show us how actors of the time stood and gestured.

Changing ideas

These days, as well as comedies, tragedies and melodramas, there are all kinds of drama to watch: plays without words, or plays where the actors themselves have made up the script; plays with actors in masks; pantomimes and musicals with enormously expensive and complicated sets; and plays with no scenery at all. Watching drama, or taking part in it, is one way of learning about ourselves and other people. ■

There is an illustration of an Elizabethan theatre building in the article on Theatres.

See also
Films
Greek ancient history
Masks
Mime
Musicals
Mystery plays
Operas
Pantomimes
Theatres

Biography
Shakespeare
Shaw

Famous actors
Ashcroft
Gielgud
Olivier

Drawing

Drawing is the making of pictures using a pointed or sharpened tool. It is related to writing, and in some ancient languages, like Chinese, the words were originally simple drawings of the things the words represented.

Humans have made drawings from prehistoric times. The first drawings were made by scratching marks on earth, rock or tree bark with pointed sticks or stones. When paper was invented many thousands of years later, a wider range of drawing tools could be used.

Today we have the choice of pencil or crayon, pen and ink, charcoal and pastels, felt and roller pens, and so on. Each of these tools gives a different effect and needs a different technique. The latest drawing tools are special computer programs which can reproduce electronically many of the qualities of traditional drawings.

There are many methods of drawing and the one chosen depends upon what the artist aims to achieve. Look at the two examples on this page. The drawing by Escher is in what we call a 'tight' style. Escher uses precise lines and extensive shading

▲ *Two Women Resting*, a drawing by Henry Moore (1898–1986). **Moore made pen-and-ink sketches similar to the one above as a basis for his famous sculptures.**

to trick the viewer's eye and make impossible perspectives seem possible. In contrast, the drawing of two women resting by Henry Moore is in a 'free' style. In this picture Moore is not interested in capturing precise detail or emphasizing the individuality of the women. He uses a loose drawing technique to explore the overall form of his subject matter. Look too at the medium (choice of drawing tool) each artist has used in order to gain the effect he wants.

We usually think of drawing as being an artistic activity, but this is not always so. Many drawings are made in order to provide information or to help people construct things. Architects' plans and engineers' drawings are two examples of these 'working drawings'. You can see examples of these in the biographies of Issigonis, who designed the Mini car, and of Smeaton, who designed a lighthouse, in Volume 6.

Working drawings usually show things from a particular viewpoint: from the front, from the side or from directly overhead. We rarely see objects like this. We see them in the round, in a particular place, and with the light coming from a particular direction. To show objects in three dimensions, and to show them in relation to other objects, artists use perspective.

▼ *Convex and Concave*, a lithograph by Maurits Escher (1898–1972). **In lithography an image is drawn onto stone or metal, and is then inked and printed onto paper. With its soft tones and fine detail this picture looks like a pencil drawing.**

◯ See also
Buildings
Calligraphy
Designers
Paintings
Writing systems
Biography
Dürer
Issigonis
Moore
Smeaton

In the Middle Ages artists did not really understand perspective, and their drawings often look odd and out of proportion to us. In the 15th century, in the early years of the Renaissance, artists such as Paolo Uccello laid down the rules of perspective, and these have been followed ever since. Today it is hard for us to imagine that they did not always exist.

Using perspective

Take some paper, a pencil and a ruler.

Begin by drawing a line across the paper to indicate the **horizon**. Lines across the paper are horizontal (like the horizon), and vertical lines go up and down.

If you were drawing a real scene from life, the horizon might be hidden from view by buildings or trees. Here we are inventing our own picture, so we can draw in the horizon where we want it.

If we draw it low down, things in the picture will seem large and we shall feel small. If we draw it high up, they will appear smaller and we shall feel bigger.

Next, mark a point anywhere along this line. This is your **vanishing point** (the point at which all perspective lines meet).

Draw two lines starting from below the horizon line, to meet at this point. Then draw two more lines starting from above the horizon line, also to meet at this point.

Now draw a vertical line on the left and one on the right, to show the end of each building.

Now, by adding more vertical and horizontal lines to connect the lines you have already drawn, you can make the drawing into anything you wish.

Instead of two buildings as have been drawn here, you may wish to draw a railway line, or a road with a fence or trees on either side. ■

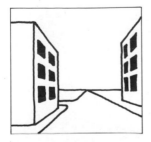

This is the same picture as above, but with a lower horizon so the buildings look larger.

Dreams

Dreams are images or thoughts that pass through your mind during sleep. Peculiar and vivid things can happen in a dream, and so they have always fascinated people.

Dreaming is usually accompanied by rapid eye movements, as though the dreamer is actually watching something. Some scientists have argued that these rapid eye movements actually create the dreams, but there are many other ideas as to why we dream. One is that dreams prevent the brain from becoming over-loaded, by 'unlearning' thoughts and memories from the day. Another theory is that the brain is like a very complicated computer which has to be reprogrammed each day.

Sigmund Freud, the founder of psychoanalysis, suggested that dreams express our subconscious desires and anxieties (those we do not know we have). He argued that some psycho-logical problems could be uncovered and solved by analysing dreams, but many scientists have not been convinced by his evidence.

Nightmares

Nightmares are frightening or ex-tremely disturbing dreams. Almost all children have nightmares, which may make them wake up suddenly in a panic or feeling upset. Adult nightmares are not so common, and often happen during periods of stress.

A few children and a very few adults suffer from night terrors. They sit up with a scream, and seem terrified or angry about something they imagine is in the room. No one knows what causes night terrors, but they are different from nightmares as they do not seem to be accompanied by a dream.

Daydreaming

When someone daydreams they allow their thoughts to wander and dwell on imaginary situations. Daydreaming is quite different from dreams during sleep. ■

Adults probably dream about four times each night, but usually do not remember doing so.

Dreams sometimes seem to last for hours, but do not usually last longer than about 30 minutes.

A 'nightmare' is a female monster that was thought to sit on the heads of sleepers, almost suffocating them.

 See also
Sleep

Biography
Freud

Dress

When you get dressed you start by putting on your underclothes. In ancient times these were a rich people's luxury. As far as we know, most people did not have underclothes.

Roman ladies wore a sleeveless undergarment, called a *tunica interior*. In Europe in the Middle Ages people wore stockings reaching to the knee, held up by garters; and petticoats were worn by some women by the 15th century. Men wore shirts and baggy drawers, called *braies*. There is evidence (from the diarist Samuel Pepys and others) that some women wore drawers (wide-legged underpants) in the 17th century, but they were not common in England till early Victorian times. Little girls then wore pantalettes, which were long pants with frills showing beneath their skirts, and wore several petticoats at once.

Children's dress

For centuries, European children from the age of about three or four wore the same kinds of clothes as their parents. As babies they were bound up like a parcel in swaddling bands (long strips of cloth). This was because people thought it would help the limbs to grow straight and strong. But there must have been many uncomfortable, distressed babies. From the time they could crawl, little children, boys as well as girls, wore ankle-length frocks and petticoats.

About 200 years ago special styles began to be made for children whose parents could afford them. In the late 18th century boys wore long trousers, buttoned under the arms onto frilled blouses, and peaked caps. Girls wore long dresses with loose skirts and straw bonnets. By the middle of the 19th century boys' fashion was for sailor suits, black velvet jackets, lace collars and knee breeches. Girls wore dresses and pinafores.

During the 20th century, clothes for children and adults have gradually become more comfortable, and the difference in dress between rich and poor is not nearly so great.

Night dress

For centuries people either slept naked or wore underclothes, if they had any. By Tudor times the rich had night clothes. Victorians wore long and heavy nightshirts. Pyjamas came into fashion for men in the 1880s; for women they were not popular until World War I.

▲ Georgian, late 18th century.

▲ Victorian, 1850s.

▲ Edwardian, 1900s.

▲ A piper plays the bagpipes. The tartan costume he wears has been a symbol of Scotland for many years. Nowadays kilts are worn mainly on ceremonial occasions or by women as skirts.

▶ Japanese mother and child wearing special festival kimonos, which are traditional robes tied with sashes.

National dress

In some countries many people wear the same style of dress as each other, which changes only very slightly with the fashion. The style is handed down from generation to generation. So everyone knows the style of dress which is worn in a certain region. Patterns for embroidery and weaving are also passed on from one generation to the next.

One country may have several different styles of traditional dress. In India, for instance, Rajasthani women wear brightly coloured long skirts and blouses. Further north in the Punjab they wear *shalwar* (loose trousers) and *kamiz* (a long shirt). In the south and east the sari is the women's normal dress, though it can be tied in different ways. All over India traditional clothes are worn for everyday work as well as for special occasions.

In European countries hardly anyone now wears traditional styles of dress for everyday use. But in some parts of eastern Europe people wear national dress (sometimes called folk costume) for festivals, weddings and other celebrations.

▼ The bride (on the right) wearing a richly embroidered white dress, surrounded by guests at a village wedding in Bukowina, Poland.

▲ A bright and sunny day in Angmagssalik, Greenland. This woman proudly wears her Sunday clothes, which are also a colourful example of Greenland's national dress.

◀ A young Ugandan mother wearing colourful cotton clothing, which helps her to stay cool in the fierce heat.

Drums

► A drum kit made by the Premier Drum Company. The large bass drum is played with a foot pedal. The snare drum is on a stand, closest to where the drummer sits. The other drums are tom-toms. The drum kit also has several cymbals. The pair of cymbals together are called a hi-hat. The hi-hat can be played with drumsticks, or the two cymbals can be clashed together by using the foot pedal.

▼ Some different drum types.

For most people 'playing the drums' means sitting behind a drum kit and playing with a group. There is the big bass drum, played with a foot pedal. This is also found in military and marching bands, where the player carries the drum strapped to the body and hits it with padded sticks. There is also a snare drum (also called side drum). This has a wire spring across the underside to give the drum a dry, rattly sound when struck. The snare drum is also seen in marching bands, where it is carried to one side of the player out of the way of his striding legs, and played with two drumsticks.

A drum kit also has tom-toms, which are deeper than side drums and have no spring. They make a thundering sound when beaten with sticks.

Kettledrums

In an orchestra or wind band there are also timpani (kettledrums). These are big copper bowls with a skin across the open end. A kettledrum plays a definite note, and an orchestra usually has three or four of them. The player can use foot pedals to tune the drums to different notes.

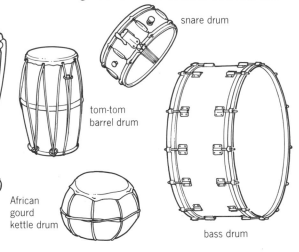

snare drum

tom-tom barrel drum

African gourd kettle drum

bass drum

timpani

▼ Musicians in Niger, West Africa, playing ganga drums. These are a type of snare drum. The drummers are using curved sticks in their right hand, but they also drum with the fingers of the left hand.

► Sri Lankan temple drummers. On the left is a *tama-tama*, a double-headed kettle drum. On the right a *gata bera* (barrel drum) with a drumhead at each end. One has a clear ringing sound; the other is heavier and more muffled.

Techniques of drumming

All cultures: Indian, African, Caribbean, Far Eastern and others, have their own drum traditions and techniques. Often drums are played with bare hands. Shaping and cupping the hands give different sounds. Hand drums, such as conga drums, are often used in Western groups and big jazz bands to add variety to the percussion. ■

Ducks, geese and swans

Wildfowl is the name we often give to this large group of birds. They are usually found near water and have webbed feet, short legs, long necks and short tails. They fly strongly, but most moult all their flight feathers at once and so become flightless for a few weeks after breeding.

Ducks

There are several groups of ducks. Dabbling ducks, such as mallards, filter the surface water to find food. Diving ducks, such as pochards, search below the surface for vegetable matter.

Perching ducks, including the colourful mandarin, both perch and nest in trees. Ducks like eiders are called sea-ducks because they dive around sea coasts.

Sawbills, like the mergansers, also dive for food. They have long, pointed bills with sharp, tooth-like edges for catching and holding slippery fish.

Stiff-tails are found in most parts of the world. Their stiff tail feathers can be raised or lowered and they often feed after dark.

In addition there is a group called shelduck which are neither true geese nor true ducks.

Most are found south of the Equator, where they take the place of the more northerly geese.

Geese

Like swans, but unlike ducks, geese often pair for life and families keep together throughout the young birds' first winter. True geese are found only in the northern hemisphere. They graze on grass and other vegetation. At night they often roost on open water. Much of the year is spent in large flocks and many undertake long migrations.

Geese fall into two groups, 'grey geese' and 'black geese'. Grey geese include the greylag goose, which is the ancestor of many farmyard geese. Among the black geese are the Canada geese of North America, which have also been introduced into Britain.

Swans

Swans feed on grass and water plants. They have long necks with more vertebrae than any other animal. This gives flexibility and allows them to reach plants up to a metre below the surface of the water.

They do not usually breed until they are four or five years old, but they do have long lives. At least one mute swan lived to be over 20 years old. Once pairs of swans are formed they tend to remain loyal for life.

Several species of swans are long-distance migrants. Bewick's swans fly from the Russian tundra to north-west Europe for the winter. The closely related whistling swan breeds in Arctic Canada and winters in the southern USA. ■

Subphylum
Vertebrata
Class
Aves
Order
Anseriformes
Number of species
143

See also
Birds
Migration
Ponds
Streams

▲ Different species of wildfowl have different ways of finding food: grazing on the bank (brent goose); filtering the surface water (shoveller); up-ending in deeper water (mallard); diving to the bottom in deep water (tufted duck); or chasing and catching fish (goosander).

brent goose

shoveller

mallard

goosander

tufted duck

Dust-bowl

▲ **The term dust-bowl is often used to refer to the removal of a great deal of soil from the high plains of the west central United States in the 1930s.**

A dust-bowl is an area of land where the wind has blown away the soil. This is most likely to happen during very dry weather. If large areas of soil are left bare after a crop has been harvested the topsoil may dry and be blown away. The same thing can happen if crops fail because of drought. Even grassland can turn to dust if too many animals eat the grass and trample the dry soil. Any part of the world which has a long dry season or which suffers from drought is in danger of becoming a dust-bowl. ■

See also
Erosion

Dyes

Dyes are used to change the colour of materials. At one time, dyes were made from plants and animals. For example, saffron, a yellow dye, came from the crocus plant. Today, the chemical industry makes thousands of different coloured dyes. Dyes produced chemically like this are called synthetic dyes. When cloth is dyed, chemicals called mordants are used to help the dye penetrate the fabric and stay fixed. If you have done any dyeing at home, you may have used salt as a mordant. When dyes cannot be washed out and do not fade, we say that they are fast.

Flashback

5,000 years ago, the ancient Egyptians were using many different berries and plants to dye wool, silk and cotton beautiful colours. 3,000 years ago, the Phoenicians were producing a magnificent purple dye from the juices of crushed sea-snails. The dye could only be made in small amounts, so it was very expensive and became the colour worn by kings. ■

The first synthetic dye, mauveine, was made by William Perkin in 1856 using chemicals obtained from coal tar.

The red colouring used in some foods is obtained from the cochineal insect found in South America. It is also used to dye some army uniforms red. Synthetic dyes are much cheaper.

See also
Chemicals
Drugs

Dynamos

The principle of the dynamo was discovered by Michael Faraday in 1831 in England. About 30 years after Faraday's death (in 1867) his dynamo principle had become the basis of massive, powerful electricity generators.

Dynamos are machines that produce electricity when turned. They are also known as generators. Large ones generate the electricity in power-stations. Small ones can run the lights on a bicycle. On many bicycles, the dynamo is turned by a tiny wheel which presses against the tyre.

Inside the dynamo, a magnet is rotated close to a coil of wire. As the magnetic field sweeps past the coil, it generates electricity. Power-station generators use the same idea, but the moving magnet is a much stronger electromagnet. In some dynamos, the magnet is fixed and the coil is turned. ■

See also
Bicycles
Electricity
Magnets
Motor cars

Biography
Faraday

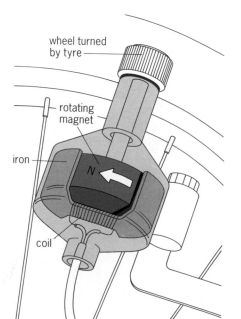

wheel turned by tyre

rotating magnet

iron

N

coil

◄ **This dynamo is turned by a bicycle tyre. Inside the dynamo, a rotating magnet generates electricity in a fixed coil.**

Before the discovery of the dynamo, electric current could only be produced by chemical batteries which were small and expensive.

Alternators are dynamos which generate alternating current (a.c.). This is electricity which flows backwards, forwards, backwards, forwards . . . and so on. Bicycle dynamos are alternators. Car engines have alternators to charge the battery.

Ears

All mammals have ears. Bats have large ears that act rather like radar aerials. Flying bats at night make high-pitched sounds that are too high for humans to hear. These sounds bounce off flying insects, such as moths, like a radar beam. The returning echoes are picked up by the bat's big ears so that it can find and catch the insect in mid-air. Some prey animals like rabbits and hares have big ears so that they can hear their enemies approaching and tell which direction they are coming from. Birds, reptiles and amphibians have good hearing, but their ears are simpler than those of mammals. Some insects can also hear, but their ears may be placed on their front legs or the sides of their bodies.

Structure of the human ear

The part of the ear that you can see is called the outer ear. As it is funnel-shaped, it collects sound waves and focuses them on the eardrum inside the head. The eardrum then vibrates, which causes the group of tiny bones (ossicles) that are attached to it to vibrate as well. The ossicles act as levers to increase the force of the vibrations moving the liquid in the snail-shaped inner ear called the cochlea. Inside this, sensitive hair cells are moved by the vibrations. As these are attached to nerves, every time they are vibrated messages are sent to the brain. These nerve messages enable us to hear and understand sounds, including speech.

The ear and brain working together can separate sounds depending on how loud they are and how high or low they are. Having two ears, one on each side of the head, helps us to tell where a sound is coming from, as it will be louder in one ear than the other unless it is straight ahead or immediately behind.

Balance

Your sense of balance is controlled in your inner ear, where sense organs detect any change in the position of your head. You are probably not very aware of this, but without it you would be unable to move without falling.

Earache

This is the commonest illness of the ear. It is usually caused by an infection in the middle, hidden part of the ear. This region is connected by a tube (the Eustachian tube) to the throat. Bacteria can pass up the tube and cause infection and earache. ■

◀ The fennec fox lives on African savannahs (grasslands). It has huge, movable ears that let it accurately find sounds of insects like termites underground. It then digs them up and eats them.

▼ Bats have large crinkled ears that act rather like radar aerials. This is a long-eared bat from Europe.

▶ Hares, like rabbits, have big outer ears and are able to pick up sounds at a distance and be warned of approaching danger.

The lowest sounds humans can hear are at 20 vibrations a second (a low hum) and the highest are 20,000 vibrations a second (a high-pitched hiss). As you get older you are less able to hear the higher-pitched sounds. Very loud sounds, such as factory machinery, gun-fire or disco music, can damage the ears and cause deafness.

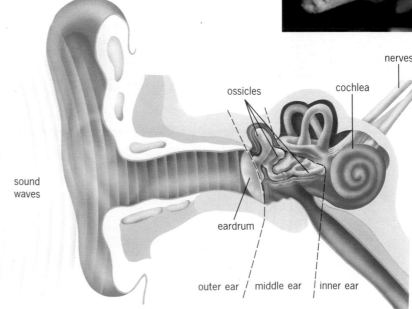

nerves
ossicles
cochlea
sound waves
eardrum
outer ear / middle ear / inner ear

▲ Sounds make the eardrum vibrate, which makes the ossicles vibrate, which makes sensory hairs in the cochlea vibrate, which sends nerve impulses to the brain where we hear the sound.

See also
Deafness
Radar
Senses
Sound

Earth

The Earth is one of the planets in the Solar System. It is different from all the others because it has an atmosphere containing oxygen and this has allowed life to evolve. The Earth goes around the Sun in a great orbit once every year. This causes the seasons. The Earth also spins round on its own axis once every 24 hours, and this causes day (when one side faces the Sun) and night (when the same side faces away).

The Earth in space

The Earth is tiny when compared with many other planets, or with the Sun. The planets Mercury, Venus, Mars and Pluto are smaller, but Jupiter and Saturn are hundreds of times bigger. The Sun is over a million times bigger than the Earth.

Since the 1960s we have been able to see the Earth from space. Satellite photographs show the Earth as a blue ball covered with great swirling masses of cloud. Closer views can show the surface features such as the shapes of the continents, the great snow-covered mountain ranges, and even rivers and cities.

Remote sensing

Satellite photography of the Earth has become very important. It allows weather forecasters to see the large-scale patterns of clouds over the Atlantic and Pacific oceans, for example, and they use this to predict the weather. It allows farming and forestry advisers to study the soil and climate of very large areas. It helps biologists to assess the effects of human activities on forests, deserts, and waterways. Geologists can study the major surface features of the Earth, and use them as a guide to finding valuable minerals.

This is called 'remote sensing' because scientists can study or 'sense' major features of the Earth from a distance. The methods have improved greatly in recent years as many more satellites are now available to carry out surveys. Nowadays photographs are so good that houses and even cars can be made out on the best pictures.

Inside the Earth

Scientists do not know exactly what the Earth is like inside. We live on the outer part which is made from hard rocks and covered with water in places. This is the crust. The inside of the Earth is very hot, and below about 70 km (40 miles) the rocks are all in the form of molten liquid. We know this because miners have found that the rocks become warmer and warmer down deep mines; and molten rock often comes to the surface through volcanoes. The main inner layer, the mantle, is made of molten rock, and the inner core of the Earth is made from solid and liquid metal.

► A cross section of the Earth showing the main layers. The crust on which we live is so thin that it only shows as a line.

Earth's crust

0
30 km
2900 km
5165 km
6385 km

solid core
molten core
mantle

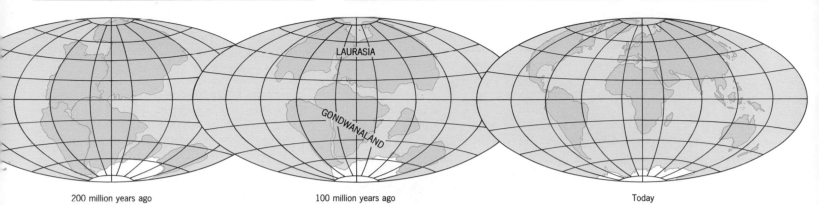

200 million years ago   100 million years ago   Today

Origin of the Earth

The Universe is said to have come into existence as much as 20,000 million years ago. We shall never really know how this happened. The most popular explanation is the 'Big bang' theory. According to this, there was an enormous explosion which sent gases and particles hurtling out in all directions. Gradually, galaxies and solar systems began to form from this swirling mass, and the Sun might have eventually formed about 5,000 million years ago.

The Earth is thought to have formed 4,600 million years ago as a ball of molten rock. It was probably as hot as 4,000°C. It took many millions of years for the Earth to cool down enough for a crust to form, and the crust must have been very thin at first. Molten rock turns into solid rock at temperatures of 800–1,500°C, so the early Earth's crust would have been too hot to stand on.

The early Earth probably had no atmosphere, just like most of the other planets now. However, gases were ejected from volcanoes all over the surface, and a primitive atmosphere developed.

This early Earth atmosphere had no oxygen. The first forms of life are believed to date from 3,500 million years ago, and they lived without oxygen. Oxygen came much later, since it is mainly produced by plants.

Continents on the move

The shape of the continents and the oceans on this early Earth is very uncertain. So many changes have taken place over the thousands of millions of years that the features formed at that time have largely been lost.

One thing is certain: in the distant past the Earth looked very different. The continents and the oceans have changed tremendously. For example, 200 million years ago, there was no Atlantic Ocean. North America, Europe and part of Asia were joined as one continent which we call Laurasia. South America, Africa, India, Australia and Antarctica formed a large southern continent called Gondwanaland. We can work out when the Atlantic began to open up, and how wide it was at different times.

This continental drift seems evident when we see how well the coastlines match up. For example, Africa and South America fit neatly together. Also, the sands and muds on the bottom of the ocean can be dated accurately, and they become younger and younger as you get nearer to the centre of the ocean. What is happening is that there is a deep fissure (crack) right up the middle of the Atlantic which is like a line of small volcanoes. Molten rock is forced up the crack and the two halves of the Atlantic are pushed apart. A new ocean floor is created in the middle with Africa gradually shifting eastwards, South America westwards. This movement is only 1 to 10 cm (⅜ in to 4 in) per year.

The surface of the Earth is divided up into several large plates, and these are all moving in different directions. North America will eventually reach Russia to the west. California (on the Pacific plate) may drift away from the rest of North America. Africa may move north and close off the Mediterranean Sea, and so on. ■

◀ Egypt and the Nile delta seen from a space shuttle.

▲ The present-day continents only began to take shape 200 million years ago. Since then the various land masses have drifted to their present location.

Area of the Earth's surface
510 million sq km
Area of land
149 million sq km (29%)
Areas of oceans and seas
361 million sq km (71%)
Volume of the Earth
1,083,230 million cubic km
Weight of the Earth
5,976 million million million tonnes
Greatest known height
8,848 m Mount Everest
Greatest known depth
11,035 m Marianas Trench
Age of the Earth
4,600 million years. Cooled to 1,000°C and first rains: 4,300 million years ago
Origin of life
3,500 million years
Temperature at the core of the Earth
5,000°C
Pressure at the core of the Earth
3·5 million atmospheres

◉ See also
Atmosphere
Continents
Earthquakes
Geological time
Geologists
Gravity
Planets
Plate tectonics
Satellites
Solar System
Universe

Earthquakes

▲ The big earthquake that shook Armenia in 1988 destroyed blocks of flats and made tens of thousands of people homeless. These Armenians at Spitak are trying to keep out the bitter cold.

Earthquakes happen when the surface of the Earth moves. Anyone who has gone through an earthquake has felt that it was one of the strangest and most disturbing things they have ever known. We feel that the Earth is solid and safe, but then it can jerk and crack; houses can disappear into great holes that did not exist a few seconds before; roads can be split by great steps many metres high; and the water in lakes can disappear into the ground.

Causes

Earthquakes remind us that the crust of the Earth is very thin in comparison to the size of the Earth. Beneath the crust are thousands of kilometres of molten rock and metal which are very hot and under very high pressure. The crust of the Earth is divided into great plates that move very slowly. The margins of these plates mark lines of weakness in the crust, lines along which we occasionally see the effects of the inner parts of the active Earth.

Earthquakes happen when two plates jerk against each other. For example, in California, the famous San Andreas fault marks the boundary between the North American plate and the Pacific plate. These two plates are moving in slightly different directions by only a few centimetres each year. However, this does not go smoothly. The weight of the crust, and the friction of the rocks, mean that the plates cannot glide easily against each other.

Famous earthquakes		
Date	Place	Richter value
1755	Lisbon, Portugal	
1906	Colombia/Ecuador	8·6
1906	Valparaiso, Chile	8·4
1906	San Francisco, USA	7·8
1911	Sinkiang, China	8·4
1920	Kansu, China	8·5
1923	Sagami Bay, Japan	8·2
1933	Japanese Trench	8·5
1955	North Assam, India	8·6
1960	Chile	8·6
1964	Alaska	8·6
1988	Armenia	6·9
1989	San Francisco, USA	6·9
1990	Iran	7·7

Damage

For years there is no movement at all, but tremendous pressures are building up. Suddenly, the pressure is too great, and the plates jump. This causes an earthquake. The size of the jump depends on the amount of pressure that has built up. A small earthquake will just feel like a distant rumble under your feet. A larger earthquake may tip ornaments and books onto the floor. A much bigger earthquake may cause chimneys and trees to fall down. The worst earthquakes of all will knock down every building in sight, shatter roads and bridges, destroy all electricity, gas, and telephone services, and often lead to great floods.

The size of every earthquake that happens is measured on a scale from 1 to 10, called the Richter scale. This measures the forces involved and the effects of the earthquake. Instruments that measure earthquakes are based on the pendulum. The base of the instrument is firmly fixed to the ground, and a small weight hanging on a string then shows how much movement is taking place in the Earth. Instruments like this can even pick up earthquakes that take place thousands of miles away, which we could not possibly feel ourselves. ■

See also

Plate tectonics
Volcanoes

Characteristic effects of shallow shocks in populated areas	Richter scale	Number of earthquakes per year
Damage nearly total	more than 8·0	0·1–0·2
Great damage	more than 7·4	4
Serious damage, rails bent	7·0–7·3	15
Considerable damage to buildings	6·2–6·9	100
Slight damage to buildings	5·5–6·1	500
Felt by all	4·9–5·4	1,400
Felt by many	4·3–4·8	4,800
Felt by some	3·5–4·2	30,000
Not felt but recorded	2·0–3·4	800,000

Earwigs

Earwigs have this odd name because people thought at one time that these insects would wriggle into their ears. Earwigs do like to squeeze into small spaces, but it is most unlikely that they ever go into human ears. Gardeners often complain that earwigs eat their plants, though in fact earwigs feed on almost anything, particularly dead animals.

Hidden wings

Earwigs are nocturnal and spend most of their time on the ground, or on plants. They can fly, although they rarely do so. Their wings, which are large and fan-like, are normally hidden under short, leathery wing cascs. They can unfold them easily, but to pack them back again is more difficult. The earwig has to use the pincers, called forceps, at the back end of its body to help. These forceps are curved in the males and straight in the females.

In the winter-time female earwigs lay about 25 eggs in a sheltered place under a stone, or in the soil. The eggs are large, and the female stays

◄ This large-pincered earwig, *Labidura riparia*, can be identified as a male by his curved forceps.

with them until they hatch in early spring. The baby earwigs, which look like tiny versions of their mother, are cared for by her until they are big enough to fend for themselves.

The female earwig constantly licks the eggs she has laid. By doing this she probably removes germs from them, for if the eggs are taken from their mother, they usually go rotten quite quickly. ■

Phylum
Arthropoda
Class
Insecta
Order
Dermaptera
Number of species
About 1,200

 See also
Insects

Easter

Easter is a Christian festival which takes place in March or April. It is a happy feast which ends 40 days of fasting called Lent.

The last two days of Lent are Good Friday, when Jesus was crucified, and Easter Eve (or Holy Saturday) when he lay in the tomb. But Christians believe that his death was not the end. On the Sunday morning some of his friends found that the stone sealing his tomb had rolled away. They believed that he had risen from the dead. Easter Sunday celebrates this event, the resurrection of Christ.

Churches are often silent and dark during the sad part of the story. This changes before dawn on Easter Day. One flame and one candle are used to light many candles, and churches fill with the light and singing of hope and joy at the victory over evil and death.

Easter and spring

The English name for Easter comes from a pre-Christian fertility celebration. Spring is the natural time for new life and hope when plants begin to grow and many animals have their

young. Easter combines this natural sense of joy with the Christian story. Many of the popular things associated with Easter are part of the events of spring. Eggs, chickens, rabbits and flowers are all symbols of new life. Chocolate and rich fruit cake covered with marzipan show that fasting is over. ■

See also
Christians
Fasting

Biography
Jesus

▼ Easter procession of monks of the Eastern Orthodox Church in Mount Athos, Greece.

Edwardian Britain
1901–1910

Population of England and Wales in 1901: 32,528,000.

▼ These homes may have been rented by prosperous people; there was plenty of accommodation for rent in Edwardian times. Motoring was popular for families who could afford it. But it was a luxury and there were few cars on the roads. Horse-drawn traffic was still common.

King Edward VII was the eldest son of Queen Victoria. Because Victoria was Queen for so long, Edward was 59 when he became King. He came to the throne in 1901 and died in 1910. Edward was very different from Victoria. He liked parties and gambling and going to the races. Most people rather liked him for this, and even now when we think of 'Edwardian times' we think of rich men in evening dress smoking cigars, and elegant ladies strolling with parasols while the new motor cars chug by. Most of the problems of Victorian times still existed, however; there was still much poverty and poor housing.

1901 Queen Victoria died
  Edward VII
1902 Boer War ended
  Balfour prime minister
1904 Rolls and Royce
  started making cars
1906 Liberals won election
  Campbell-Bannerman
  prime minister
  Suffragettes first
  jailed
1907 Boy Scouts formed
1908 Asquith prime minister
  Olympic games in
  London
1909 Old-age pensions
  Blériot flew Channel
1910 **George V**

Wealth

Britain was a powerful and rich country in Edwardian times. Much of the wealth came from business abroad. British money was invested in many countries. British ships carried goods on all the world's oceans. British banks and insurance companies had customers and did business all over the world. Other countries were catching up, though, and British industry was slow to take up new ideas. For example, the first cars in Britain came from Germany and France. Germany especially was modernizing its industry, and working hard to be the equal of Britain. America, too, was rapidly becoming a modern industrial country.

Changes

In Edwardian Britain, there were important changes in the way that people lived and were governed. The Labour Representation Committee, which soon became the Labour Party, was formed in 1900. Its aim was to see working people represented in Parliament. It was supported by powerful trade unions.

In 1902 the Government began providing secondary education. Only a small number of children could go to secondary school, however. You either had to pay, or be clever enough to pass a scholarship exam. Most working-class children still left school at 13, and many only went to school part-time after 11.

A Liberal government was elected in 1906, and began to provide some of the things which we now take for granted. The first old-age pensions were drawn in January 1909, and Employment Exchanges, where unemployed people could go to find work, also started in that year. Women still did not have the vote and the suffragettes were agitating for this reform.

Technology

The first powered aeroplane flew in America in 1903. By 1910 flights over Britain were common. Cars started to appear on the roads. The telephone came into an increasing number of homes. Radio, or 'wireless telegraphy', was increasingly used, especially by ships at sea.

Public film theatres began to open in Edwardian times, the first one in America in 1905. However, they were rare novelties and most people still went to the theatre or music-hall. Gramophones became popular despite the scratchy quality of Edwardian recordings. ■

◄ An Edison standard phonograph.

See also
Aircraft
Boer War
Motor cars
Poor Laws in Britain
Radio
Recording
Suffragettes
Telephones
Trade unions
Twentieth-century history

Biography
Edward VII
Lloyd George
Pankhursts

Eggs

▲ Guillemot eggs are about 8 cm long and are laid on narrow cliff ledges. Their pointed shape makes them roll in a circle if knocked, rather than in a straight line over the cliff.

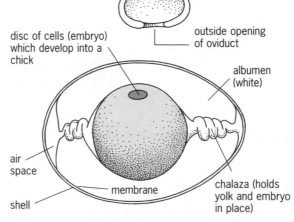

◄ Ostriches lay up to ten eggs at a time, but several hens often lay them in one place, making a pile of as many as 50.

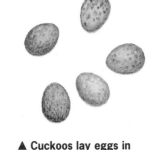

◄ Hummingbird eggs weigh about one-fifth of the adult bird's weight.

▲ Cuckoos lay eggs in the nests of other birds. Their eggs are usually about the same size as the host bird's, but not always the same colour.

An egg is the cell made by which, when fertil... a new animal. A... Most animals lay... are normally co... jelly or a tough... or in lakes and... in the sand, fro... birds' eggs in m... ...ntain food in the form of ... ...hen enables the young animal (embryo) to grow.

Most mammals, like ourselves, do not lay eggs. Instead they have tiny eggs without yolk, which are fertilized inside the mother's body. The embryo becomes attached to the mother's womb (uterus) by a placenta. This nourishes the growing baby, so that yolk food is not needed. Platypuses and spiny anteaters (echidnas) are the only mammals that lay eggs. Their eggs are soft-shelled, like those of snakes and lizards.

How bird eggs are made

A bird's egg has many layers. It has a hard shell on the outside for protection, which lets oxygen pass inwards. Inside is a membrane, and inside that the white. This is a store of water and protein food. Right in the centre of the egg is the yolk, made of fat and proteins to feed the growing chick.

Inside a mother bird the parts of an egg are put together from the inside outwards. An egg starts as a large, yolky cell (an oocyte) in the bird's ovary. It breaks free and passes along a tube called an oviduct, where it is fertilized. The fertilized oocyte is the egg's yolk, and on its

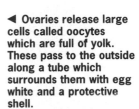

ovary

developing egg cells (oocytes)

egg tube (oviduct)

outside opening of oviduct

◄ Ovaries release large cells called oocytes which are full of yolk. These pass to the outside along a tube which surrounds them with egg white and a protective shell.

disc of cells (embryo) which develop into a chick

albumen (white)

air space

shell

membrane

chalaza (holds yolk and embryo in place)

◄ The chick sits on a ball of food called yolk. This floats in a 'pond' of jelly, the egg white, which gives it moisture. The shell gives protection and lets in air.

surface the embryo begins to grow. Moving down the tube, the yolk is covered by white, then by the membrane, and finally by the shell itself.

When an egg is laid, the young bird inside continues to grow using the yolk and white as food. It needs to be kept warm all the time, and the parents manage this by taking turns sitting on eggs in the nest. This is called incubation. At the end of incubation the bird hatches by breaking out of the egg. Incubation can take eleven days for small birds such as sparrows, and 80 days for the largest birds such as ostriches. ■

See also
Birds
Crocodiles (photo)
Platypuses
Pregnancy
Reproduction
Slugs and snails (photo)

Egypt

Area
1,002,000 sq km
(386,900 sq miles)
Capital
Cairo
Population
49,560,000
Language
Arabic
Religion
Muslim, Christian
Government
Parliamentary republic
Currency
1 Egyptian pound = 100
piastres

Land height in metres

more than 2000
1000–2000
500–1000
200–500
less than 200

Land below Sea Level

main roads
railways

0 kilometres 200
(124 miles)

CYPRUS

Mediterranean
Sea

ISRAEL

JORDAN

Alexandria

Port
Said

Suez Canal

El Gîza Cairo Suez

Qattara
Depression El Faiyûm

SAUDI
ARABIA

LIBYA

El Minya

Asyût

Red
Sea

L I B Y A N

El Khârga

Luxor

D E S E R T

Aswân

Nile

Lake
Nasser

S U D A N

▶ The view from the Al
Azhar Mosque over the
old bazaar district shows
the traffic of Cairo today.

⊙ See also

Africa
Arabs
Canals
Egyptian ancient history
Middle East
Muslims
Ottoman empire
Pyramids

Biography
Nasser

Egypt is a large and lively country in the centre of the Arab world. More people live here than in any other Arab country and the population is rising fast. The vast majority of Egyptians live close to the River Nile which flows north into the Mediterranean Sea. The peasant farmers, called fellahin, have little modern equipment. Buffaloes are used for turning wheels to pump water into the fields, and donkeys are used for transport. Away from the Nile, most of the country is desert.

The centre of Egyptian life is Cairo, which is also on the Nile. It is noisy and dirty and its streets become clogged with traffic. But it is full of colour. About 15 million people live in Cairo and there is not enough room for them all. The rich live in splendid villas and eat at luxury restaurants. But the rich are few. Most people in Cairo have to find homes where they can, some crammed into crumbling old houses, some in bleak blocks of flats, and others in the shanty-towns on the edges of the city. The basic food for Egyptians consists of flat loaves of bread and beans, with dates, olives, water-melons, onions and tomatoes.

Egypt receives money from ships passing through the Suez Canal which connects the Mediterranean with the Red Sea. But there is great poverty and unemployment. Many Egyptians emigrate for work.

Flashback

After the centuries of ancient civilization, Egypt has had many different rulers. It was conquered by Persians and by Greeks and then became a part of the Roman empire. By AD 200 many Egyptians had become Christians and the Church, called the Coptic Church, was strong. But when the Arabs invaded in the 7th century, Egypt became mainly Muslim, though a Coptic Christian community survives.

From the early 16th century Egypt was part of the huge Ottoman empire. Then in 1882 after serious anti-foreign riots, Britain occupied Egypt to protect the Suez Canal which they partly owned. Egypt gained independence in 1922. In 1952 the king was forced to abdicate and Egypt became a republic. In 1956 President Nasser nationalized the Suez Canal. ■

Egyptian ancient history

Egypt became a kingdom in about 3100 BC when King Menes conquered the northern part of the country. This makes it one of the oldest states in the world. The Egyptians became famous for their great buildings, their statues and their ability to farm a land which was largely desert. The Egyptians used pictures (called hieroglyphs) for their writing, which we can translate today. They conquered other countries and established an empire. However, in 30 BC the Romans invaded and Egypt became part of the Roman empire.

The wealth of the Nile

Egypt could never have become a prosperous and powerful country without the River Nile. The Greek historian Herodotus called Egypt 'the gift of the Nile'. He was right, because each year the Nile flooded the land around. This yearly flood brought water to a land which has very little rainfall. The river also washed fertile mud onto the soil in which the crops could grow. The Egyptians were able to grow corn for bread, and lettuces, onions, peas, cucumbers and other vegetables. Once the crops were growing, the Egyptians were able to water the soil by digging irrigation channels from the Nile. The Egyptians saw their River Nile as a god, called Hapy, who was generous to them. It was not always reliable though, and there were years of drought and sometimes floods.

The Egyptians were famous for using a reed, papyrus, to make writing materials. They were also good at engineering. They built special 'Nilometers' to measure the height of the flood waters in July, to work out how much water they could use when ploughing began in October. Officials kept careful records, if only to be able to collect taxes from the farmers.

The king and the government

The rulers of Egypt were called 'pharaohs'. The pharaoh was a king but was also thought to be a god after death. He was the High Priest of the Egyptians, the chief judge and also the commander-in-chief of the army. The king usually married his own sister and their son would become the next pharaoh. A large number of officials, appointed by the king, ran the government. Some would have been relatives of the king. These officials looked after government departments such as the treasury, the civil service, the foreign office and the records.

Egyptians used papyrus to write on and for painting pictures. They invented a method of making this writing material from a reed, also called papyrus.

◄ **The construction of a great dam at Aswan to provide hydroelectricity threatened the temples of Abu Simbel. From 1959 to 1965 the two temples were cut out and rebuilt on a new site. At the entrance of the Great Temple are these colossal seated statues of the pharaoh, Rameses II. He is wearing the double crown of Upper and Lower Egypt. The smaller figures represent his wife, princes and gods.**

◄ Map of ancient Egypt.

Mediterranean Sea

Alexandria

LOWER EGYPT

Giza ▲ ● Heliopolis
Saqqara ▲ ● Memphis

Heracleopolis ●

SINAI

● Tell el Amarna

Nile

Red Sea

UPPER EGYPT

Abydos ■
Valley of the Kings ■
● Thebes

SAHARA DESERT

Hieraconpolis ●

■ Aswan

NUBIA

● city
▲ pyramid
■ temple or tomb

Abu Simbel ■

0 kilometres 150
(92 miles)

▲ **Rameses II holding an offering table. This sculpture was made in about 1250 BC.**

Ordinary Egyptians

A lot of ordinary Egyptians worked on the land as farmers. The farmers not only planted crops but kept cows, sheep, goats and pigs. They also hunted animals such as deer, and trapped birds and fished, sometimes just for sport.

There were also a large number of special jobs to be done. Some Egyptians were fishermen, or boat-owners moving goods up and down the Nile. Builders were needed for the towns, palaces and the tombs. As many as 100,000 people might have been needed to build the largest pyramids. Craftspeople were trained to be tomb-painters or statue sculptors, or to make objects like jewellery.

Buildings

Very important buildings, such as pyramids and temples to the gods, were built of stone cut from quarries. All the other buildings (people's houses, palaces and government buildings) were made of mud bricks. Earth was mixed with straw and water and put into wooden moulds. Once it had dried hard in the sun it could be used as a building brick. Bricks were fairly easy to make and they lasted for a long time because the climate in Egypt is dry and hot.

Egyptian gods and the afterlife

The Egyptians were very religious and believed that gods played a great part in their lives. They also believed that there was life after death. They thought that the dead person made a journey to the next world and continued to live the same sort of life there. The king would still be a king; a farm labourer would still be a farm labourer. To help in this journey, the rich were given a painted tomb with a variety of their possessions. The Egyptians buried food and drink in the tomb because they thought an actual journey was made at death. ∎

▶ **This painting comes from a tomb in Thebes. It shows the nobleman Nebamun as a hunter throwing a special stick at birds. Notice the great variety of birds and fish in the River Nile below his boat of reeds.**

▶ **This scene painted on papyrus is part of *The Book of the Dead*. It shows what the Egyptians believed happened when a person died. Here the dead person's heart is being weighed against the Feather of Truth. If his heart was heavier this meant he had led a wicked life and was punished in the underworld.**

👁 See also
Egypt
Egyptian myths
Hieroglyphics
Nile
Paper
Pyramids

Biography
Cleopatra
Tutankhamun

Egyptian myths

The Egyptians worshipped over 750 gods. The people thought of their gods as giant human beings, with birds' or animals' heads. The gods ruled the upper world where humans lived, and the underworld where souls went after death.

Ra

The world began with a baby god, asleep in a lotus-flower. His name was Ra, and he was the Sun. He woke up and opened his eyes, and at once light-rays streamed out to fill the sky. In that instant, Ra sprang from being a baby to a full-grown god. He soared across the sky, and sent light glittering into every corner of the world. The seas and rivers reflected his light, and dazzled him. His eyes watered, and the water-drops made plants, people and animals.

Most of Ra's new creatures lived together in peace and happiness. Only human beings were discontented. They argued and fought until Ra was so angry that he took out one of his fiery eyes and threw it at them. The eye flashed across the world like a fireball, and human beings cowered. From that moment on, Ra ruled unchallenged.

Every day he sailed serenely in his Sun-ship, east to west across the sky. Every evening he plunged below the horizon, and began a night-long voyage through the caves and tunnels of the underworld. At dawn each day he returned to the upper world, where his worshippers were waiting with hymns of joy.

Why the Nile floods: Osiris and Isis

The River Nile floods every year, leaving a layer of rich, muddy soil, ideal for crops. To explain why it happened, the Egyptians told the myth of Osiris and Isis.

In the myth, Osiris and Isis were gods, the king and queen of all human beings. Their brother, Set the storm-god, realized that he would never have power so long as Isis and Osiris ruled. He plotted to end their reign. He murdered Osiris, cut his body into fourteen pieces and floated them down the Nile. Isis had to sail after them, gather them one by one from the river and reassemble them for burial. Osiris went down to the underworld, where he became ruler of the dead, and every year, on the anniversary of his murder, Isis wept for him. Her tears filled the River Nile to overflowing and caused the floods.

The underworld

The ancient Egyptians believed that as well as a mortal body, every human being had a *ka*, or spirit-self. When the body died, the ka lived on. Horus, the falcon-headed messenger-god, led the ka to the underworld for judgement. Before the throne of Osiris, lord of the dead, 42 judges questioned the ka about its behaviour in the upper world. Jackal-headed Anubis, god of tombs, weighed each ka's heart on a pair of scales, balancing it against the Feather of Truth. Wicked kas were handed over to Ammut, the crocodile-headed Eater of Corpses. Horus led good kas to Osiris, who gave them eternal happiness. ■

Gods and goddesses

Amun
King of the gods. He was the lord of fertility; it was by his power that crops grew, animals produced young and human beings had children. He had a human body and a ram's head with curling horns. His worshippers built huge stone temples in his honour.

Bes
God of marriage, dancing and cheerfulness. He was hideously ugly, with twisted limbs, a crooked spine and a lolling tongue.

Ptah
God of arts and crafts. He was gentle and kind, a patron god of doctors and healers. He was married to Sekhmet, and protected people from her attacks.

Sekhmet
Goddess of war, half woman and half lioness. She prowled over battlefields, greedy for human flesh.

See also

Egyptian ancient history

▼ This painting was made in about 1250 BC. Osiris is seated in a kiosk with columns decorated with papyrus reeds. Isis stands behind him with Nephthys, her sister.

Eid

It can also be spelt Id.

Eid is the Muslim word for festival. There are two main eids in the religion of Islam. Eid ul Adha, the Festival of Sacrifice, comes at the end of the month of pilgrimage. This festival commemorates Abraham's willingness to sacrifice Ishmael and the fact that God provided an animal in his place. Pilgrims to Mecca slaughter and share a sheep or goat as part of the pilgrimage. At the same time, Muslims all over the world do the same with their families and friends. They also give each other eid cards and exchange presents of clothes and food.

The other eid is Eid ul Fitr, the festival to mark the end of the fasting month of Ramadan. The month of Ramadan commemorates the giving of the Koran to Muhammad. In order to concentrate on the importance of this, Muslims fast from dawn to dusk throughout the month. At the end, the fast is broken in a festival when Muslims feast with their friends, buy new clothes, send greetings cards and exchange presents. During both festivals attendance at mosques is particularly high. ■

See also

Fasting
Festivals
Koran
Mosques
Muslims

Biography
Abraham
Muhammad

▶ A greetings card celebrating the festival of Eid. The message inside reads: 'With Hearty Greetings and Every Good Wish on the Auspicious Day of Eid'.

Eisteddfod

This is a Welsh word meaning a 'sitting' or gathering. Eisteddfodau, held in towns and villages in Wales throughout the year, are events where people come together to compete for prizes by singing, reciting and writing poetry.

The National Eisteddfod of Wales is the largest and is held in a different town in Wales each year. It lasts over a week and all the competitions are held in Welsh. There are competitions of every kind from folk singing, classical music and pop groups to competitions in science, technology, arts and crafts, and first aid. The highlights are the ceremonies of crowning and chairing the bard (poet).

The crown is given to the best poem written in a free metre, without rhyme, and the chair is awarded for a poem written according to strict rules originally developed in the Middle Ages, called *cynghanedd*. These ceremonies are led by an Archdruid and the Gorsedd of the Bards dressed in their colourful robes of green, blue and white. The white robe, the highest honour, is awarded for outstanding service to Wales and its culture.

The Gorsedd of Bards claims to follow the ways of the old Celtic Druids, although the modern Gorsedd ceremonies are largely the idea of a rather eccentric Welshman, Edward Williams (1747–1826), usually known by his bardic name 'Iolo Morganwg'. He 'reinvented' both the modern Gorsedd of Bards and the idea of holding eisteddfodau where the bards could meet.

In addition to the National Eisteddfod, another very popular annual eisteddfod is held in the town of Llangollen in North Wales. This eisteddfod first began after World War II and has been held every year to bring together singers and dancers from all over the world and build international peace and understanding. ■

The plural is 'eisteddfodau'.

From 1950 Welsh became the official language of the Eisteddfod.

The National Eisteddfod is held every year in North and South Wales in turn.

See also

Druids
Welsh history

Elastic

Elastic materials are materials which return to their original shape after they have been stretched, squashed or bent. We sometimes say that materials like this are stretchy or springy. A rubber band is elastic. Stretch it and then let it go, and it shortens again. Materials like wood, steel and plastic are much less stretchy than rubber bands but they are still elastic. A plank of wood sags when you walk on it and straightens when you get off. A steel spanner bends slightly when you turn it, though by so little that you do not notice.

Using elastic materials

Elastic materials have many uses. Elastic tape holds clothes round your waist. Tennis balls and footballs are elastic. They change shape when they hit something, but regain their shape when they bounce off. Car engines are mounted on rubber blocks to absorb vibrations. Passenger seat cushions are elastic to give a comfortable ride. And car bodies are mounted on steel springs so that a bumpy road will not shake the car to bits. Even our bodies have elastic fibres in them. Try pinching the skin on the back of your hand. As soon as you let go, the skin returns to its original shape.

Storing energy

Elastic materials can be used to store energy. Some model planes use the energy stored in a coiled-up length of rubber to turn the propeller. A wind-up clock has a steel spring inside which drives the clock as it slowly unwinds. Air is elastic. The energy stored in compressed (squashed) air is used to drive pneumatic drills and hammers.

Over the limit

If too much force is used on an elastic material it may stay out of shape. Scientists say that it has passed its elastic limit. This happens when a car is dented or a screwdriver gets bent. If a material goes too far past its elastic limit, it may break altogether. Materials such as china and chalk, which are hardly elastic at all, break very easily because they cannot bend or stretch. We say that materials like this are brittle. ■

◄ If tennis balls were not elastic a game of tennis would be very short indeed.

◉ See also

Plastics
Rubber
Skin
Springs

Elections

Elections are the way in which a group of people can choose one person to represent them or lead them. Members of groups and clubs often hold elections to choose an organizing committee.

Elections may also be held to choose a trade union official, a local councillor, or a member of a parliament or congress. In a democratic election, the voters have a choice of candidates and voting takes place in secret so that no one can be forced to vote for someone they do not want. In elections to parliaments and local councils, candidates are often organized into rival political parties.

In the simplest form of election, each elector has one vote, and the candidate who receives the most votes is elected. This is called the 'first past the post' system. Another system of voting is proportional representation (PR). Under this system, the total numbers of votes are added up and the political parties have as many members elected as their share of the votes. This can give a fairer result than the 'first past the post' system. ■

In 1990 voters in the Soviet Union were allowed to vote for candidates from different parties. For over 70 years all the candidates had to be communists. Free, democratic elections were also held in Czechoslovakia and Hungary after over 40 years of communist rule.

◉ See also

Democracy
Government
Parliaments
Political parties

Electricity

Electricity

▶ Lightning over the town of Tamworth in New South Wales, Australia.

Typical voltages

torch battery	1½ volts
car battery	12 volts
mains power-point (UK)	240 volts
underground train	600 volts
power-station generator	25,000 volts
overhead power line	400,000 volts
lightning flash	100 million volts

It makes cling-film stick to your hands and it crackles when you comb you hair. It can power TVs, tumble-driers and trains. It can even light up the sky in a flash.

What is electricity?

Electricity is lots of tiny particles called electrons. Electrons are much smaller than atoms. In fact, they are parts of atoms. Everything is made of atoms, so there is electricity in everything. However, you do not notice any of its effects until something makes the electrons move from their atoms.

Rubbing makes electrons move. When cling-film rubs on your hand, it pulls electrons away from atoms in your skin. The atoms try to pull the electrons back again, so the cling-film sticks to your hand. The same thing happens when you rub a balloon on your sleeve. The balloon will stick to your body or to a wall.

Batteries make electrons move. They can push electrons through wires made of copper and other metals. Materials like copper which let electrons flow through are called conductors. The tiny electrons squeeze between the atoms in the wire. Some materials stop electrons passing through. These are called insulators. Plastics and rubber are insulators. Air is an insulator most of the time. But if electrons are pushed hard enough, they can even jump through air. Then you see sparks.

Circuits

A battery has two terminals. Electrons only flow out if these terminals are joined by a conductor. This happens if you connect a small bulb between the terminals with wires. The battery pushes the electrons from the − (negative) terminal round to the + (positive) terminal. The bulb lights up as the electrons flow through.

The complete loop through the wires, bulb and battery is called a circuit. The flow of electrons is known as a current. You can put a switch in the circuit to turn the current on and off. Switching off pulls two contacts apart. This breaks the circuit and stops the flow of electrons.

▼ Electrons flow from one terminal of a battery round to the other, but only if the circuit is unbroken.

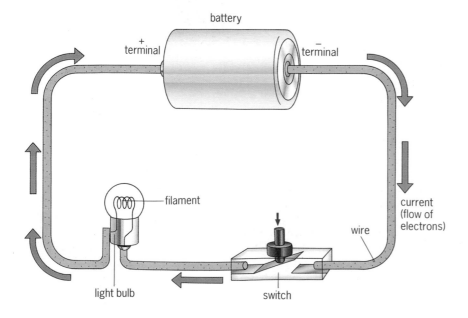

battery

+ terminal

− terminal

filament

current (flow of electrons)

wire

light bulb

switch

Using electricity

Heat, light, magnetism, sound and movement are just some of the things which we can get from electricity.

Wires warm up when a current flows through. Thin wires warm up much more than thick ones, and some types of wire warm up more than others. In an electric fire, wire made of an alloy called nichrome becomes red-hot when a current flows through. In a light bulb, a thin tungsten wire (a filament) gets so hot that it glows white.

Every current has a magnetic field around it. If a current flows through a coil of wire, the coil behaves just like a magnet. Electromagnets are a special type of magnet which you can switch on and off. They have a coil of wire in them. Electric motors also have a coil in them. It rotates between the ends of a bent magnet. When a current flows through the coil it becomes magnetized. The pull of the magnet makes the coil spin round. In a loudspeaker, a varying current makes a coil vibrate near a magnet. The vibrations make the sound.

Volts, amps and watts

Batteries and generators all push out electrons. The higher their voltage, the harder they push. Scientists measure voltage in volts.

A current is a flow of electrons. The higher the current, the more electrons flow round the circuit every second. Scientists measure current in amperes ('amps').

Electrons carry energy. The energy comes from a battery or generator. It is spent when the electrons pass through a lamp, a kettle or some other electrical appliance.

The power of an appliance is measured in watts. The higher the power, the more energy the appliance takes every second.

There is a connection between power, voltage and current:

Power in watts = voltage × current.
       (volts)   (amperes)

So a 200 volt kettle taking a current of 10 amperes has a power of 2,000 watts (2 kilowatts).

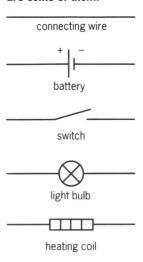

▼ Electricians use special symbols for drawing circuits. Here are some of them:

connecting wire

battery

switch

light bulb

heating coil

◄ In many power-stations, the generators are turned by steam turbines. The generators produce alternating current (a.c.).

Direct current (d.c.)
Current which always flows the same way. Electricity from a battery is like this.

Alternating current (a.c.)
Current which flows backwards, forwards, backwards, forwards . . . and so on. Mains electricity is like this.

Mains frequency
Measured in hertz (Hz). Tells you how many times the alternating current from the mains flows backwards and forwards every second:
UK   50 Hz
USA 60 Hz

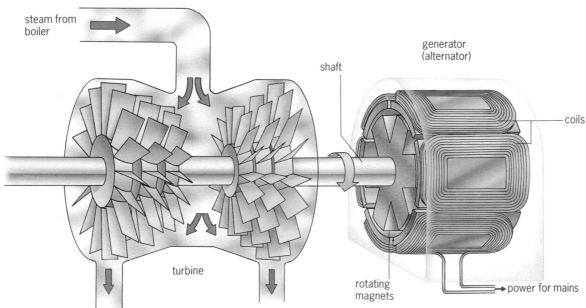

steam from boiler

shaft

generator (alternator)

coils

turbine

rotating magnets

power for mains

Generating electricity

Batteries cannot store enough energy to keep cookers, washing machines and electric fires supplied with electricity. The electricity for these has to come from the mains.

Mains electricity comes from huge generators in power-stations, turned by turbines driven round by the force of water or high-pressure steam. The steam is made using the heat from burning coal, oil or gas or from a nuclear reactor.

Each generator has a ring of copper coils round the outside. Inside this, huge magnets are turned by a shaft from a turbine. As the magnets rotate, they make electrons move in the coils. The current flows backwards and forwards, as first one end of a magnet and then another sweeps past. Current which flows like this is called alternating current (a.c.). The generators are known as alternators. Current from a battery is different; it flows only one way. It is known as direct current (d.c.). ■

Electricity supply

Scientists are investigating new non-polluting ways of generating electricity, including harnessing the power of tides and winds.

Hydroelectric plants generate electricity when water flows down from lakes or reservoirs. These projects are very expensive because large dams have to be built to contain the water.

When you plug in a kettle, the power can come from a generator miles away. At the power-station, electricity from the generator passes along thick cables to a transformer. Here, the voltage is stepped up, before the power is fed to the transmission lines which carry it across country. Increasing the voltage cuts down the current. The electrons are pushed harder, so fewer are needed to carry the power. Most transmission lines hang from tall pylons, but in areas of great natural beauty, they are buried. The lines are part of a network of power-stations and cables called the Grid. If one area needs more power, it can be supplied by generators in other areas.

Distributing the power

Power from the transmission lines goes to the substations. Here, the voltage is stepped down by transformers; the lines divide to go to smaller substations . . . and so on. You may have a small substation in your street. If so, it will have a steel fence round it and a notice saying something like 'Electricity Board: keep out'. The final connection to your house is usually made by a cable buried under the road, though in country areas, poles and overhead wires are sometimes used.

Where the cable comes into your house, you will find three things: a main switch, a main fuse which automatically switches off the current if the circuits become overloaded, and a meter so that the Electricity Board knows how much to charge you.

▼ Power is carried across country by overhead transmission lines. The voltage is stepped down in stages as the power is distributed to towns and factories.

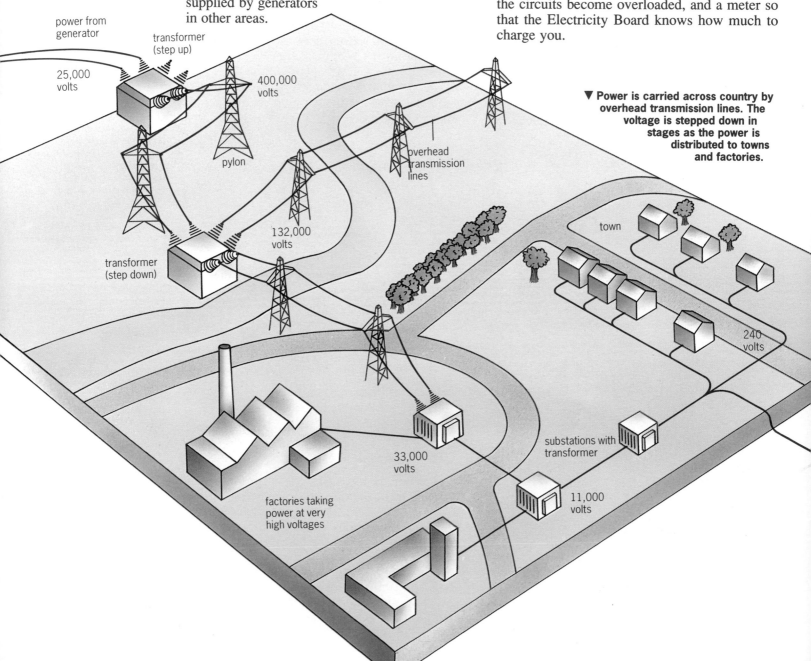

power from generator

transformer (step up)

25,000 volts

400,000 volts

pylon

overhead transmission lines

132,000 volts

transformer (step down)

town

240 volts

factories taking power at very high voltages

33,000 volts

substations with transformer

11,000 volts

Power around the house

The wiring in the house divides into several branches. There are circuits for the lights and power points. And there are circuits for the electric cooker and the water heater. The wires divide at a box called the consumer unit ('fuse-box'). Here, each circuit has its own fuse or circuit-breaker.

In many houses in Britain, the power points are connected to a single cable which runs round the house and back to the consumer unit again. The cable is called a ring main. Each item you plug into it has a fuse in its plug. It is important that a fuse of the correct value is fitted. If the fuse value is too high, the fuse may not 'blow' if a fault develops. In many countries, the plugs do not have fuses. Instead, each power point has its own cable and a fuse or circuit-breaker in the consumer unit.

Danger!

Mains electricity is dangerous. Touching 'live' (high voltage) wires can cause shocks, burns and even death. For safety, overhead power lines are kept high above the ground, but it is still extremely dangerous to use kites or fishing lines close to them.

At home, appliances such as hair-driers and lamps have a double layer of insulation to protect you from the high voltages inside. Metal appliances like kettles and toasters have an earth wire connected to them. It stops the metal becoming 'live' if a wire works loose.

Frayed cables are very dangerous. Not only can they give you a shock; they can overheat and catch fire. Faulty TV sets are especially dangerous. You should never take the back off a TV, because parts inside may be at 20,000 volts or more. And you should always pull out the plug overnight. A faulty set can overheat and catch fire even with the switch on the front turned off. ■

Mains cables
Each cable has three insulated wires in it. In many countries, standard colours are used in cables connected to plugs: Live wire (brown) is at mains voltage. Neutral wire (blue) completes the circuit. Earth wire (green and yellow stripes) is a safety wire.

Power per person
In industrialized countries, power-stations have to provide about half a kilowatt of power for every person in the country. That is enough to keep five light bulbs alight.

Electricity Board engineers watch TV
When popular TV programmes end, extra generators have to be ready. The demand for power can rise by 10 per cent or more as people start to make hot drinks.

Large power-stations can generate a 1,000 MW (1 MW = 1 megawatt or one million watts). Light bulbs used in your home use between 40 and 150 watts. Fluorescent lights, although very bright may use only 25 watts.

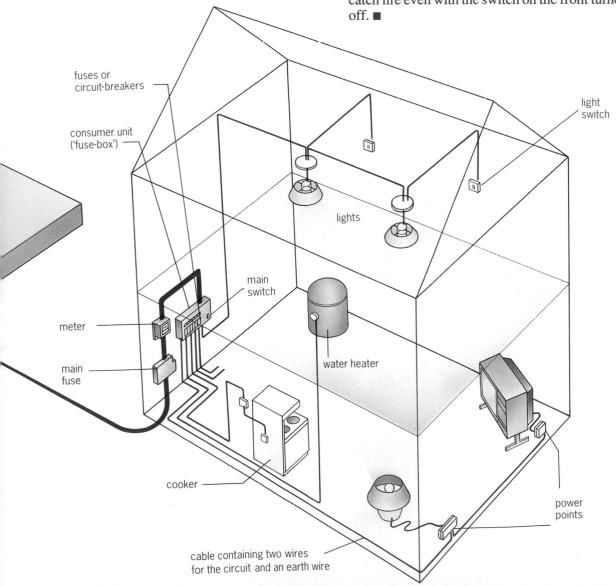

fuses or circuit-breakers

consumer unit ('fuse-box')

light switch

lights

main switch

meter

main fuse

water heater

cooker

power points

cable containing two wires for the circuit and an earth wire

◄ **The main cable branches out into several cables at the consumer unit ('fuse-box'). In many houses in Britain, the power points are all connected to the same cable, called a ring main.**

 **See also**
Cables
Electricity
Power

Electronics

Most of us use electronic equipment at some time. Radios, TVs, disc players and video recorders all use electronics. So do computers, digital watches and calculators. Electronic circuits change and control the flow of tiny electric currents. These tiny, changing currents are called signals. They can make loudspeakers give out sounds and TV screens show words or pictures. They can control machines or carry information.

Electronics in use

Electronic equipment is used everywhere, in and out of the home. Modern cookers have electronic timers to control the cooking. Many kettles use electronics to switch themselves off when they boil. Shop doors can open and shut automatically by electronics. Some cameras focus and set the correct exposure electronically.

Television depends from start to finish on electronics. The cameras and sound equipment work electronically. So does the transmitter which sends out the radio waves. Your television set uses electronics to turn the information in the radio waves back into sounds and pictures.

All the computers in the world use electronics. In factories, machines can be controlled by electronics instead of humans. Radar is electronic. Aircraft navigate by electronics, and their engines and controls are checked electronically.

In hospitals, electronic equipment tests heartbeats and keeps a check on seriously ill patients. X-ray machines are controlled by electronics. Hearing aids and heart pacemakers all work electronically.

Electronic circuits

There are four main jobs which electronic circuits can do:

Switching In some circuits, a tiny electrical signal is used to switch another circuit on or off. The automatic doors in shops work like this. When someone comes close, an infra-red detector sends a signal to an electronic circuit. This switches on an electric motor which opens the door.

Amplification This means making weak electrical signals stronger. The signals coming into a radio aerial are very weak. In the radio, an amplifier boosts the signals so that they are strong enough to make the radio give out a sound.

Rectification There are two types of electric current. Current from a battery is direct current (d.c.); it always flows the same way. Current from the mains is alternating current (a.c.); it flows backwards, forwards, backwards, forwards... and so on. Rectifier circuits are electronic turnstiles. They let the current through only in one direction. This changes a.c. into d.c.; it rectifies the current. Portable radios run on d.c., but with a rectifier fitted, they can be run from the a.c. mains.

Oscillation The signals picked up by a radio aerial are a.c. The current oscillates (wobbles) backwards and forwards. To handle some of these signals, radios need to produce their own a.c. But the problem is that radio batteries cannot supply it because they are d.c. An oscillator solves the problem. It is an electronic circuit which makes d.c. 'wobble' back and forth so that it becomes a.c.

▼ In an electronically-controlled simulator like this, pilots can practise their flying skills without ever leaving the ground.

Electronic components

If you look inside an old radio you will see lots of electronic components. These are the bits and pieces which connect together to make up the electronic circuits. Usually, the components are mounted on a special circuit board. This has copper strips on it to make the connections. The components are fixed to the strips by solder. Here are some of the components you might see:

Resistors These reduce the flow of current. They make sure that all the other components get the right amount of current to work properly.

Capacitors Some capacitors smooth out the flow of current. Others pass on signals. They are especially useful for this because they do not treat all signals alike. Using capacitors, a radio can be tuned to select signals from one station rather than another.

Diodes These are electronic turnstiles. They let current through in only one direction. They are used for rectification.

Transistors These are electronic taps. In a transistor, a tiny current can control the flow of a much larger current. It can make the flow stronger or weaker, or can turn it off altogether. Transistors are used for switching, amplifying and oscillating.

Most diodes and transistors are made from a material called silicon. Silicon is a semiconductor. It is not a good conductor of electricity, but it is not an insulator either. To make a diode or transistor, a tiny crystal or chip of silicon is treated with special chemicals. This changes the way the crystal conducts electricity.

Integrated circuits

Nowadays, electronic circuits with thousands of parts can be formed on a single chip of silicon no bigger than your finger-nail. The chip is treated with chemicals so that

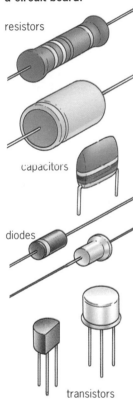

▲ This old radio has lots of separate electronic components soldered to a circuit board.

resistors

capacitors

diodes

transistors

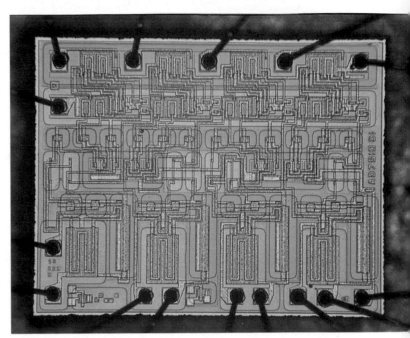

different parts behave like resistors, capacitors, diodes, transistors or connecting wire. The result is an integrated circuit or i.c. It can be the timer in a digital watch, the amplifier in a radio or the 'brain' in a calculator. Microprocessors are the most advanced chips of all. They are used in computers. They can run car engines and drive trains. They can fly aircraft and control artificial limbs.

Flashback

The first electronic component was the rectifier valve invented by Ambrose Fleming in 1904. It did the same job as a modern semiconductor diode but was much bigger and heavier. In 1906, Lee de Forest developed the triode valve. This did the same job as a modern transistor. It looked rather like a light bulb and used lots of power. Valves like these were to be used in radios for more than fifty years. The first transistor was made by John Bardeen, Walter Brittain and William Schockly in 1947. They used a semiconductor called germanium. The first integrated circuit was made by Jack Kilby at Texas Instruments in 1958. ■

▲ Circuits on a silicon chip, magnified 140 times. The chip is inside a package like the one shown below. Tiny wires connect the chip to the pins ('legs').

integrated circuit

See also
Computers
Radio
Television
Transistors
Video

Electronic music

There are two main groups of electronic instruments. In one you start with a mechanical sound, such as the ping of a guitar string or the toot of a flute, and then you change it electronically. In the other, even the original sound is made electronically.

Guitars

In electronic guitars the sound is changed into a varying electric current by things like microphones fixed under the strings. This current can then be altered in all sorts of ways by electronic circuits and finally fed to an amplifier and loudspeaker. This might just make the sound louder, but it can also change it so much that it sounds like a completely different instrument.

Sampling

Recently, electronic systems have been made that record any sound in digital form (as a series of numbers). These numbers are the samples that give the system its name. The sound can then be played back using a keyboard and changed by electronics into sounds of different pitch and quality. For example you could record one bottle being broken, and then use the sampler keyboard to play a tune that sounds as though bottles of many different sizes are being used.

Keyboards

There are many sorts of electronic keyboards available. In some, by pressing different buttons, you can change the sound to that of a piano, harpsichord or other instrument. One of the most important improvements in keyboards is that they can now be made so that you can change their sound by pressing the keys heavily or lightly, as in a mechanical piano with hammers and strings.

Synthesizers

On many keyboards the possible sounds are programmed in advance by the manufacturer, and though there may be hundreds of possible sounds you cannot invent new ones. In a synthesizer (which may look like a keyboard) there is the extra possibility of making new sounds of your own. You can mix a whole lot of simple sounds together. You can change the way they start and stop. You can even make them change quality during the note, like the way the sound of a bell changes, for example.

Computers

The most complicated of all electronic instruments can use a computer to make the sounds and to change them, or it may simply use a computer to 'drive' a synthesizer. A new computer language called 'MIDI' (Musical Instrument Digital Interface) has now been invented that allows computers, synthesizers and other kinds of electronic instruments to 'talk' to each other. It makes it much easier for composers who do not understand the electronics, to use very complicated synthesizers to make interesting sounds. For example, you could compose a piece of music by simply typing in on the computer keyboard the names of the notes (A, B, C and so on); how many beats each note is to last; which instrument is to play it, and so on. Then MIDI will take over and tell the computer how to print out the written music and then play it on a synthesizer. MIDI can also help to control a synthesizer with an electronic device that looks and plays like a real instrument such as a guitar or clarinet. ∎

See also
Computers
Electronics
Music
Musical instruments

The first really useful synthesizers were made in the 1960s.

One of the first computers to make 'music' was one that produced its answers as holes punched in a paper tape. By varying the speed at which the punch worked it could play *God Save the Queen*.

The first electronic organs were made round about 1932.

▼ **Jean-Michel Jarre playing in an open air concert in London.**

Elements

The elements are the basic materials that everything on the Earth and in the whole Universe is made of, including us. Everything is made of tiny atoms, much too small to see, and though many materials contain different kinds of atoms, each element contains only one kind of atom. So an element cannot be split up into different materials. There are about 90 different elements found in nature. Scientists have given each one a name and a chemical symbol. You can use the symbol if you do not want to write the name in full. Most of these elements are rare. About 99 per cent of the Earth is made of only eight elements.

Elements and compounds

You will not have heard of many of the elements in the chart here. In fact most familiar everyday materials are not pure elements but combinations of elements, called compounds. To make a compound the atoms of two or more elements join together to make a completely different material. Water is a compound. It is made from atoms of hydrogen and oxygen. Hydrogen and oxygen are both gases and water is nothing like either. Sugar is another compound. It is made from atoms of hydrogen, oxygen and carbon.

Isotopes of elements

Although the atoms of any element all behave the same way, they are not always identical. At the centre of each atom there is a nucleus containing particles called protons and neutrons. All the atoms of an element have the same number of protons but they may not all have the same number of neutrons. These different versions of the same element are called isotopes. A few elements have radioactive isotopes whose atoms tend to change into different atoms by throwing out tiny particles. These materials change into a different isotope of the same element or into a different element. The atoms of most elements never change.

The most common elements
On Earth, oxygen is the commonest element followed by silicon. Both are found in sand and rocks. In the whole Universe, hydrogen is the most common element and next is helium.

Solids, liquids and gases
At ordinary temperatures most elements are solids. Only 2 elements are liquids, 11 are gases, and 81 are solids.

Elements made by scientists

Scientists have made new elements in their laboratories by shooting tiny atomic particles at some heavy elements. So far they have made at least eleven new elements, though tiny amounts of two of these were later found in nature. They think that it may be possible to make over a hundred more new elements. However, most elements made in laboratories do not last very long, sometimes less than a second. They have large atoms which split up very easily into smaller atoms. ■

See also
Aluminium
Atoms
Carbon
Chemists
Helium
Metals
Oxygen
Silicon
Biography
Mendeleev

▼ There are over 100 known elements. Each has its own chemical symbol. Most exist in nature, but some (those in *italics*) have been made in laboratories.

When discovered	The elements: names and chemical symbols						
Prehistoric times	Carbon	C	Iron	Fe	Silver	Ag
	Copper	Cu	Lead	Pb	Sulphur	S
	Gold	Au	Mercury	Hg	Tin	Sn
Before AD 1650	Antimony	Sb	Arsenic	As		
1650–1699	Phosphorus	P				
1700–1749	Cobalt	Co	Platinum	Pt	Zinc	Zn
1750–1799	Bismuth	Bi	Nickel	Ni	Titanium	Ti
	Chlorine	Cl	Nitrogen	N	Tungsten	W
	Chromium	Cr	Oxygen	O	Uranium	U
	Hydrogen	H	Strontium	Sr	Yttrium	Y
	Manganese	Mn	Tellurium	Te	Zirconium	Zr
	Molybdenum	Mo				
1800–1849	Aluminium	Al	Iodine	I	Rhodium	Rh
	Barium	Ba	Iridium	Ir	Ruthenium	Ru
	Beryllium	Be	Lanthanum	La	Selenium	Se
	Boron	B	Lithium	Li	Silicon	Si
	Bromine	Br	Magnesium	Mg	Sodium	Na
	Cadmium	Cd	Niobium	Nb	Tantalum	Ta
	Calcium	Ca	Osmium	Os	Terbium	Tb
	Cerium	Ce	Palladium	Pd	Thorium	Th
	Erbium	Er	Potassium	K	Vanadium	V
1850–1899	Actinium	Ac	Helium	He	Radium	Ra
	Argon	Ar	Holmium	Ho	Rubidium	Rb
	Caesium	Cs	Indium	In	Samarium	Sm
	Dysprosium	Dy	Krypton	Kr	Scandium	Sc
	Fluorine	F	Neodymium	Nd	Thallium	Tl
	Gadolinium	Gd	Neon	Ne	Thulium	Tm
	Gallium	Ga	Polonium	Po	Xenon	Xe
	Germanium	Ge	Praseodymium	Pr	Ytterbium	Yb
1900–1949	*Americium*	*Am*	Francium	Fr	Promethium	Pm
	Astatine	*At*	Hafnium	Hf	Protactinium	Pa
	Berkelium	*Bk*	Lutetium	Lu	Radon	Rn
	Curium	*Cm*	Neptunium	Np	Rhenium	Re
	Europium	Eu	Plutonium	Pu	*Technetium*	*Tc*
1950–1954	*Californium*	*Cf*	*Einsteinium*	*Es*	*Fermium*	*Fm*
1955–1960	*Mendelevium*	*Md*	*Nobelium*	*No*		
After 1960	*Lawrencium*	*Lr*	*Rutherfordium*	*Rf*		

Elephants

For centuries Asian elephants have been used as beasts of burden, carrying or dragging timber and other heavy materials. Elephants are also trained to perform in circuses. African elephants are far more difficult to tame because they are fiercer.

The Asian elephant (below) differs in many ways from its African cousins (right). Asian elephants have small, triangular ears; African elephants have large, rounded ears. Asian elephants have rounded backs; African elephants have concave (hollowed) backs. Asian elephants have two bulges on their foreheads; African elephants have rounded foreheads.

▼ Asian elephant.

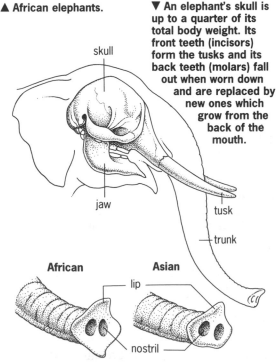

Elephants are the biggest living land animals. There are two types of elephant, African and Asian. Both types live in herds, and have poor eyesight, but very good senses of hearing and smell. If one animal detects danger, the whole herd is alerted.

Elephants do not defend the home range over which they wander; instead they seem to know and be on friendly terms with their neighbours. Each herd is led by an old female who is followed by her young offspring and her adult daughters and their families. The elephants in a herd remain together for many years. Its members keep close to each other and look after and even suckle each other's babies if need be. Sometimes a herd splits, and a younger female leaves with some of the others, but they remain close to the parent group and may rejoin it briefly.

Young males leave the herd when they reach puberty, at the age of about twelve years. Males may form herds, but these do not have any constant members and change from one day to the next. There is no special breeding season, but if a female is ready to mate, her group will be joined by males though they will not remain permanently.

Trunks and tusks

As well as their size, the two things which set elephants apart from other mammals are their trunks and their tusks. The trunk is the elephant's nose. It is boneless but muscular and has one or two finger-like points at the tip. The elephant uses it to breathe, and to drink, which it does by sniffing water up and then blowing it down its throat. It is also used as a hand, strong enough to break down a branch if there are choice leaves on it, and delicate enough to pick a single fruit the size of a raspberry.

▲ African elephants.

▼ An elephant's skull is up to a quarter of its total body weight. Its front teeth (incisors) form the tusks and its back teeth (molars) fall out when worn down and are replaced by new ones which grow from the back of the mouth.

skull

jaw

tusk

trunk

African   Asian

lip

nostril

▲ An elephant's upper lip and nose form its trunk. It is a sense organ of smell and touch; it can squirt water and dust, is strong enough to lift trees, but has one or two finger-like lips which can pick up a pebble.

An elephant's trunk is very sensitive; courting elephants twine trunks, and mother elephants spend a lot of time using their trunks to touch and fondle their babies. This 'elephant cuddling' is important to the calf. One which is deprived of it does not make such good progress as one which has plenty of contact.

An elephant's tusks are its second upper incisor teeth. When they begin to grow they have a cap of enamel, like human teeth. But as they get larger the enamel does not continue to cover them. The greater part of a tusk is made of dentine (ivory). Elephants use their tusks for defence, and in feeding. They continue to grow throughout the elephant's whole life, so one with very large tusks is likely to be an old animal. Females have smaller tusks than males, and Asian elephant tusks are smaller than those of African elephants.

Feeding

An elephant's size means that, when it is fully grown, it is safe from all predators other than humans. To support its large size it needs huge amounts of food. An adult elephant eats about 150 kg (300 lb) of grass, leaves, twigs and fruit each day.

Such tough food needs to be thoroughly chewed, and elephants have grinding teeth in the back of their mouths. This is the position in which the teeth have the most force, but they do wear out. When this happens they are replaced by others which push in from behind. As a result, elephants spend all of their life teething. In all they have six sets of grinding teeth, but when the last of these wears out, the animal is probably about 55 years old. It becomes weakened by lack of food and dies of starvation or disease.

Endangered species

In the past there were many species of elephants, which lived over most of the world apart from Australia. Some were much bigger than the elephants of today, but they are now all extinct. There is no doubt that elephants belong to a group that is dying.

Unfortunately, human beings are helping elephants into a quicker extinction. As a result of hunting for ivory and poaching and taking over the elephants' environment, there are far fewer elephants today than there were even 20 years ago. Many people feel that it is not possible for such large and demanding animals to survive in a world of expanding human populations. In 1989 the African elephant joined the Asian elephant as an officially protected endangered species. ∎

Distribution
Africa south of the Sahara, and south-east Asia
Asian elephant
Head and body length 5·5–6·4 m; shoulder height 2·5–3·0 m; weight up to 5,000 kg
African elephant
Head and body length 6·0–7·5 m; shoulder height 3–4 m; weight 2,200–7,500 kg
Heaviest single tusk
Weight 107 kg
Number of young
1, very rarely twins. Calf begins to be weaned at about 1 year, but takes some milk until it is about 4 years old.
Lifespan
50–70 years
Elephants are pregnant for 22 months.

Subphylum Vertebrata
Class Mammalia
Order Proboscidea
Number of species 2

◉ See also
Domestication
Endangered species
Ivory
Prehistoric animals
Smugglers
Teeth

El Salvador

El Salvador is a small country on the Pacific coast of Central America. The sea coast is hot and humid. Inland the landscape is dominated by two chains of volcanoes and the climate here is cooler. Some of these volcanoes are still active, like the volcano that towers above the capital San Salvador. It last erupted in 1917. San Salvador is also in an earthquake zone and the modern city has many low buildings designed to withstand future earth tremors.

El Salvador has the densest population of the Central American countries. Most people are mestizo (descended from both Indians and Spaniards).

The country was part of the Spanish colonial empire and became independent in 1821. Poverty and repression led to a civil war which started in 1979 and has caused great suffering and loss of life. ∎

Area 21,393 sq km
Capital San Salvador
Population 5,480,000
Language
Spanish, Indian languages
Religion Christian
Government
Parliamentary republic
Currency
1 El Salvador colón = 100 centavos

◉ See also
American Indians
North America
Spanish colonial history

Embroidery

See also
Bayeux Tapestry
Sewing
Textiles

Running stitch is used for making outlines and creating simple line effects. Pass the needle over and under the fabric at regular intervals.

Backstitch is used for outlining. Make a stitch backwards, bringing the needle out some way in front of the starting point. Then make another stitch backwards to meet the beginning of the last stitch, and so on.

Stem stitch is used for outlines, lines and fillings. Bring the needle out to the left half-way along the previous stitch and then in half-way along to the right. The stitches should overlap each other.

French knots are used for decoration. Bring the needle up through the fabric, wrap the thread round the needle point once, and insert the needle again. Hold the thread firmly with your thumb and pull the needle through smoothly.

Chain stitch is used for decoration. Take the needle through the fabric and insert it in the same hole. Then bring the needle out a little farther forward. Wrap the thread round the needle and pull the needle through the fabric. Repeat to form a chain of stitches.

Cross stitch is used for fillings and decoration. Bring the needle up at the bottom right-hand corner, go down at the top left-hand corner, coming out at the bottom left corner. Go down again at the top right-hand corner and up again to start the next stitch.

Couching is used as a filling or to outline a pattern. Lay a thread on the fabric and sew it down with tiny stitches made at regular intervals along its length.

Satin stitch is used for fillings. Stitches are worked to varying lengths to fill a shape, and they should lie flat and be even.

Embroidery is a way of decorating fabric with stitches. Here are some of the basic stitches you can use.

These instructions are for a right-handed worker. Left-handed workers should read 'left' for 'right' and 'right' for 'left' in each instruction. ■

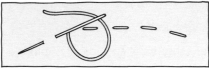
running stitch

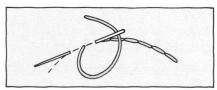
backstitch

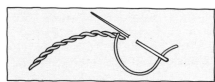
stem stitch

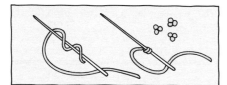
French knots

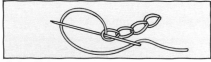
chain stitch

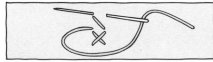
cross stitch

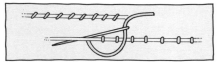
couching

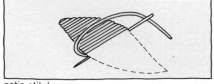
satin stitch

Empires

An empire is a group of countries ruled by an emperor or an empress. Most empires begin when one country conquers others, or sets up colonies in distant lands. The British empire was one of the biggest. The rulers of some countries, such as Japan, have used the title emperor although they reign over just one country. ■

See also
British empire
Byzantine empire
Japan's history
Ottoman empire
Roman ancient history
Russia's history

Enclosures

In the lowlands of England in the Middle Ages people used to farm the land on the open field system. A farmer would have several strips of land in different fields.

'Enclosure' was putting a hedge or a wall or a fence round part of the land. Lords of the manor began enclosing land in the 13th century. The main periods of the enclosures were from the 15th to the 17th century, and from about 1750 to 1850. The last period of enclosure was helped by a series of Acts of Parliament allowing the changes.

The new system of smaller fields meant that the landowner could control what was grown on his land. The commoners, people who had held rights 'in common', received small amounts of land for growing crops, but lost their rights for their animals to graze on common ground. The present-day commons near some old towns and villages are all that is left of the old common lands.

In some parts of the country enclosures took place with little difficulty, but in others there was great hardship. Many cottagers lost their independence and had to work for other farmers. Enclosures took place in other countries besides England. In Italy it began in the Middle Ages, but in Germany and the Scandinavian countries most enclosures happened in the 19th century. ■

Many people who disagreed with enclosures because it robbed people of the common land used to recite this verse:

The law doth punish man
or woman
That steals the goose from
off the common,
But lets the greater felon
loose,
That steals the common
from the goose.

See also
Highland clearances

Endangered species

Endangered species of plants and animals are those which are so rare that it is likely that, unless they are specially protected, they will soon become extinct. The International Union for the Conservation of Nature keeps a watch on the numbers of animals. It publishes *Red Data Books* with details of the rarest animals and plants, which are listed as being endangered, threatened or vulnerable. Today more species of plants and animals are endangered than ever before because human numbers and activity are increasing throughout the world.

Human beings can live in many sorts of environments. Most kinds of animals can live successfully in only one sort of environment. When humans change the face of the earth, by cutting down forests, for instance, the animals and plants which lived there cannot survive, and most of them die out. Once this has happened we cannot bring them back, and in many cases we do not know exactly what has been destroyed.

The World Wide Fund for Nature has produced a list of the twelve species most likely to become extinct in the near future. Some have had their habitat destroyed by human activity. The clearance of the forests of Madagascar for farming threatens the survival of the greater bamboo lemur and the big-leaf palm.

Sometimes humans thoughtlessly introduce foreign species to areas where they can seriously harm native species. The far-northern flax snail of New Zealand has been reduced to only 200 individuals, because the snails are prey to blackbirds, thrushes and rats introduced by Europeans.

Sometimes greed can bring a species to the brink of extinction. The horn of the African black rhino is used to make dagger handles in the Middle East. These handles are so valuable that poachers have reduced the rhino population by 95 per cent in the last fifteen years, just to get more horn.

Even our love of nature can be harmful. So many salmon-crested cockatoos have been collected for the pet trade that it is now almost extinct in its native Indonesia. The Chiapas slipper orchid and the green pitcher plant are disappearing because of plant collectors.

Why should we bother about endangered species? One reason is that many, especially the plant species, may contain substances which could be useful to all mankind, as the basis of new drugs for example. More importantly, for every known species that goes extinct, there may be a hundred other species sharing the same habitat that will disappear without ever being known to us. All this means a great loss to the planet Earth. ∎

Most endangered species, 1990

Species	Range	Threat to survival
Black rhinoceros	Sub-saharan Africa	Poaching for horn
Kouprey	Indo-China	Hunting and forest clearance
Greater bamboo lemur	Madagascar	Forest clearance
Highland guan	Central America	Hunting and forest clearance
Philippines eagle	Philippines	Hunting and forest clearance
Salmon-crested cockatoo	Indonesia	Collection for pets
River terrapin	SE Asia	Hunting and river pollution
Far-northern flax snail	New Zealand	Introduced predators and bush clearance
Homerus swallowtail butterfly	Jamaica	Forest clearance
Chiapas slipper orchid	Mexico	Forest clearance and collecting
Green pitcher plant	USA	Collecting
Big-leaf palm	Madagascar	Forest clearance

WWF

◄ The aye-aye is a small lemur which lives in the forests of Madagascar. Forest clearance to make more land available to farmers destroys the habitat and the aye-aye is an endangered species.

See also
Butterflies
Conservation
Elephants
Extinct animals
Pandas
Population: animal
Prehistoric animals
Survival

▼ The humpback whale is one of the species that have suffered from whaling in the 19th and 20th centuries. The hunting of these whales is now banned by the International Whaling Commission but not all countries observe the ban.

Energy

▲ **Powered by the Sun. These cyclists are turning energy stored in their bodies into kinetic (movement) energy. The energy came from their food, and the energy from their food originally came from the Sun.**

Measuring energy
We measure energy in joules. Power, the amount of energy used every second, is measured in watts.

Energy for people
We measure food energy in kilojoules (kJ). One kilojoule equals 1,000 joules. An average 11-year-old needs about 10,000 kilojoules of energy every day.

Energy for action
A child weighing 30 kg uses about 700 joules of energy walking upstairs.

Nothing can live, move or work without energy. Plants need it to grow. We need it just to keep alive. Our energy comes from the food we eat. Machines need a supply of energy to work. Some use electricity, while others burn fuels which contain stored energy. We all use energy and almost all of it originally came from the Sun.

Different types of energy

There are many different kinds of energy. **Heat**, **light** and **sound** are all kinds of energy which move around. Light and heat are **radiant** energy, often called radiation. Other kinds of radiation include microwaves and X-rays. Every time we turn on an electric switch we use **electrical** energy. It provides lighting and heating and makes many things work. **Chemical** energy is stored in foods and fuels. It is released when fuels are burned, or chemicals get to work on the food in our bodies.

When some atoms split or join to make different atoms, huge amounts of energy may be released. This is called **nuclear** energy. We can use it peacefully to make electricity, or destructively in bombs.

Anything that moves has **kinetic** energy. The larger the moving thing and the faster it moves, the more kinetic energy it has. If you throw a ball up in the air, you give it kinetic energy. As it goes up, it slows down and loses kinetic energy. But it gains a kind of stored energy called **potential** energy. When the ball stops at the top of the throw, it has no kinetic energy

because it is not moving; but it has potential energy. As it falls down again, its potential energy is changed back into kinetic energy.

Keeping energy

Sometimes energy seems to be used up. But it is never lost. It just changes into another kind of energy. A ball rolling along the flat ground slows down and stops, losing its kinetic energy. It slows because it rubs against the ground; we say there is friction between the ball and the ground. The friction heats up the ball and the ground. The ball's kinetic energy has changed into heat, but the total amount of energy has not changed.

Storing energy

Lots of things store energy, including food. Our food is either plants or animals which have been fed on plants. When plants grow, they take in and store energy from the Sun. The Sun's energy has also been stored in the fossil fuels: coal, oil and gas. Millions of years ago these were living trees and tiny sea creatures storing energy from the Sun as they grew. Once fossil fuels have been taken from the ground they are never replaced, so we must use them carefully and not waste them.

Energy for living
The food we eat gives us energy. We need it, even when we are asleep, to stay warm and keep the organs of our body working. When we are active, we need more energy to move our muscles.

Energy in plants and animals
Green plants use the Sun's energy to make their food from simple materials like water, and carbon dioxide gas in the air. Like other living things, plants need food to live and grow. We get our energy by eating plants, or eating meat from animals which have fed on plants. So our energy really comes from the Sun.

Energy from the Sun

Almost all our energy originally came from the Sun. At the Sun's centre, nuclear reactions give enormous amounts of energy which radiate from the surface as heat and light. There is enough nuclear energy left in the Sun to keep it shining for another 5,000 million years.

Energy from the Sun

On average, each square metre of the Earth's surface receives the same energy from the Sun as it would do from a one-bar electric fire.

Energy in fossil fuels

Millions of years ago, plants and tiny creatures took in energy from the Sun as they grew. When they died, they became buried under layers of rock which slowly formed above them, and were gradually turned into coal, oil and natural gas. These fossil fuels now store energy which once came from the Sun.

Bottled gas is a useful way of storing energy. So is a battery. When a battery is properly connected, chemical changes inside it produce electricity. A dam across a river is another way of storing energy. The water which collects in a lake behind the dam has potential energy. When electricity is needed, some of the water trapped by the dam flows down a channel and turns a turbine to make electricity. The stored potential energy becomes kinetic energy in the flowing water before changing to electrical energy.

Energy for machines

Everything that moves or does work needs energy to run it. Most of the machines in our homes and many machines in large factories use electricity to make them work. This comes along cables from power-stations to houses and factories. These machines cannot be moved away from an electricity supply. When you want to carry small things like torches and radios around with you, it is often more convenient to use the electricity stored in batteries. Other moving things such as cars, aircraft and some trains get energy by burning fuels made from oil, such as petrol or diesel oil. They have to carry enough fuel to get them to another supply at a petrol station or at an airport.

Using electrical energy

An ordinary electric light bulb uses 100 joules of energy every second (100 watts). A colour TV uses about 200 joules every second (200 watts).

An average hotplate on an electric cooker uses 1,500 joules every second (1,500 watts).

Energy for transport

The engine in a small car can deliver about 30,000 joules of energy every second.

Energy in fuels
Coal
1 g contains about 25 kilojoules of energy.
Oil
1 g contains about 45 kilojoules of energy.
Nuclear
1 g contains about 1,400,000 kilojoules of energy.

Energy from fossil fuels

To get the energy in fossil fuels, we mine coal, and pump oil and natural gas from underground. The oil is refined to make other fuels, including petrol, kerosene (jet fuel) and diesel fuel. We release the energy from fossil fuels by burning them. This happens in heating systems, in power-stations, and in the engines of cars, trucks, trains, ships and aircraft.

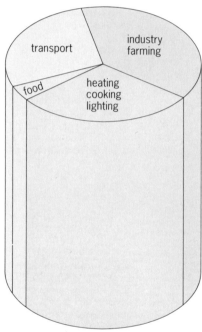

How energy is used for each person in an industrialized country

How energy is used for each person in a developing, Third World country

▲ *Solar Challenger* has special panels on its wings to absorb the energy in sunlight and make electricity for its motor. But all aircraft use energy which originally came from the Sun.

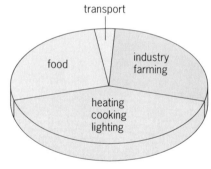

▲ Compare the size of the pie charts. Each person in an industrialized country uses over ten times as much energy as someone in a developing, Third World country.

⊙ **See also**

Food
Fuel
Geothermal power
Greenhouse effect
Hydroelectric power
Nuclear power
Solar power
Water power
Wind power

How much energy do we use?

Everyone needs energy just to keep alive. However, we also use a lot of energy running machines to help us in our work and play. Almost all homes in Europe, North America, Australia and other industrialized countries have a supply of electricity for lighting and heating and to run the TVs, washing machines and other electrical machines. Pipes usually bring a supply of gas as well for cooking or heating. We also have cars which get their energy from petrol. In many developing countries, including China, India, most of Africa and parts of South America, people use a lot less energy. Not so many can afford cars and machines and fewer homes have a supply of electricity and gas.

Alternative energy

Most of the energy we use today comes from the fossil fuels: coal, oil and gas. But these will not last long because they are not being replaced. Also, burning them is slowly harming the atmosphere. Engineers are now looking for other ways of supplying energy. Modern windmills are being built in groups to produce electricity from the wind. In some places, the sea water flowing to and fro with the tides will also turn turbines, and even waves on the sea can produce electricity. The Sun's energy can be collected by solar panels which heat water, or by solar cells which produce electricity when light falls on them. Geothermal energy comes from the hot rocks inside the Earth which can heat water and make electricity. All these methods can supply our energy and they do not harm the atmosphere. But people go on using fossil fuels because they are still the cheapest and most convenient way to get energy.

Flashback

Thousands of years ago people had only the Sun's energy and their own energy. They burnt wood for heat, and animals provided energy to carry things and work on the farms. Then they learnt to use energy in rivers to turn water wheels, and the energy in the wind to drive windmills and sailing ships. About 200 years ago coal-burning steam-engines began to drive factory machines and then railway locomotives. And people started to use gas for heating and lighting. Now with petrol-driven cars and planes that give us fast, convenient transport, and electricity providing clean energy for homes and factories, we are using more and more energy. ■

Engineers

Engineers design, make and mend machinery and other equipment. There are many different types of engineer.

Mechanical engineers work with engines and machines.

Electrical engineers are responsible for power-stations, generators and electronic equipment like radio and TV transmitters.

Civil engineers supervise the construction of tunnels, roads, dams and railways.

Structural engineers deal with the concrete and steel structures of large buildings and bridges.

Chemical engineers are responsible for the chemical plants which make things like fertilizers, plastics and petrol.

Nuclear engineers deal with nuclear power-stations.

Marine engineers design ships and submarines.

Aeronautical engineers work with aircraft.

Computer engineers deal with computers and all the equipment connected to them.

Engineers will have worked on lots of the equipment you have at home. For example, this is what happens when a company decides to make a new washing machine. A **design engineer** decides how the machine is going to work, how the parts should fit together, the best materials to use and how to keep the costs down. Then a **production engineer** works out how the design can be made on a production line. The production engineer has many decisions to make. What is the easiest, quickest and cheapest way to manufacture the machine? How can lots of them be made one after another so that they all work properly? Finally, when the machines are sold, they have to be serviced and maintained. The person who comes to your house to do this is called a **service engineer**. ■

Great engineers
Sir Isambard Kingdom Brunel designed and built the largest and most successful steamships of his day. He was also responsible for the construction of the Great Western Railway.

Sir Alec Issigonis was the engineer who designed some of Britain's most famous small cars, including the Morris Minor and the Mini.

See also

Designers
Mass production
Materials
Technology

Biography
Brunel
Issigonis
McAdam
Stephenson
Telford
Trevithick
Watt
Whittle

Engines

Engines are used to make things move. They can power anything from a lawnmower to a space rocket. There are many different types of engine but they all work in the same basic way. They burn fuel to give heat. The heat makes gas or steam expand. The force of the expansion produces movement.

Most steam-engines use coal or oil as their fuel. The heat from the burning fuel turns water into steam in a boiler. The steam is trapped under pressure in a metal cylinder. It expands and pushes a piston along the cylinder.

Petrol engines also have pistons and cylinders. But the combustion (burning) of the fuel takes place *inside* the cylinders themselves. So petrol engines are called internal combustion engines. The burning fuel produces lots of hot, high-pressure gas which moves the pistons. Diesel engines work in much the same way.

Most steam, petrol and diesel engines have pistons which move up and down in their cylinders. Engines with this type of movement are called reciprocating engines. To drive vehicles or machinery, the up-and-down movement has to be changed into round-and-round movement. This is done using a crank. The pedals on a bicycle are fixed to cranks. They turn the up-and-down movement of your legs into the round-and-round movement of the chain wheel.

Steam turbines do not have pistons and cranks. They have huge fans which are blown round by jets of high-pressure steam. Engines which rotate like this are called rotary engines.

Jet engines do not have pistons and cranks either. When their fuel burns, the expanding gases rush out of the back at high speed. This forces the engine forward. Rocket engines use the same idea. ■

Powerful engines
The world's most powerful engines are the rocket engines which lift spacecraft into orbit. They produce as much power as 500,000 large car engines, but only for a few minutes at a time.

The steam turbines in large power-stations produce as much power as 5,000 large car engines.

The world's biggest jet engines produce as much power as 500 large car engines.

See also

Internal combustion engines
Jet engines
Rockets
Steam-engines
Turbines

England's history

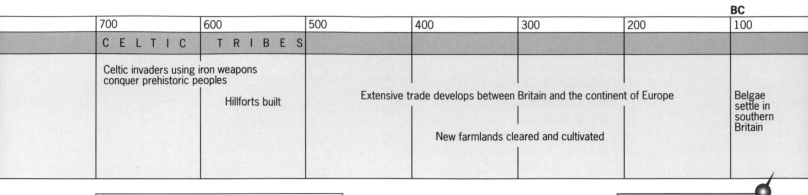

	700	600	500	400	300	200	**BC** 100
	C E L T I C	T R I B E S					

Celtic invaders using iron weapons conquer prehistoric peoples

Hillforts built

Extensive trade develops between Britain and the continent of Europe

Belgae settle in southern Britain

New farmlands cleared and cultivated

← Stonehenge had been completed 1,000 years earlier

Julius Caesar invades 55 BC

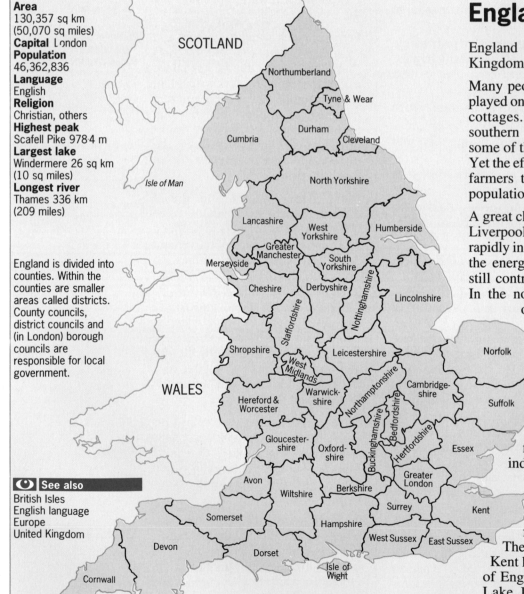

Area
130,357 sq km
(50,070 sq miles)
Capital London
Population
46,362,836
Language
English
Religion
Christian, others
Highest peak
Scafell Pike 978·4 m
Largest lake
Windermere 26 sq km
(10 sq miles)
Longest river
Thames 336 km
(209 miles)

England is divided into counties. Within the counties are smaller areas called districts. County councils, district councils and (in London) borough councils are responsible for local government.

See also
British Isles
English language
Europe
United Kingdom

SCOTLAND

Northumberland
Tyne & Wear
Durham
Cumbria
Cleveland
Isle of Man
North Yorkshire
Lancashire
West Yorkshire
Humberside
Greater Manchester
South Yorkshire
Merseyside
Cheshire
Derbyshire
Nottinghamshire
Lincolnshire
Staffordshire
Shropshire
Leicestershire
Norfolk
West Midlands
Warwickshire
Northamptonshire
Cambridgeshire
Hereford & Worcester
Bedfordshire
Suffolk
WALES
Buckinghamshire
Hertfordshire
Gloucestershire
Oxfordshire
Essex
Avon
Berkshire
Greater London
Wiltshire
Surrey
Kent
Somerset
Hampshire
Devon
Dorset
West Sussex
East Sussex
Isle of Wight
Cornwall

England

England forms the largest part of the United Kingdom, a country in north-west Europe.

Many people's picture of England is of cricket played on a village green surrounded by thatched cottages. There are scenes like this in the southern counties, but England also contains some of the most crowded regions in the world. Yet the efficient use of its fertile land has enabled farmers to grow almost enough food for the population.

A great chain of cities stretches from London to Liverpool. The industrial cities of the north grew rapidly in the 19th century. Nearby coal provided the energy for their factories. Today there are still contrasts between the north and the south. In the north, unemployment is higher as the older industries have declined. In the south, particularly around London, houses are more expensive because more and more people want to live there. London is one of the world's oldest and greatest capital cities and is a focal point for modern manufacturing industry and tourism. It is an important financial centre and part of the industrial centre of Europe.

Not all the differences between the north and the south have been made by people. Southern England has fertile lands and gently rolling hills. The fields and orchards in the county of Kent have led to its being called the 'garden of England'. The northern landscapes of the Lake District and the Pennines are more rugged. ■

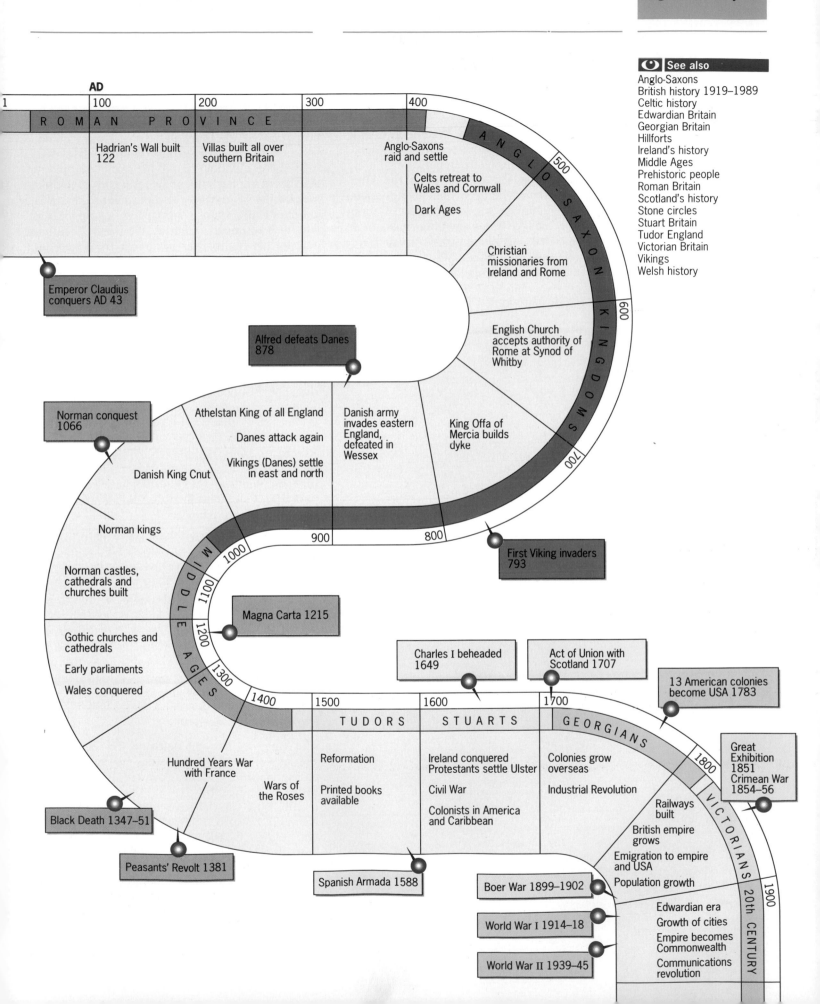

See also
Anglo-Saxons
British history 1919–1989
Celtic history
Edwardian Britain
Georgian Britain
Hillforts
Ireland's history
Middle Ages
Prehistoric people
Roman Britain
Scotland's history
Stone circles
Stuart Britain
Tudor England
Victorian Britain
Vikings
Welsh history

AD

1   100   200   300   400   500   600   700

R O M A N   P R O V I N C E

A N G L O - S A X O N   K I N G D O M S

Hadrian's Wall built 122

Villas built all over southern Britain

Anglo-Saxons raid and settle

Celts retreat to Wales and Cornwall

Dark Ages

Christian missionaries from Ireland and Rome

English Church accepts authority of Rome at Synod of Whitby

King Offa of Mercia builds dyke

Emperor Claudius conquers AD 43

Alfred defeats Danes 878

Athelstan King of all England

Danes attack again

Vikings (Danes) settle in east and north

Danish army invades eastern England, defeated in Wessex

Norman conquest 1066

Danish King Cnut

First Viking invaders 793

800   900   1000   1100   1200   1300   1400

M I D D L E   A G E S

Norman kings

Norman castles, cathedrals and churches built

Gothic churches and cathedrals

Early parliaments

Wales conquered

Magna Carta 1215

Hundred Years War with France

Wars of the Roses

Black Death 1347–51

Peasants' Revolt 1381

1500   1600   1700   1800   1900

T U D O R S   S T U A R T S   G E O R G I A N S   VICTORIANS   20th CENTURY

Reformation

Printed books available

Ireland conquered Protestants settle Ulster

Civil War

Colonists in America and Caribbean

Colonies grow overseas

Industrial Revolution

Charles I beheaded 1649

Act of Union with Scotland 1707

13 American colonies become USA 1783

Great Exhibition 1851 Crimean War 1854–56

Spanish Armada 1588

Railways built

British empire grows

Emigration to empire and USA

Population growth

Boer War 1899–1902

World War I 1914–18

World War II 1939–45

Edwardian era

Growth of cities

Empire becomes Commonwealth

Communications revolution

English Civil War
1642–1649

The English Civil War was fought to decide who should have the most power in England, Parliament or the king. Parliament wanted more say in governing the country, but the king, Charles I, believed that his right to rule came from God. There were disagreements about religion. People took sides, but not in any simple way. Some families were split by war, with brothers on opposing sides. Many people kept out of the fighting altogether. Supporters of Parliament were nicknamed Roundheads, and the Royalists were called Cavaliers.

See also
Cavaliers
Roundheads
Stuart Britain
Weapons

Biography
Charles I
Cromwell

Army size
This varied. At Naseby the King had 9,000 men, whereas at Marston Moor Parliament had around 28,000.

Weapons used
Pike A long (4·5 to 5·5 m) iron-headed spear on an ash shaft, used against cavalry.
Musket A foot soldier's weapon loaded with powder, ball and wadding down the muzzle. It took about a minute to load a musket, a long time if you were facing a cavalry charge.
Cannon Clumsy and difficult to move. A 20 cm cannon that fired a 29 kg shot took a team of sixteen horses to move it.

Areas controlled by Royalists, 1644

Areas controlled by Parliament, 1644

Battles
✕ Parliamentary victory
✕ Royalist victory
✕ Draw

Marston Moor 1644 ● York

Newark ●

Naseby 1645
Edgehill 1642 ✕ ✕ Cropredy Bridge 1644

Oxford ●
Turnham Green 1642

Bristol ●
Newbury 1643, 1644
Roundway Down 1643

Langport 1645

Lostwithiel 1644

How the war started

The real trouble began when Charles I needed money. Only Parliament could provide enough money for an army, and Charles needed an army to put down rebellions in Scotland and Ireland. Parliament tried to make the king share his power with them. Charles gave in for a time, but many Members of Parliament were afraid he would not keep his promises. Then, in January 1642, he personally tried to arrest five leading MPs, but they escaped. Charles then left London, fearing his family was in danger from London mobs. Both sides prepared for war.

The fighting

To win the war, the king needed to capture London. He recruited a sizeable army. His cavalry, commanded by his forceful nephew Prince Rupert, was formidable. The Earl of Essex, who was slow, methodical and rather dull, commanded Parliament's main army. Some landowners on both sides trained their own regiments in their local areas. The first battle was at Edgehill on 23 October 1642. The Royalist cavalry had the best of the fighting but there was no clear winner. After the battle, the king marched on London, but was stopped by the defences at Turnham Green. He then made Oxford his headquarters.

There were local battles in many parts of the country. At first the Royalists did better. In 1643 they besieged and captured the important port of Bristol, and they controlled most of the north and west of England. But they still did not get near London. Then, in 1644, a Scottish army joined in on Parliament's side. That summer, the king's main army was badly beaten at Marston Moor. Oliver Cromwell's cavalry and the determination of the Scottish infantry helped win the battle for Parliament.

Parliament's victory

The king was not yet defeated. So Parliament got rid of its old and inefficient commanders and set up a New Model Army to finish the war. In 1645, at Naseby, it was victorious. Eleven months later Charles surrendered to the Scots at Newark. Cromwell and the army leaders soon got hold of Charles, and tried to make a deal with him. But fighting started again in 1648. They eventually decided that they could never trust the king, and he was beheaded in 1649. ∎

English language

English is spoken all over the world. More than 300 million people use it as their main language, and many more learn it as a second language. English is based very much on idiom: the grouping of words together to mean much more than the words mean by themselves. For example, words such as 'make' and 'get', although very simple in themselves, produce all sorts of meanings when they are put with other words. Just think of all the different things 'get on' and 'make up' can mean. People who are brought up to speak English learn these naturally, but idiom makes English a difficult language for foreigners to speak really well.

English has many different forms or varieties. Even within the British Isles there are dialects and regional variations. Dialects have many local words and phrases that are understood only in the area in which they are spoken. There are also different local ways of pronouncing words, called accents. In the north-east of England 'work' is often pronounced in the way that 'walk' is in the south.

English, like other languages, has words that are very informal as well as words that are formal. The most informal words are known as slang and are used in casual speech, such as when you are speaking to friends or people you know very well. Think of a machine breaking down. In normal English you would say 'the machine has broken down', but using slang you might say 'it's gone and bust'. At the other extreme is the formal English you might read in a book of instructions: 'if the equipment ceases to function properly'. The important thing is to choose the best words for the occasion.

Flashback

The oldest form of English was spoken by the Anglo-Saxons about 1,500 years ago. It is called Old English. You would not recognize much of it today. English has been changed over the years since then by the other peoples who have come to the British Isles to conquer or settle in them, especially the Vikings from Denmark, and the Normans who conquered England in 1066.

The Normans spoke a form of French with many words that came from Latin, the language of the ancient Romans, and they gave us many of the longer official-sounding words such as 'connection' and 'inhabitant'. The form of English that arose from this is called Middle English. It is the language used by the poet Chaucer in the 14th century. Unlike Old English, you would be able to understand a good deal of it today.

In modern English there are words from the older Anglo-Saxon and words from Middle English that mean the same thing, such as 'shut' and 'close', and 'buy' and 'purchase'. Sometimes we have a choice of three, as with 'start', 'begin', and 'commence'. If you think about it, you will realize that each word has its own 'ring' and is used in special ways. You would never normally say 'I am just going to purchase some crisps' or 'I'd better commence my homework'. In fact, you could say that words such as 'commence' and 'purchase' are not needed at all, except in very stuffy or pretentious English.

There are also words that have come from other languages in more recent times, such as 'kiosk' from Turkish and 'yacht' from Dutch. Modern English is a rich mixture of words from many places, and this explains why some of them are rather difficult to spell. Most of the very basic words, however, such as 'book' and 'eat', survive from Old English. ■

British and American English

Familiar things with different names

British	American	British	American
autumn	fall	pavement	sidewalk
biscuit	cookie	petrol	gasoline
bonnet (of car)	hood	post	mail
dustbin	garbage can	pushchair	stroller
holiday	vacation	queue	line
lift	elevator	railway	railroad
lorry	truck	rubber	eraser
motor car	automobile	sweets	candy
nappy	diaper	tap	faucet

The same word with different meanings

	British	American
homely	warm and friendly	plain and dull, or even ugly
mean	stingy	nasty
nervy	nervous	cheeky
pants	underpants	trousers
public school	private fee-paying	ordinary

Different spellings

British	American	British	American
analyse	analyze	mould	mold
catalogue	catalog	pyjamas	pajamas
colour	color	sulphur	sulfur
defence	defense	theatre	theater

Australian English

There are many special slang and informal words and phrases in Australian English.

Australian	British	Australian	British
beaut	very good	ropeable	angry
crook	unwell	she's right	all is well
dinkum	right, genuine	tube	can of drink
gibber	a large stone		

English is spoken as a main language in Britain, North America, the Caribbean, Australia, New Zealand, India and parts of Africa, and in each area special words and meanings have developed.

Dialect words meaning 'stupid' or 'stupid person':
chucklehead (many places)
doughball (Glasgow)
dunny (Herefordshire)
mump-aid (Devon)
saggy-head (Staffordshire)

Pidgin and Creole
These forms of English are spoken in the Caribbean and elsewhere. They often include words from English, French, Portuguese, Spanish and West African languages. Parts of the verb 'to be' are often left out, and sentences simplified.

Di boy sick
  (the boy is sick)
Di cat no fat
  (the cat is not fat)
Dat must true
  (that must be true)
Rain falling
  (it is raining)

Some words in Australian English, often from the Aboriginal languages, are familiar in Britain, usually because the things they name are familiar, for example:
boomerang, budgerigar, walkabout, wallaby

A special feature of Australian slang is the number of words ending in -o, shortened from other words, for example:
aft**o** afternoon
comp**o** compensation
smok**o** a rest for a smoke

See also
Grammar
Languages

Biography
Chaucer

Environments

▲ A farm in the northern part of New Jersey, USA. This area is on the eastern seaboard of the continent of North America, less than 100 km from New York City. The environment provides a very different space for living from the street scene at the bottom right of the page.

▶ A street in Harlem, New York City, USA, during a hot summer. Children make the best of a difficult environment by cooling off in water from fire hydrants.

◔ See also
Atmosphere
Deserts
Erosion
Forests
Landforms

Environment means 'surroundings', especially the conditions which affect people's lives. We often use the term to mean our natural surroundings. These include the biosphere, the hydrosphere, and the atmosphere.

The **biosphere** exists on or very close to the surface of the Earth. It is the region where living things can survive. Plants, fungi, bacteria and animals, including human beings, are all part of the biosphere.

The **hydrosphere** consists of the oceans, seas, lakes, rivers, ponds: all the water on the surface of the Earth.

The **atmosphere** surrounds the biosphere and protects it from harmful rays from the Sun. It helps to keep the surface of the Earth at a fairly constant temperature and it shields it from solid particles from space.

The shape of the land is another part of the natural environment: mountains, hills and plains, river valleys and sea coasts are some of the different landforms.

The environment can be natural, but can also be made by people. Unless you live in a very rural area, you will find that most of your environment has been made by people. The village, suburb, town or city is the environment where you live. Your country is also your environment, and planet Earth is the global environment.

Environmental problems

Although people are part of the biosphere, we have a far greater ability than other living things to adapt and alter the environment to suit our own needs. We can make it more comfortable and convenient, but in some areas of the world the environment has been damaged by the activities of people.

Deforestation

Tropical rainforests help to control the amount of carbon dioxide in the atmosphere and these forests are also home to a huge variety of plant and animal species. In 1950, 15 per cent of the land surface of the Earth was covered by rainforests. By 1985 only 10 per cent of the land supported forests because trees had been felled for timber and to free land for cattle ranching.

Erosion

Soil erosion happens naturally, but it can also be caused by cutting down trees on hill slopes so that soil is washed away downhill by heavy rains and storms. In the Himalayas much of the natural forest has been felled for firewood and to increase land for farming. The bare soil is unprotected from the wind. Use of chemical fertilizers instead of organic manure and compost exhausts the soil so that it crumbles into dust and is easily blown away.

Many people are now more conscious of the need to protect the natural environment and to preserve the balance of the biosphere where we all live. ■

Enzymes

Life would be impossible without enzymes. They are substances which speed up the chemical changes which all life depends upon. Without enzymes these changes would go very slowly or not happen at all, and life would come to an end.

Each enzyme is a special protein adapted to one particular chemical process. Digestive enzymes change food into liquids which can pass into the blood and travel around the body. Other enzymes change digested food so that it releases energy, and more enzymes use energy to build food into the substances living bodies are made of. Enzymes also turn any poisons in the body into safe substances. If enzymes get too hot, they stop working, which is why heating kills bacteria and other organisms. ■

See also
Digestive systems
Proteins

Epidemics

Epidemics are outbreaks of disease that affect a large number of people in the same place at the same time. Some epidemics are caused by pollution, or by people's behaviour: cigarette smoking has led to an epidemic of lung cancer this century. But most epidemics are caused by infectious diseases passed from person to person.

Epidemic diseases

Epidemics are caused by many infections that spread in different ways. Some, including cholera and typhoid, spread when people eat food or drink water that contains germs.

Others are spread by animals: rats can pass plague to humans, and mosquitoes can pass on malaria. And some epidemic diseases, like influenza and measles, are caused by viruses which are spread through the air by coughing and sneezing or caught by touching infected people.

Scientists who study epidemics and other diseases are called epidemiologists.

Epidemics can affect a continent or even the whole world. Then they are called pandemics.

Famous epidemics and pandemics
The Black Death (plague): began in western China and the infection was carried along to the Middle East and Europe 1347–1350. Killed one in three, about 25 million people.

The Great Plague of London, 1665: killed 60,000 of the city's 450,000 inhabitants.

Influenza pandemic, 1918–1920: spread around the world, killed about 20 million people, including almost one million in the USA.

Stopping epidemics

Epidemic diseases that spread through water or food can be stopped by keeping hands and kitchens clean, and by proper disposal of rubbish and sewage. They are no longer common in Europe, North America and Australia, but are still a problem in poor countries that cannot afford proper sanitation. Diseases spread by animals can be slowed down if the animals are killed off or confined.

Some diseases that are caused by viruses can be prevented if people are given a vaccine to protect them. In 1977 a disease called smallpox vanished from the world after millions of people were given vaccines.

But viruses are very complicated, keep changing, and can come in several different types. New viruses can appear, like the HIV virus that causes the disease of AIDS. So, despite our discoveries, epidemic diseases remain a puzzle and are not likely to disappear. ■

See also
AIDS
Black Death
Diseases
Health
Hygiene
Immunity
Malaria
Quarantine
Vaccinations
Viruses

Epilepsy

A person has epilepsy if they have repeated epileptic fits. There are many types of fit; from major convulsive fits when a person falls to the ground and shakes, to an 'absence' where they simply look blank.

Epilepsy is a condition not an illness. Fits occur when the brain, or part of the brain suddenly stops working properly for a few moments. Once the brain starts working normally again the fit stops and the person returns to normal.

Epilepsy is quite common. In the United Kingdom 300,000 people have epilepsy. You do not see many people having fits because those who have this condition take drugs prescribed by a doctor; such drugs prevent fits from occurring. ■

Equations

In mathematics there are many types of equation. One of the simplest uses a box (❑) for a number that is as yet unknown. For instance:

$❑ + 4 = 10$.

What number can you put in the box to get the right answer?

If the equation were

$❑ + ❑ = 10$,

what are the possibilities then?

In algebra letters such as x and y are used to stand for the unknown numbers. So another equation is $6x + 4 = 28$ (which can be read as 'six times some number plus four equals twenty-eight'). What number can x stand for? Often x can stand for several different numbers:

$$x^2 + y^2 = z^2.$$

This can be read as 'one number squared (multiplied by itself) plus another number squared is equal to a third number squared'. One trio which works is $x = 3$, $y = 4$ and $z = 5$. Can you find any more sets of numbers which work?

An equation is usually formed by two mathematical expressions connected by an equals sign (=).

Equations form a very important tool for scientists. Most of the laws of science can be written in a mathematical form as equations. For example there is a law called Newton's First Law of Motion which tells us that things do not accelerate (which means they start to move or change their speed) unless there is a net force acting on them. Mathematically this is written as $P = m \times f$. P represents the force, m the mass, and f the acceleration.

Other equations tell us how rays of light behave, how electricity behaves, how chemicals behave when they are mixed and so on. Without equations scientists would not be able to predict what is likely to happen in their experiments. ■

One of the most famous equations is Einstein's

$$E = mc^2.$$

E stands for energy, m for mass and c for the speed of light (3×10^8 m per second). Many people are familiar with this equation but this does not mean that they understand it.

⊙ See also
Algebra
Arithmetic
Mathematics

Equator

The Equator is an imaginary line round the Earth, half-way between the North and South Poles. It is 40,077 km (24,903 miles) around the Earth at the Equator. At any place on the Equator the Sun is directly overhead at midday on 21 March and 23 September. Between these dates, the Sun is almost overhead at midday, so it is very hot all through the year. Places at the Equator have twelve hours of daylight and twelve hours of darkness. ■

⊙ See also
Latitude and longitude

Equatorial Guinea

Equatorial Guinea is a hot country in west-central Africa. It is made up of an area on the mainland called Rio Muni and several islands. The largest island, Bioko, contains the country's capital, Malabo.

Most people work on farms or in the forests and cocoa, coffee and timber are the main products. Spain ruled Equatorial Guinea from the mid-19th century until the country became independent in 1968. ■

Area 28,051 sq km (10,830 sq miles)
Capital Malabo
Population 392,000
Language Spanish, Fang, Bubi, Portuguese Patois, others
Religion Christian
Government Republic
Currency 1 (CFA) franc = 100 centimes

⊙ See also
Africa

Equinoxes

Equinox means 'equal night' and it is a name given to two special days in the year when the hours of daylight and darkness everywhere in the world are equal. The two days fall on or near 21 March and 23 September. At midday on the equinoxes, the Sun is directly overhead at places on the Equator.

Day and night are not the same length at any other times but change regularly with the seasons. The days when the number of hours of daylight is greatest and smallest also have a special name. They are called the solstices, and fall on about 21 June and 21 December. Sometimes these days are called midsummer or midwinter day. ■

In Latin *aequus* means equal and *nox* means night.

March 21 is called the spring or vernal equinox. September 23 is called the autumnal equinox.

Solstice comes from the Latin meaning 'Sun standing still'. The solstices occur when the Sun reaches its most northerly and southerly position among the stars (namely latitudes 23½° north and south).

⊙ See also
Day and night
Seasons

Erosion

All around us, the Earth's surface is being worn away by water and by wind. This process is called erosion. The word comes from the Latin for 'to gnaw', a very good description of the slow action that keeps on wearing away the rocks. Moving water includes mighty rivers and little streams, the sea and also ice which moves over the land as glaciers and ice-sheets. Water, ice and wind not only wear away the land, they also carry away eroded material and deposit it in other places, especially in the sea.

Weathering

Erosion is the work of moving water, ice or wind. The action of snow and frost, sun and rain on rocks is called weathering. When rocks are exposed to the atmosphere, they are affected by the weather. Constant heating and cooling can split some rocks. When water in the rocks freezes and then melts, it cracks them. Rain-water is a weak acid and can dissolve or change the chemicals in rocks. Weathering can also be speeded up by plant roots and burrowing animals.

Rock pieces that have been broken up by weathering are moved away by water, ice and wind. When wind, water and ice are armed with pieces of rock, however small, they can erode even more powerfully. Although weathering and erosion are different, they both work together to reshape the landscape.

The speed of erosion

Erosion is usually a slow process. But during storms, water and wind are much more powerful. They carry bigger fragments of rock and erode the land more quickly. Rivers are deepening and widening their valleys all the time, but a river in flood can erode the land faster in a few hours than it would normally do in years. The floodwater is armed with pieces of rock and fallen trees. It can roll great boulders along the river bed, and alter its course to cut new channels.

The rocks of the Earth's surface also affect the speed of erosion. Soft rocks are eroded more quickly than hard ones. Faults and folds make weaknesses that can be attacked. Whether the rock layers are flat or dipping also affects erosion. Hard rocks may make a waterfall along a river or headlands at the seaside. ■

▲ Erosion has cut deeply into this hillside in Cyprus, washing away the soil and sending the rocks tumbling down. These broken rocks are called scree.

See also
Deserts
Glaciers
Icebergs and ice-caps
Mountains
Rivers
Rocks
Soil

Escalators

An escalator is a continuously moving staircase. A modern one can carry up to 10,000 people an hour. You simply step on, hold the handrail while you are taken to another floor or level of a building, and then step off at the other end.

The modern type of escalator was developed in the 1930s. An electric motor provides the power for an endless chain of steps. The chain is turned by toothed wheels at the top of the escalator, where the drive for the handrail is also situated.

At the bottom of the escalator toothed wheels carry the chains round and back up to the top. A curved rail guides the steps from the horizontal, up the slope, then back to the horizontal again at the top. ■

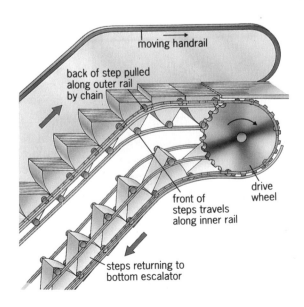

moving handrail

back of step pulled along outer rail by chain

front of steps travels along inner rail

drive wheel

steps returning to bottom escalator

The world's longest escalator is at Lenin Square on the St Petersburg Underground, Russia. It has 729 steps and a vertical rise of 59·68 m.

▲ In an escalator, an electric motor drives an endless chain of steps. The same motor also moves the handrails.

Europe

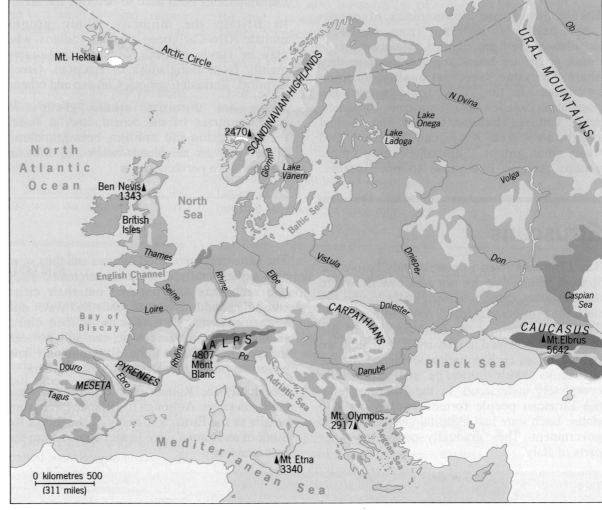

Land height in metres

- more than 2000
- 1000–2000
- 500–1000
- 200–500
- less than 200
- land below sea level
- ▲ highest peaks with heights given in metres
- ice cap

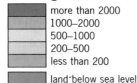

Excluding Russia, Europe has about 6 million sq km (2½ million sq miles) of land for about 600 million people to live on. If you include the European parts of Russia, there are about 10 million sq km (4 million sq miles) of land for about 700 million people.

From the north of Europe (in Norway) to the south (in Greece) is nearly 4,000 km (2,500 miles). From the west (in Portugal) to the east (in Russia) is over 5,000 km (3,000 miles).

Europe is the smallest continent, yet it is the most crowded, with about one-eighth of all the world's people. Over the past 500 years Europeans have settled in every other continent, and today European languages can be heard all over the world: English in North America and Australia; French in Canada and south-east Asia; Spanish and Portuguese in Central and South America; English, French, Portuguese and Dutch in Africa.

Landscapes

Europe is a continent of peninsulas and islands. In fact, the whole continent is really a westward extension of Asia.

There are two main inlets of the sea: the Baltic Sea to the north and the Mediterranean Sea to the south. The main mountains are the Alps, a line of jagged, snow-capped peaks stretching from southern France to Austria. The Pyrenees, between Spain and France, and the mountains

of Norway, Greece and the Balkans are not so high. The North European plain, from Brittany in France to Russia, is low and mainly flat. It is littered with clay and boulders that were left behind after the Ice Age glaciers had melted.

Climate

Most winds in Europe come from the west. They are wet because they have blown over the Atlantic Ocean. The arrangement of the peninsulas, mountains and seas in Europe allows these wet winds to blow far inland, bringing rain.

Depressions move over Europe all the time, bringing quick changes in the weather. In winter, warm Atlantic ocean currents keep the coasts free from ice. Far from the sea, though, winters can be calm, clear and very cold. The Mediterranean region has warm, wet winters and hot, dry summers. There are long periods of sunshine and clear, blue skies in summer.

ICELAND

Faeroe Islands
(Denmark)

Shetland Islands

Orkney Islands

NORWAY

SWEDEN

FINLAND

RUSSIA

ESTONIA

LATVIA

LITHUANIA

RUSSIA

BELARUS

IRISH
REPUBLIC

UNITED
KINGDOM

DENMARK

NETHERLANDS

Channel Islands

BELGIUM

GERMANY

POLAND

UKRAINE

LUXEMBOURG

CZECHOSLOVAKIA

FRANCE

LIECHTENSTEIN

SWITZERLAND

AUSTRIA

HUNGARY

MOLDOVA

AZERBAIJAN

SLOVENIA

ROMANIA

GEORGIA

MONACO

CROATIA

YUGOSLAVIA

ARMENIA

PORTUGAL

ANDORRA

SAN
MARINO

BOSNIA-
HERZEGOVINA

SERBIA

BULGARIA

SPAIN

Corsica

ITALY

MONTENEGRO

MACEDONIA

Balearic
Islands

Sardinia

ALBANIA

GREECE

Gibraltar (U.K.)

Sicily

MALTA

CYPRUS

Crete

Area
10,498,000 sq km
(4,053,300 sq miles)
Highest peak
Elbrus 5,642 m
Lowest point
Caspian Sea
28 m below sea-level
Largest lake
Caspian Sea
371,000 sq km
(143,205 sq miles)
Longest rivers
Volga, Danube
Largest country
(by area)
(excluding Russia)
Ukraine 603,700 sq km
(233,090 sq miles)
Largest country
(by population)
(excluding Russia)
Germany 79,000,000

Countries and languages

The borders of European states have changed many times. Several countries which are on the map today did not exist separately a hundred years ago. Yugoslavia and Czechoslovakia became nation states after World War I. Hungary regained its independence at the same time and Austria shrank in size. The Baltic states of Estonia, Latvia and Lithuania became independent states in 1920 but in 1940 they became republics within the USSR as a result of a treaty between Hitler and Stalin. In 1991 they declared their independence again, the first to break away from the Soviet Union.

The languages spoken in Europe can tell us something of the early history of the continent, and of the waves of invaders from Asia who settled in prehistoric times. German, Dutch, Danish, Swedish and English are all Germanic languages. Polish, Bulgarian, Czech, Slovak and

Serbo-Croat are Slavonic languages related to Russian. Italian, Spanish, Romanian and French developed out of the Latin language which was spoken all over the Roman empire. These are called Romance languages.

Religion

In southern Europe and Poland most Christians belong to the Roman Catholic Church. In northern Europe the churches are mainly Protestant. Greeks, Bulgarians, some Yugoslavs, and Russians belong to the Orthodox Church. There are Jews living in most European countries, though few in Germany and eastern Europe where they were exterminated by the Nazis in the Holocaust. Since World War II, immigrants from Africa, the Caribbean, Turkey, India and Pakistan have settled in parts of France, Germany, Scandinavia and Britain. Now there are mosques for Muslim worshippers and temples for Hindus in several large cities. ■

There is no clear boundary between eastern Europe and western Asia. The Ural Mountains in Russia make a convenient line on the map so Russia is partly in Europe but has much larger territories in Asia. The countries between the Black Sea and the Caspian Sea are usually counted as part of Europe. But many people consider Azerbaijan and Armenia to be Asian. Turkey is usually counted as part of west Asia.

See also

Alps
Christians
Depressions
European Community
European history
Languages

European Community

After World War II a number of countries in western Europe began to co-operate more closely with each other. Then in 1957 the European Economic Community, commonly known as the Common Market, was founded by the Treaty of Rome. Goods could be sold between these six countries without extra import taxes and people were free to take jobs in any of the other countries.

In order to make decisions and administer the Community, new institutions had to be set up. By 1967 there was a Council of Ministers, a Commission, a European Parliament and a Court of Justice. The **Council of Ministers**, made up of ministers from each country's government, have the final say on the policies and programmes of the Community. The **Commission** is made up of two people from each larger country and one from each smaller country. They take decisions on routine matters and propose new laws.

The members of the **European Parliament** are directly elected by voters in each member state. The Parliament is able to comment on proposals put up by the commissioners and influence the budget, and it is slowly gaining more powers.

The **Court of Justice** has the power to enforce Community law on member states. This Court has sometimes overturned a decision made by the British law courts. All citizens of Community countries have the right to appeal to the European Court of Justice should they feel a decision is against Community law.

Between 1973 and 1986 Denmark, the Irish Republic, the United Kingdom, Greece, Spain and Portugal all joined. So the Community increased from the original six to twelve member states. In 1987 these twelve member states passed the Single European Act. This meant that from the end of 1992 money, goods, services and people could move freely within the Community without customs and other controls at the frontiers. Any citizen of a member state can start a business, hire workers and sell products as easily in another member country as in their own. Workers too are able to use their skills to find jobs anywhere throughout the Community.

For many people the main purpose of the European Community is to create a continent whose countries need never go to war with each other again. ■

Belgium, France, West Germany, Italy, Luxembourg and The Netherlands came together in 1952 in the European Coal and Steel Community.

The **commissioners** work in Brussels and are supported by a staff of civil servants.

The **Parliament** meets partly in Strasbourg, France, and partly in Luxembourg. In 1991 it had 518 members. The UK, France, Germany and Italy had 81 Euro MPs each. Spain had 60, The Netherlands 25, Portugal, Belgium and Greece 24, Denmark 16, Ireland 15 and Luxembourg 6.

The **Court of Justice** meets in The Hague, The Netherlands.

1973
Denmark
Irish Republic
United Kingdom
1981
Greece
1986
Portugal
Spain

Austria, Sweden and Switzerland applied for membership in 1991.

See also
Europe
European history

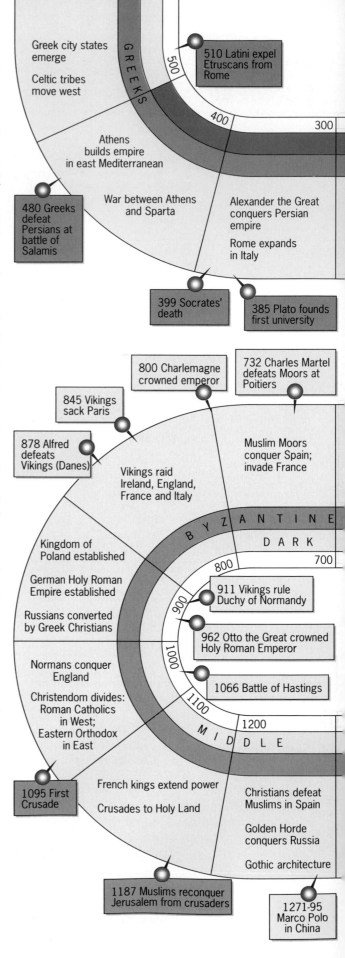

European history

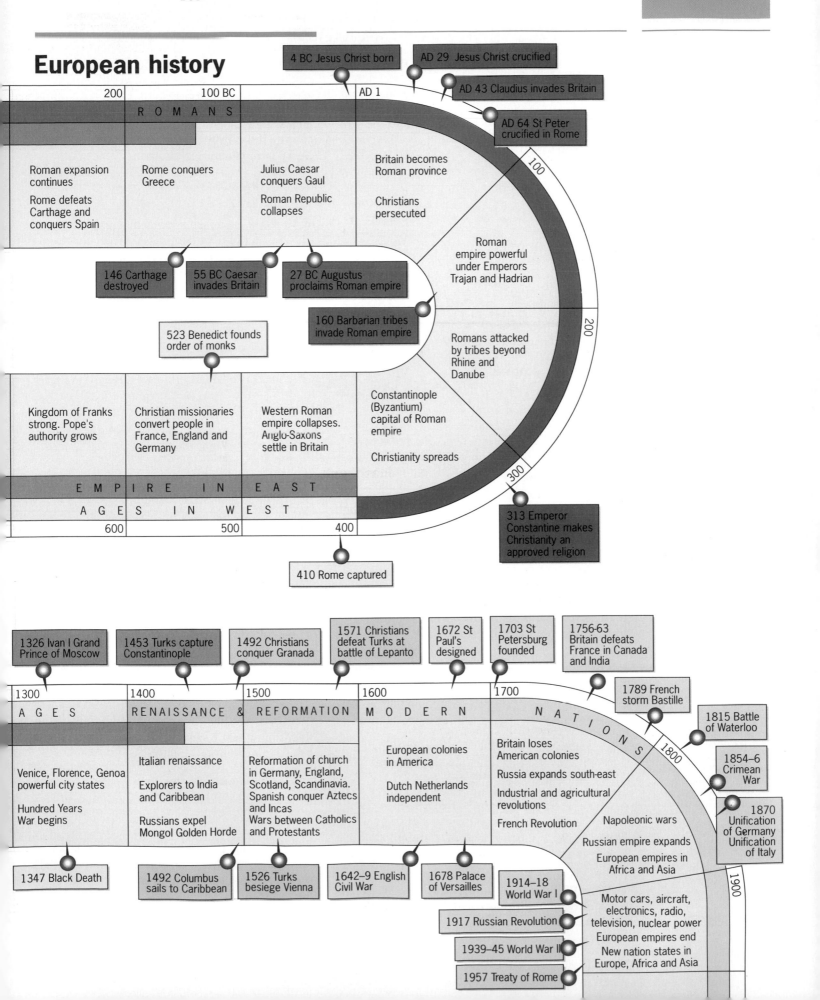

4 BC Jesus Christ born

AD 29 Jesus Christ crucified

AD 43 Claudius invades Britain

AD 64 St Peter crucified in Rome

200   100 BC   AD 1   100

R O M A N S

Roman expansion continues

Rome defeats Carthage and conquers Spain

Rome conquers Greece

Julius Caesar conquers Gaul

Roman Republic collapses

Britain becomes Roman province

Christians persecuted

Roman empire powerful under Emperors Trajan and Hadrian

146 Carthage destroyed

55 BC Caesar invades Britain

27 BC Augustus proclaims Roman empire

160 Barbarian tribes invade Roman empire

Romans attacked by tribes beyond Rhine and Danube

523 Benedict founds order of monks

Kingdom of Franks strong. Pope's authority grows

Christian missionaries convert people in France, England and Germany

Western Roman empire collapses. Anglo-Saxons settle in Britain

Constantinople (Byzantium) capital of Roman empire

Christianity spreads

200

300

E M P I R E   I N   E A S T

A G E S   I N   W E S T

600   500   400

313 Emperor Constantine makes Christianity an approved religion

410 Rome captured

1326 Ivan I Grand Prince of Moscow

1453 Turks capture Constantinople

1492 Christians conquer Granada

1571 Christians defeat Turks at battle of Lepanto

1672 St Paul's designed

1703 St Petersburg founded

1756-63 Britain defeats France in Canada and India

1300   1400   1500   1600   1700

A G E S

RENAISSANCE &

R E F O R M A T I O N

M O D E R N

N A T I O N S

1789 French storm Bastille

1815 Battle of Waterloo

Venice, Florence, Genoa powerful city states

Hundred Years War begins

Italian renaissance

Explorers to India and Caribbean

Russians expel Mongol Golden Horde

Reformation of church in Germany, England, Scotland, Scandinavia. Spanish conquer Aztecs and Incas
Wars between Catholics and Protestants

European colonies in America

Dutch Netherlands independent

Britain loses American colonies

Russia expands south-east

Industrial and agricultural revolutions

French Revolution

Napoleonic wars

Russian empire expands

European empires in Africa and Asia

1800

1854-6 Crimean War

1870 Unification of Germany Unification of Italy

1900

1347 Black Death

1492 Columbus sails to Caribbean

1526 Turks besiege Vienna

1642-9 English Civil War

1678 Palace of Versailles

1914-18 World War I

1917 Russian Revolution

1939-45 World War II

1957 Treaty of Rome

Motor cars, aircraft, electronics, radio, television, nuclear power

European empires end

New nation states in Europe, Africa and Asia

There is another explanation of where the name 'Europe' comes from. The Assyrians used to speak of 'asu' (meaning land of the rising Sun) and 'ereb' (meaning land of the setting Sun, or mainland). They passed these names on to the Greeks, and eventually they became Asia and Europe.

▶ The Romans excelled as engineers, architects and builders. Aqueducts were constructed in Italy, North Africa, Spain, France and other parts of the Roman empire. This drawing is of the Pont du Gard in southern France.

▶ Gothic churches and cathedrals were built in western Europe from the late 12th to the 15th century. The drawing is of the great cathedral of Chartres in France.

▶ Byzantine churches were built in Greece, Russia, the Balkans and parts of eastern Europe where Christians followed the practices of the Greek (Eastern) Orthodox Church. This drawing is based on a church in Greece.

Europe is named after a legendary Phoenician princess Europa. The Greeks then gave her name to the islands and mainland of Greece. A Greek historian, Herodotus, when writing about the war between the Greeks and Persians in the 5th century BC, called all land west of the Bosporus Europe and all land east of it Asia. And so it has remained.

The Roman empire

By about AD 100 the Romans had conquered many of the lands that now make up countries of modern Europe, including Spain, France and Britain. However, their power did not extend beyond the river Rhine; here there were German tribes whom the Romans called 'barbarians'.

The Roman empire gradually split into a western half and an eastern half (the Byzantine empire). The West accepted the Pope in Rome as head of the Church and called itself Christendom. In eastern Europe and Russia, people were gradually converted to Christianity by missionaries from the Greek Orthodox Church in Constantinople, the capital of the Byzantine empire. From then on the Ural Mountains were regarded as the European eastern border with Asia.

Dark Ages

As the Roman empire declined and collapsed, many tribes crossed the Rhine and moved into western Europe. By about AD 500 there were as many as twenty different tribes, including Franks, Saxons, Visigoths and Ostrogoths, controlling

particular areas of Europe. These peoples gradually came to accept the power of the Church and, throughout Christendom, Latin became the official language of church services, of governments, and of lawyers and scholars. Educated people travelling across the continent could easily understand one another.

Muslim invaders

The followers of the prophet Muhammad, known as Muslims, launched a series of wars in southern Europe after his death in AD 632. They conquered much of the Byzantine empire, without managing to take Constantinople. They also invaded Spain and France in the west. Charles Martel ('the Hammer') defeated a Muslim army at a battle near Poitiers in 732 and they were driven out of France. But Muslim Moors from North Africa settled in Spain and for hundreds of years southern Spain was Islamic not Christian. The Muslims ruled Granada right up to 1492, the year Columbus sailed to the Caribbean.

Nation states emerge

Gradually, during the Middle Ages, people in western Europe who spoke different languages began to separate into nations. The first strong, united country was Francia (France) ruled over by Charlemagne (Charles the Great), grandson of Charles Martel. England became a united country even before the Norman invasion of 1066.

Later Spain, Portugal, Sweden and other countries gradually established themselves. Many German-speaking people were ruled by the Emperor of Austria, who for centuries used the title Holy Roman Emperor. Italian-speaking people did not unite until 1860.

Renaissance and Reformation

Between the 14th and 17th centuries great advances took place in learning and the arts. Italian artists, sculptors and architects studied the writings and ruined buildings of the ancient Romans and were inspired by this classical civilization. Their ideas spread all over Europe. Printing made it possible for books and pamphlets to be produced so that more people had the chance of learning to read.

Many people wanted to read the Bible in their own language and, for this and other reasons, they split from the Roman Catholic Church. This 'Reformation' created Protestant churches which became powerful in northern Europe, particularly in England, Scotland, Sweden and northern Germany. Terrible wars between Catholics and Protestants followed in the 16th and 17th centuries. The Thirty Years War from 1618 to 1648 caused enormous loss of life and damage right across central Europe.

France

After the religious wars, France emerged again as the strongest European country. King Louis XIV built the magnificent palace at Versailles, and for a century, from about 1660, France was the centre of European civilization. But Britain, her old rival, began to challenge her power overseas and build an empire. In the Seven Years War from 1756 to 1763 Britain defeated France in both India and Canada. The new inventions of the Industrial Revolution were also helping to make Britain economically powerful. In 1789 the French Revolution took place and France became a republic.

The Napoleonic wars

After the Revolution, the French general Napoleon came to power and crowned himself Emperor. He wanted France to rule all Europe, and between 1803 and 1812 his armies entered Germany, Austria, Italy, Holland, Prussia, Poland, Spain and Russia. After retreating in defeat from Moscow, Napoleon was finally defeated at Waterloo in 1815.

Colonies and wars

The influence of Europe spread throughout the world. Many Europeans came to feel superior to all other peoples in the Americas, Africa, India and China. During the 19th century most west European countries took over as many colonies as they could. Britain, France and Holland built the biggest empires. Rivalry between these nations, particularly after the unification of Italy and then Germany, led to war between France and Germany in 1870–1871 and then to the two great world wars.

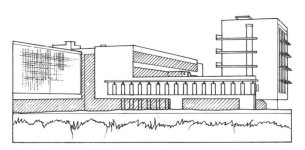

The twentieth century

In World War II Britain, the USA, the USSR and their allies defeated the Axis powers of Germany, Italy and Japan. After this war the USSR dominated the countries of central and eastern Europe, including East Germany, for over 40 years. It was as if an iron curtain had split Europe down the middle. While the eastern European countries were ruled by communist governments, western Europe recovered from the destruction of the war and grew prosperous. As the new institutions of the European Community developed, the gap between the wealthy, democratic countries of the Community and the economically backward countries under communist dictatorships increased.

In 1989 the communist governments lost power in Poland, Hungary, East Germany and Czechoslovakia. During 1989 and 1990 free elections were held for the first time in over 40 years. The power of the USSR collapsed and the republics that had made it up became independent states. ■

◄ Renaissance architects admired the classical temples of the Greeks and Romans. The drawing is of a palace, the Villa Rotonda, designed by Palladio, a famous Italian architect, in the 16th century.

◄ The Bauhaus was designed by Walter Gropius in Germany in the 1920s. His geometrical and functional style of design greatly influenced modern architecture.

◄ The palace of Versailles, built by Louis XIV in the 17th century.

Evolution of living things

▲ Stromatolites are made up of layers of blue-green algae and rock. These live stromatolites are in Australia. The oldest known fossils are of stromatolites 3,500 million years old.

When the Earth was first formed, there was no life at all. The surface of the Earth was very hot then, and nothing could have lived. It took about 1,000 million years for the Earth to become suitable for life. It is very hard to imagine how life could arise from non-living things. For years, biologists could not understand how the very complicated plants and animals, including ourselves, could have come from simple chemicals.

However, some very simple microscopic forms of life have been discovered and these seem to be partly like living things and partly like chemicals which are not alive. For instance, viruses can reproduce but are so simple that they can be made into crystals like other chemicals.

Scientists think that life arose from chemicals that entered the atmosphere from volcanoes, thousands of millions of years ago. Geologists can tell from ancient rocks that these chemicals included hydrogen, methane, ammonia, and water, but no oxygen. Experiments have shown that these chemicals will form into molecules called amino acids quite easily.

Amino acids are the building blocks of proteins, and proteins are the main substances of living things. Experiments in laboratories have suggested that lightning and radiation from the Sun triggered the formation of amino acids. These dissolved in the oceans where, over millions of years, they formed proteins and then simple cells.

These simple cells were like small bags of protein with an outer membrane which could take in other chemicals (feed) and divide to form new cells (reproduce). The oldest fossils that have been discovered are 3,500 million years old. They support these ideas.

▶ *Pteraspis*, one of the first fish, had no jaws and had to suck food from the sea-bed. It was heavily armoured, probably to protect it against sea scorpions which grew up to 2 m.

Life in the sea

The first fossils are of very simple organisms made up of one cell, like bacteria. After many hundreds of millions of years, the cells gradually changed and became bigger. They had a special structure called a nucleus in the centre which controlled the whole cell. Simple creatures made up from several cells eventually appeared about 850 million years ago. At first, these were just strings of cells, like chains of beads.

The first real animals are known to have lived from about 670 million years ago. There were worms and jellyfish and other simple sea creatures. Their fossil remains were found first in Australia, in the Ediacara Hills. But fossils of these sea animals have now been found from all parts of the world.

A major change took place about 570 million years ago, at the beginning of the Cambrian period of geological time. The first animals with hard parts, like shells, appeared. From that date there were more fossils, because the hard parts are much more often preserved than soft parts. Many new groups appeared in the sea: shellfish of various kinds and trilobites, which were animals with jointed legs, related to crabs and insects.

Near the end of the Cambrian period, 505 million years ago, some new kinds of animals appeared in the sea. These included the corals, the graptolites (floating creatures that have since died out), and the fish. We know that fish were living then because fossil scales have been found.

First fish

Fish have bony backbones, just like us and all other vertebrates (backboned animals). The development of backbones was a very important step in the evolution of life. During the next 100 million years, little is known of the history of the fish since their fossils are not very common, but by about 400 million years ago, the major living groups had come on the scene: sharks, bony fish (ancestors of such fish as the cod, herring and goldfish), and lungfish.

Plants on land

The next major stage in the history of life was the move onto land. Simple plants had evolved in the seas, where they drifted around with the bacteria, the worms and jellyfish, trilobites, corals, fish and other animals. Perhaps plants grew and formed a greenish slime on seaside rocks as much as 800 million years ago. But nobody can be sure.

The first true land plants are known to have lived about 410 million years ago, from the end of the Silurian period of geological time. The fossils show simple reedy stems with rounded spore cases at the top of each stem. This type of plant had no leaves or flowers. But it did have simple roots. Roots are essential for land plants to take in water and minerals. Water plants do not need roots. Stems are not needed in the water either, where plants like seaweed simply float.

During the next 100 million years, the land plants became more advanced and complex. They also became much bigger and the first 'trees' appeared. These spread over large parts of the world, forming the great 'coal swamps'

of the Carboniferous period, 300 million years ago. The coal that we burn on our fires comes mainly from those early trees.

Animals onto land

As the plants spread over the lands, they created many new places for animals to live. The fallen leaves built up layers of soil, and the stems and leaves formed sources of food, as did the spores and fruits. The first land animals are known from the beginning of the Devonian period, 400 million years ago. The small insects, spiders and mites were first. They lived in the soil and burrowed into the juicy stems of the plants.

The backboned animals were not far behind. Groups of fish, related to the modern lungfish, already lived in freshwater ponds which often dried up. They could breathe air if necessary, and they had strong roundish fins which they could use to drag themselves over land for short distances.

The first amphibians are called *Ichthyostega*, which means 'fish-scaled'. They evolved from such fish near the end of the Devonian period, 370 million years ago. These animals still had fish-shaped heads and fins on their tails. But they also had four legs for walking, and lungs for breathing air. During the Carboniferous period, the amphibians became important land animals. There were many kinds living amongst the damp trees, and feeding on insects and fish.

As the number of plants increased the amount of oxygen in the atmosphere increased. Oxygen is produced when plants make their own food by photosynthesis. The increase in oxygen aided the evolution of animals.

◀ *Cooksonia*, one of the first land plants. The illustration on the left shows how scientists think it looked. The photograph on the right shows a fossil of the plant. *Cooksonia* had a waxy outer layer (cuticle) to prevent drying out, and tubes in the stems to transport food and water.

▼ The Carboniferous period saw the evolution of amphibians. *Ichthyostega* was one of the first amphibians. Its ancestors were probably very much like lungfish.

1 Ichthyostega
2 Eusthenopteron (lobe-finned fish)
3 Rhynchodipterus

▲ During the Permian period the continents moved together to form one land mass called Pangaea. This was ruled by mammal-like reptiles. At the end of the Permian there was a great mass extinction.

The age of the reptiles

The first reptiles were small lizard-like animals that could live in really dry land conditions. They evolved from the amphibians and appeared about 300 million years ago, near the middle of the Carboniferous period of geological time.

Reptiles, like amphibians, lay eggs. But the reptiles produced eggs with shells which stopped them from drying up, and so they could move out of the damp swamps and lay eggs on land instead of in water.

One large group of reptiles were the mammal-like reptiles which lived on Earth during the Permian and Triassic periods between 286 and 180 million years ago. Some of these reptiles ate insects, but others became larger and ate plants. Another group evolved long sharp teeth, and ate the plant-eaters. Some of the mammal-like reptiles became as large as rhinoceroses.

The most varied and most successful group of reptiles to evolve were the dinosaurs, which first arose in the Triassic period and soon took over from the mammal-like reptiles. Dinosaurs flourished for the next 160 million years and spread all over the Earth.

Mammals and birds

Although the mammal-like reptiles had disappeared, they had given rise to the true mammals. These were very small and managed to survive quietly beneath the feet of the mighty dinosaurs. These little animals had evolved a warm covering of hair, and they had large eyes and keen brains. When the dinosaurs died out 65 million years ago, the hairy little mammals took their chance. All kinds of mammals evolved: horses, deer, mice, dogs, cats, whales, bats and monkeys. Eventually, of course, human beings evolved, but very recently in the history of life on Earth. Modern humans (*Homo sapiens*) appeared only about 150,000 years ago. We now live in the age of mammals.

The other main group of backboned animals on land are the birds. They all have feathers and warm bodies just like the mammals. The birds are now thought to have evolved from small dinosaurs of the late Jurassic period, about 150 million years ago. The oldest known bird, *Archaeopteryx*, has the skeleton of a dinosaur, except for its wings. It also clearly has feathers. Birds gradually became more common at about the same time as the mammals did. ■

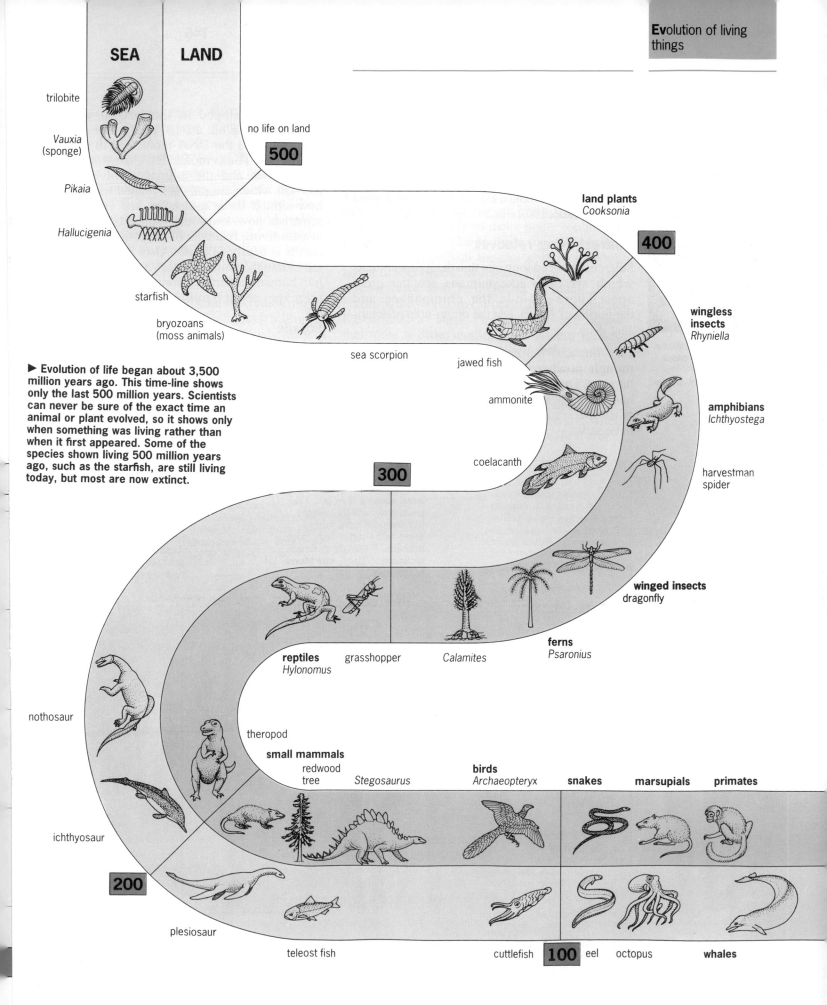

SEA **LAND**

trilobite

Vauxia
(sponge)

Pikaia

Hallucigenia

no life on land

500

starfish

bryozoans
(moss animals)

sea scorpion

jawed fish

land plants
Cooksonia

400

wingless insects
Rhyniella

amphibians
Ichthyostega

ammonite

coelacanth

harvestman
spider

▶ Evolution of life began about 3,500 million years ago. This time-line shows only the last 500 million years. Scientists can never be sure of the exact time an animal or plant evolved, so it shows only when something was living rather than when it first appeared. Some of the species shown living 500 million years ago, such as the starfish, are still living today, but most are now extinct.

300

winged insects
dragonfly

ferns
Psaronius

reptiles grasshopper *Calamites*
Hylonomus

nothosaur

theropod

small mammals

redwood
tree *Stegosaurus*

birds
Archaeopteryx **snakes** **marsupials** **primates**

ichthyosaur

200

plesiosaur

teleost fish

cuttlefish 100 eel octopus **whales**

▶ The skull of the Neanderthal (left) is larger than the Cro-Magnon skull. Some people believe this is because Neanderthals had larger brains.

The Neanderthal people

The remains of a human skeleton were discovered in the Neander Valley in Germany in 1856. It was a member of *Homo sapiens*, but was a bit shorter and stockier than most modern people and had a more sloping forehead. Similar fossils have since been found in many parts of Europe. They are called the Neanderthals. They lived from about 150,000 years ago until about 30,000 years ago. We know from the objects found with them that they had several kinds of tools such as scrapers and flint knives. They also buried their dead, so maybe they believed in some form of god. They seem to have been well able to live during the ice ages. Nobody knows why they gradually died out. Perhaps they were driven out by the more modern people.

Prehistoric people

As the Neanderthal people were disappearing, a new, more modern kind of *Homo sapiens* was spreading in Europe. These people are named the Cro-Magnon people, after the place in France where they were first found. They were taller and more slender than the Neanderthals but did not have bigger brains. Some experts believe

that the Cro-Magnon people evolved from the Neanderthals but others think this could not have happened in such a short time. Instead they think the Cro-Magnons descended from earlier people in Africa who lived at the same time as the Neanderthals in Europe and had migrated. Cro-Magnons made more delicate stone tools, such as fine knives. They also made wonderful cave paintings of the animals that they hunted for food. Clay models can also sometimes be found in the caves they lived in.

Many scientists now believe that the modern kinds of people, such as Cro-Magnon people, evolved in Africa. Their build was very like that of the many peoples who live in very hot climates today, even though the Cro-Magnon skeletons found have been discovered in regions with cold climates. They gradually spread throughout the world from Africa. Some groups spread to Asia and from there reached Australia. Others went north through China and Siberia and then crossed into Alaska and spread through the Americas. Still others entered Europe.

The fossil record is not good enough to make us sure of all the details, but by 10,000 years ago, modern people lived almost everywhere. ■

Neanderthals were the first people to bury their dead. They seem to have performed some kind of burial ritual; one skull (found in Italy) was surrounded by a ring of rocks.

Experiments

Scientists spend a lot of time asking questions. When they do experiments they are really saying 'I wonder what would happen if I tried this?' Then they do it to find out. Sometimes they try several different ways to see which works best. You are doing experiments of this kind when you cook your own recipes or play a new computer game.

Starting with a guess

Scientists often think they know what will happen when they start an experiment. They do the experiment to find out if their guess is right. Their guess is called a hypothesis. To test the hypothesis properly, the experiment has to be done many times.

For instance, you might think that a certain fertilizer will help seeds to grow. This is your hypothesis. To test this idea by experiment, you plant two seeds in separate pots, giving water to one, and water mixed with fertilizer to the other. Then you wait to see which grows best. But supposing the seed with the fertilizer does grow more quickly? You still cannot be sure that the fertilizer is having any effect. The other seed might have been bad and might not have grown well in either pot. That is why it is better to plant, say, two groups of six seeds using twelve separate pots. Then, if the six seeds with the fertilizer grow best, you can be fairly certain that the fertilizer is helping them.

Fair tests

In all experiments, you must make sure that your tests are fair. The seed experiment would not be a fair test if the pots had different types of soil in. Nor would it be fair if the pots were kept in different places while the seeds were growing. With an experiment like this, many things can change. The temperature and the amount of light can change. As time goes on, the height of each growing seedling changes. And of course the amount of fertilizer can be different from one pot to another.

Scientists have a name for things in an experiment which can change. They call them variables. In any experiment, you have to decide which variables you want to measure and which you need to keep the same. You might want to measure the amount of fertilizer used in each pot and the height of each plant after a certain time. For a fair test, the pots must get the same amounts of water, warmth and light.

Recording your measurements is important. Usually, it is best to write them down in a table. With a simple experiment, you may be able to draw conclusions just by looking at the figures. But with more complicated experiments it may help to show your results as a graph or chart.

Surprising discoveries

With some experiments, you may get a surprise when something unexpected happens. The discovery that penicillin could kill germs came about in this way. Sir Alexander Fleming was growing some germs on a plate of jelly when he noticed that there were patches on the jelly where the germs would not grow. He found that a little spot of mould had accidentally landed on the jelly. It seemed that something from the mould was killing the germs. He wondered what was happening and did some careful experiments to find out. This is how he discovered penicillin. ■

Something to do

Experiment 1: dissolving sugar

Take three barley-sugar sweets. Leave one as it is. Crack the second into three or four pieces. Wrap the third in a clean handkerchief and carefully crush it to powder with a hammer. Now put the three in separate cups of water and see how long each takes to dissolve. What result did you get? Can you explain your result? How did you make sure that your test was fair?

Experiment 2: floating

Some people think that ships and swimmers float best in salty water. Test this idea by experiment. Find out if things float better in salty water than in ordinary water. Start by making a small float. To do this, cut a drinking straw so that you have a piece about 6 cm long. Fix a round lump of Blu-Tac (about 7 mm across) to one end so that the end is sealed. You have now made a float. Check that it floats upright in a beaker of water. You may have to cut bits from the straw until it does.

You are almost ready to test your float in ordinary water and then in salty water. But first, make sure that you have thought about the answers to these questions. How will you be able to tell which water is best for floating? How can you make your observations as accurate as possible? Now do your experiment. Is salty water best for floating? Finally, you could try checking how cold water compares with warm water.

Most of the 'Something to do' sections in this encyclopedia are experiments.

The Royal Institution of Great Britain
Thousands of children and adults come to hear science lectures at the Royal Institution in London and many more watch the Christmas Lectures on television. The Royal Institution was founded by Count Rumford in 1799, and Davy and Faraday were two of its most famous professors. Many scientists work in its laboratories, and others travel to different parts of Britain and the world to help people to understand more about science.

Explorers

There have always been people who wanted to explore. In prehistoric times people looked for new lands when food became scarce, the climate changed or other groups of people threatened them. Over time, many areas of the world were populated by these movements.

Explorers of the ancient world

Many explorers of the ancient world travelled by sea. During the thousand years before Christ, Phoenician and Greek traders explored the Mediterranean Sea and settled the lands around it. The stories they told of Greek hero explorers, such as Jason and Ulysses, are still told today. The Chinese too sailed to the lands and islands of south-east Asia in search of trade.

These explorers of long ago left few written records. Once they started to keep records and draw maps we learn a great deal more about their travels and what they found. Hanno, a Phoenician, sailed from Carthage in the 5th century BC through the Straits of Gibraltar, and part of his story survived. Other Greek writers tell of long forced marches; kings, such as Cyrus of Persia and Alexander the Great, led conquering armies through the lands of south-west Asia. The Roman armies, too, sent their explorers and mapmakers ahead of them as they conquered Europe, the eastern Mediterranean and North Africa, and traded with India and China.

But the explorers with the longest voyages were the Polynesians who settled the thousands of tiny islands in the Pacific. Probably coming from Indonesia, their journeys by boat began around 2000 BC and covered huge distances of the Pacific Ocean, finally reaching New Zealand in about AD 950.

Arab explorers

From the 9th century AD, many Muslim cities in North Africa and the Middle East had universities where men studied to find out about the world around them. Explorers travelled far afield and recorded what they found. Some of their stories have survived as fantastic tales, like Sinbad the Sailor. Ibn Battuta's travels in the 14th century give us reliable descriptions of North and West Africa, India and China.

The oldest maps that have been found are Babylonian ones drawn on clay tablets more than 2,000 years BC.

Many modern explorers have tried to recreate the journeys of the earliest explorers. Thor Heyerdahl's *Kon-Tiki* expedition is a famous example of this.

Compasses were not used by explorers until people discovered that a magnetic lodestone would line up in a north–south direction. The first known compasses were used by sailors in China in the first century AD. European sailors had them by the 12th century. Before then, explorers had to rely upon the winds, the Sun and the stars to give them their direction.

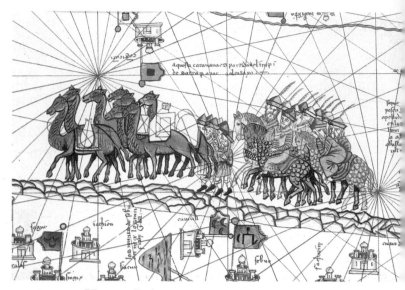

Marco Polo

One explorer who had great influence for hundreds of years was Marco Polo. He was born in Venice in 1254 and he went overland to China. He was away for over 20 years and wrote a book describing all the wonders of the cities and emperors he had seen. But the overland route to Asia was not easy, particularly as the Islamic (Muslim) countries formed a barrier between Christian Europe and the rest of Asia.

Portuguese and Spaniards

The first great sea explorers from western Europe were the Portuguese. By the 15th century, ship and sail design as well as ways to navigate across the ocean had developed to make exploration easier. Europeans had also developed guns which gave them superiority in battle. Prince Henry of Portugal sent off expeditions which explored the western coast of Africa, rounded the Cape of Good Hope and reached India and the East by 1498. They went to discover gold, spices and other riches and they conquered Arab and Indian traders and cities to take the trade for themselves. The Spanish soon followed the Portuguese but sailed westwards, hoping to reach Asia by that route. Columbus sailed from Spain across the Atlantic in 1492 and landed in the West Indies. He thought he had reached Asia, but others soon realized that a new continent had been discovered. Some Spaniards and Portuguese made the voyage to America because they wished to take the Christian faith to new peoples, but usually they simply wanted to become rich. The Spaniards explored the Aztec and Inca lands in Central and South America while the Portuguese went to the Amazon forests.

In 1522, one ship from an expedition led by Magellan sailed right round the world and showed that all the world's oceans were connected. Five ships had set out three years earlier with 268 men. But only 35 men survived the whole voyage. Magellan himself was killed in the Philippines.

Once some European nations had found wealth overseas, others did not want to lose out. Through the 16th and 17th centuries the French, Dutch and English joined the search for new lands. Most exploration was dangerous. Disease, lack of proper food, shipwreck, mutiny, hostile peoples, cold and heat meant that many ships and men never returned. Some of the most dangerous voyages were made trying to find a new way to China, through the frozen seas off northern Canada and Russia.

▼ This French map of South and Central America was made in 1550. The coastlines of the Gulf of Mexico and the Caribbean islands are fairly accurate. But the interior of the continent of South America is uncharted and the southern coastline by the Straits of Magellan had not then been fully surveyed.

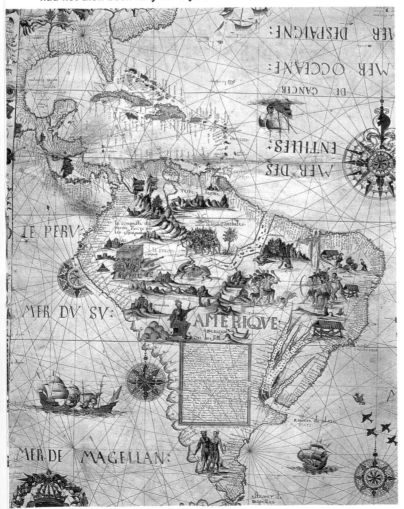

Scientists and mapmakers

Not all explorers wanted to find treasure. From the 18th century onwards many wanted to find out more about the geography and biology of the world. Many places have bays, mountains, rivers, or islands, named after their explorers. Gradually the gaps on the map of the world were filled in. Bering explored the wild northeast coast of Siberia, died there and gave his name to the Bering Strait. Captain James Cook sailed round New Zealand and up the eastern coast of Australia.

France, Britain, the Netherlands, Spain and Portugal all became rulers of large parts of the world. The explorers by sea were followed by settlers, soldiers and governors, who sent men to explore inland. In 1804 Lewis and Clark explored the American West and found a route from the Missouri River over the Rocky Mountains to the Pacific.

In Australia Edward Eyre explored the desert north-west of Adelaide. Twenty years later, in 1860, Burke and Wills led an exhibition to cross Australia from south to north. They succeeded in nearly reaching the north coast but died of exhaustion on the return journey.

With the world mainly mapped, explorers in the 20th century turned to more difficult challenges. The North and South Poles were reached by Americans and Norwegians; high mountains were climbed for the first time; ocean and space craft explored the depths of the sea and began to venture to the Moon and beyond. ■

▲ The crew on many voyages of discovery in the 18th and 19th centuries included artists to record the unfamiliar animals and plants they saw. These paintings are of duck-billed platypuses, natives of Australia.

Factories

See also
Businesses
Industry
Recycling

Factories make things; there are 'materials' going into factories and 'products' coming out. As well as the materials used to make the products, other things are needed for factories. These include a workforce of people, energy to run the machines and provide heat and light for the factory, and money. All these things are called 'inputs' by people in industry. The product is called the 'output'.

The making of things in factories also produces wastes. In a shoe factory, for example, soles made of plastic are cut by a machine from giant sheets. The waste bits from these cut sheets may be thrown away, or melted down to produce another sheet. Reusing waste in this way is called 'recycling'. ∎

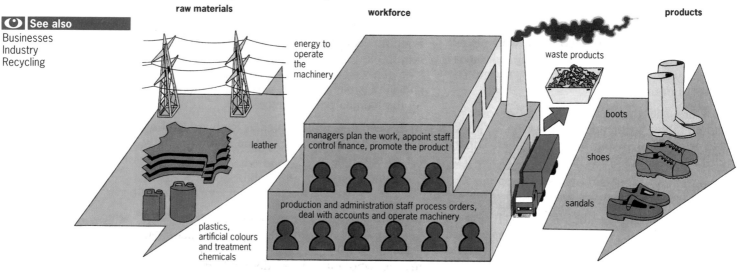

raw materials · workforce · products · energy to operate the machinery · waste products · boots · shoes · sandals · leather · managers plan the work, appoint staff, control finance, promote the product · production and administration staff process orders, deal with accounts and operate machinery · plastics, artificial colours and treatment chemicals

Factory reform in Britain

See also
Children
Industrial Revolution
Victorian Britain

Biography
Cadbury
Owen, Robert
Shaftesbury

The factories and cotton mills of the Industrial Revolution provided many jobs for ordinary people. But factory owners could run their factories exactly as they liked. They could employ five-year-olds and adults for a fourteen-hour day, and they did not have to protect their workers from dangerous moving machinery, or hot dusty air which might damage their health. So in many factories, people worked in very bad conditions.

Some factory owners such as Robert Owen provided good wages and conditions, and still did well. Not many copied them. It was obvious that Parliament would have to pass laws to stop children working in factories, and to provide reasonable hours and conditions. This was difficult. Most Members of Parliament were landowners or factory owners themselves. Also, laws are no good if people do not obey them. Employers (and parents needing extra cash) could cheat over a child's age in the days before everyone had birth certificates. Parliament appointed inspectors to check on factory owners, but at first there were not enough inspectors, and few punishments for disobeying them.

However, reformers such as Lord Shaftesbury campaigned successfully to change things. And George Cadbury later built a model factory in Birmingham. Now everyone in Western countries takes it for granted that children do not work in factories. ∎

Fairies

The word 'fairy' means 'enchanted being', and there are many different kinds: pixies, goblins, elves and leprechauns. They live in woods and fields, or in magic kingdoms humans never see. A fairy who likes human beings uses magic to help them. A fairy who dislikes mortals makes their lives a misery.

Pixies

Pixies (or 'fair folk') are like tiny, winged human beings. Sometimes, when you look at a shaft of sunlight streaming into a room, you see dust-specks dancing in it. Maybe some grown-ups and children used to think that those were pixies. Most pixies in stories are friendly towards human beings. Sometimes they cluster round a new baby, shaking stardust from magic wands to give it good luck, beauty and happiness. Many people in fairy tales have pixie friends, or 'fairy godmothers', who use magic spells to help them. Some children still believe in this kind of fairy. They say that if your tooth comes out and you leave it under your pillow while you sleep, the 'tooth fairy' will take it and leave a silver coin instead.

Goblins, elves and leprechauns

'Goblin' (or 'hobgoblin') is another word for imp (that is, a miniature, mischievous devil). 'Elf' is an old English word for 'spirit', and in folk tales, the good elves have nothing to do with human beings, so that evil elves are all mortals ever see. Goblins and elves are ugly, and hate human beings. When a human baby is born, they try to steal it and replace it with a child of their own. The human grows up in goblin-land, and the goblin grows up among humans, grumbling, sour-faced and mischievous. Goblins and elves like to play tricks on human beings. They turn milk sour, nibble cakes left out to cool, and make wailing noises to scare people in bed at night.

Leprechauns come from Ireland. They are shoemaker-elves. They bury gold in holes, and mark the place with a rainbow; where the rainbow ends, there is the gold. Anyone who manages to catch a leprechaun, and hold it still, can make it lead the way to the rainbow's end and so to the treasure. But leprechauns are much cleverer than mortals. No human being has ever managed to find a leprechaun's gold-hoard.

Fairy rings

Sometimes, when people walk in woods or fields, they find circles of grass, greener than all the rest. They call these 'fairy rings', and they say that they are caused by fairies dancing. The fairies dance at night, and if you creep up on them you can hear their music and watch their dance. But anyone who joins in is doomed. Fairies live outside human time; our minutes, hours and days mean nothing in fairy time. When you finish dancing and go home, you might find that what you thought had been one night has really been 50 or 100 years. Your house, family and friends will all have disappeared, and no one will recognize the wrinkled, snowy-haired old person you have become.

'Fairy tales' sound as if they all ought to have fairies in them. But many do not. You can find out why in the article on 'Folk tales and fairy tales'. ■

See also
Folk tales and fairy tales

Famine

When a large number of people are starving because they do not have enough to eat we say there is a famine.

Causes

Famines may be caused by climatic disasters such as drought or flooding as well as by pests and diseases. A drought can destroy crops that need the rain-water to grow properly, and floodwaters can drown crops and sweep them away. Both droughts and floods helped to cause famines in African countries such as Sudan, Ethiopia and Mozambique, during the 1980s.

Human action can cause famine or make it worse. In these countries the famines occurred during civil wars. These wars disrupted farmers' work and made the distribution of food difficult. Other causes have been suggested for famine. Sometimes traditional farming methods cannot produce enough food while population is growing fast. One basic cause of famine is poverty. People may not have enough money to buy food when it is available in their markets.

Flashback

Famines have been common throughout human history. Famines happened in ancient Egypt; there is a story in the Book of Genesis in the Bible about seven lean years of famine in Egypt that came after seven fat years of good harvests.

A terrible period of famine occurred in Europe during the early 17th century. In Britain at that time towns were growing fast and in years of poor harvests the townspeople were fed while peasants in the countryside starved.

In 1845 the Great Famine began in Ireland. Before that time half of the Irish population of 8 million had lived mostly on potatoes which they grew themselves, but Ireland's potato crop failed for several years as it was attacked by a disease. By 1848 Ireland had lost one million people. Many had died of starvation or disease, while others had emigrated to North America.

In 1974 Bangladesh suffered famine after disastrous floods destroyed the rice harvests. About 300,000 people died of starvation. Not everyone agrees that, in this case, famine resulted only because there was not enough food. Labourers who did not own their own land could not work in the fields and therefore were not paid. Many could not afford to buy the food that was available. ■

▲ An Ethiopian mother with her child. Both suffered from famine caused by the disruption of war as well as failure of food crops due to drought. The child is emaciated and very weak.

There were a number of famines in parts of Europe during World War II. In The Netherlands, for example, towards the end of the war, British aircraft dropped food supplies which prevented greater numbers dying.

◉ **See also**

Drought
Floods
Ireland's history
Refugees
Sahel
Starvation

Farming

Most types of farming produce food for people to eat. Farmers make the best use they can of natural resources (such as soil and climate) to produce crops and rear animals. Different types of plants and animals need different conditions to grow well in, so that there is a variety of types of farming around the world.

Dairy farming produces milk, butter and cheese from cows that graze in grassy fields. Dairy farms are usually quite close to large cities so that fresh milk can quickly reach people's kitchens.

Mixed farming involves both crops and livestock. The main area is the cornbelt of the midwest USA. Here farmers grow corn to feed to hogs (pigs) and cattle. Oats and hay are also grown as feed, as well as other crops such as soy beans and wheat. Mixed farming is found in Europe, too, in a region that stretches from northern Portugal and Spain across France, Germany and Poland and into the Ukraine. In Britain mixed farms are found from Devon across the counties of the Midlands.

▲ Watering a vegetable plot by hand on a farm in the Gambia, a country in West Africa. Most of the planting, weeding, and harvesting would also be done by hand, and much of this work would be done by women and children.

Mediterranean farming is found in areas with a Mediterranean climate where winters are mild, summers long and dry and rainfall is quite low. These areas are around the Mediterranean Sea, and also in California, Chile, South Africa and Australia. Winter crops include wheat, barley and broccoli. Summer crops include peaches, citrus fruits, tomatoes, grapes and olives.

In many tropical countries **shifting cultivation** is a common type of farming. It is different from settled farming because shifting cultivators raise crops in a place for only as long as the soil allows the crops to grow well. After a year or so in one place the farmer moves on, chops away the natural vegetation from another area, and leaves the first plot to return to its natural state. Shifting cultivation is practised in the tropical forests of Central and South America, Africa and south-east Asia. Farmers grow maize, rice, manioc, yams, millet and other food crops.

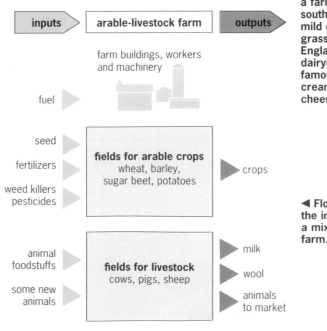

| inputs | arable-livestock farm | outputs |

farm buildings, workers
and machinery

fuel

seed
fertilizers
weed killers
pesticides

fields for arable crops
wheat, barley,
sugar beet, potatoes

crops

animal
foodstuffs

fields for livestock
cows, pigs, sheep

some new
animals

milk

wool

animals
to market

▲ Dairy cows grazing on a farm in Somerset, south-west England. The mild climate and rich grass make south-west England just right for dairying, and the area is famous for its milk, cream, butter, and cheese.

◄ Flow diagram showing the inputs and outputs on a mixed arable-livestock farm.

▶ A feeding yard for beef cattle in Colorado, USA. The cattle are fattened up very quickly and then killed for their meat.

Pastures and cattle ranges

Much of the beef in hamburgers eaten in North America comes from cattle that graze in Central and South America. To expand cattle-ranching, tropical forests have been cut down to provide grasslands for 'hamburger cattle'. Cattle also graze on natural grasslands such as the pampas of Argentina, where cattle have been herded by 'gauchos' on horseback for more than a hundred years.

In countries where intensive farming is practised, such as Britain, some cattle are not only fattened on pastures, they are also injected with drugs that make their bodies produce more meat. Where this is not done the farming is 'extensive' rather than 'intensive', as quite large areas of grassland are needed to fatten one cow. In parts of East Africa where grasslands are not good enough to feed cattle all the year round, farmers have to move their herds with the seasons to find new grazing.

Farm animals

Sheep, cattle, pigs, chickens and goats are all farm animals. Sheep are kept both for their meat and for their wool. A farmer or shepherd leaves sheep to graze on grasslands. Dogs often help to round up the sheep and to protect them and their lambs from wild animals such as wolves and eagles. Sheep are often reared on grasslands that cannot be used for other types of farming because they are too steep or too dry. Lamb and mutton are popular meats in many regions of the Middle East. There, some parts of the sheep, such as the eyes and brain, are considered great delicacies. You would rarely see pigs kept on farms in the Middle East, however, because most people there are Muslims and do not eat pork. Chickens are found on farms in many regions of the world. In western Europe and North America large numbers of chickens are kept indoors in row upon row of small cages, often never seeing the light of day. The farmer feeds these 'battery hens' each day and collects their eggs.

Intensive farming

Battery hens are an example of intensive farming; farmers organize their animals and crops to get the maximum food from them. Intensive farming uses lots of machinery to make it more efficient. Tractors are used to plough fields and plant seed, and chemical fertilizers make plants grow stronger, while pesticides kill pests and herbicides kill weeds. In North America the wheat belt, stretching from the USA into the Canadian prairies, is a large area of intensive farming where the wheat is harvested with combine harvesters.

▶ Battery hens on a factory farm. Chickens that are allowed to roam free, unlike these, are said to be 'free range'. Some people believe that factory farming is cruel to the animals. Others say that it makes food cheaper in the shops.

Grain farming

Grain (cereals) is the most important food source for most people in the world. The main types of grain are wheat, corn (maize), and rice. Grain is eaten in all sorts of ways. Wheat is mainly eaten as pasta in Italy and as bread in North America and elsewhere. The USA, Argentina, Australia and the Ukraine are the main world areas of wheat production. Farming in these countries is mostly intensive. Farmers use machines, fertilizers, pesticides and herbicides on large wheat fields. This intensive farming means that the amount of grain produced from a hectare of field (its 'yield') in North America is over four times that produced from a hectare in Africa. The USA is the world's biggest exporter of grain. Nearly every African country imports grain. Grain is also used for animal fodder.

The Green Revolution

In the 1960s special international efforts were made to breed new crop varieties that would produce better yields. This would produce more food from an average field to feed the fast-growing populations of tropical countries. Scientists were successful in breeding high-yield types of wheat and rice. This has become known as the 'Green Revolution'. In India, China, Mexico, the Philippines and other parts of south-east Asia the production of these foods has risen quickly. Some of the new rice types, for example, yield three times as much rice per hectare as traditional types. They also grow more quickly, allowing two or three crops a year from land that formerly produced only one.

There are problems, however. The new varieties of plants need fertilizers and pesticides if they are to grow well and resist diseases. Not all farmers can afford these chemicals, which also cause pollution of soil and water.

▲ Rows of tea bushes on a large plantation in Japan. The leaves are often picked by hand, although machines are increasingly used. The land here is used very intensively. Tea is an important and valuable cash crop.

◄ Farmland in the Hunza valley in the mountains of Pakistan. The floor of the valley is terraced and a variety of crops grown including wheat, rice and vegetables. The valley is famous for its apricots.

▲ Threshing wheat in the traditional way on the Mediterranean island of Crete. Threshing separates the grain from the straw, and on modern farms this job is done by combine harvesters.

Organic farming

Farmers who choose to farm organically do not use chemicals on their land. Fertilizers, pesticides and herbicides can cause problems. They kill plants and animals that the farmer does not want to kill, and very small traces of the chemicals may be left in crops, which can make them dangerous to eat. Organic farming uses compost and manure from farm animals to fertilize the land, and other plants, such as garlic, to control insects. Animals kept on organic farms are allowed to roam in the open air and are not locked up in cages for long periods. Organic farming has grown in the USA and Europe as farmers have realized some of the problems of intensive farming. Many people believe that food grown organically tastes better and is safer than food produced by intensive methods.

The farming year

Farmers in most parts of the world have different jobs to do at different times of the year. Springtime is the season when lambs are born, while in winter sheep may have to be protected from harsh weather. Autumn is harvest time for such crops as wheat. Wheat farmers plough their fields after harvesting, and sow their seed for next year's crop. In areas like the steppes of central Asia the harvest must be brought in before the snow and bad frosts of winter set in. Here, people from cities often take a week or two off from their work at harvest time to help in the fields.

Farms of the future

Some of the problems of poor weather can be solved by breeding special new crops that are not so spoiled by frost or certain pests. This sort of breeding, using 'plant genetics', is going to become more and more common in farming in the future. In laboratories, scientists take samples of the crops they want to improve and cross them with wild varieties that have a certain quality that is beneficial to the new plant. It is a long and tedious business; scientists may work for many years before they come up with a good new plant. The battle against crop pests and diseases will always continue, because although a new plant can resist a disease, it is usually attacked by a different disease just a few years after it is introduced to the fields.

Feeding the world

One problem that happens again and again through history is famine. When people cannot get enough to eat it seems obvious that farming is not producing enough food. Sometimes this is true, such as when climatic disasters ruin harvests, but this is not always the case.

The world produces enough food to feed everyone on the planet, but the problems arise when the food is not always in the right place at the right time. In the 1980s in Europe, for example, farmers were encouraged by governments to produce so much food that the countries did not know what to do with it. The result was 'food mountains' that cost a lot of money to store. Some of the food could have been sold or given to people who needed it; but this did not always happen.

Flashback

Farmers first started growing crops some time before 9000 BC. The first areas where farming was carried out on a large scale were probably in the Middle East. People changed from finding food by hunting and gathering wild plants to organizing certain plants into fields. This meant that the farmer had to settle down and live in one place, near the fields. As farmers became better at growing crops and raising animals, so settlements could develop where people could do other jobs, buying their food from farmers. ■

Farm machinery

Many of the jobs on the farm that used to be done by hand are now done by machines. These make the work far easier. Early machines were simple tools like spades and small ploughs to turn the soil, or scythes to cut corn. Today's more complicated farm machines can do almost everything from milking cows to spraying weeds.

Moving things

Often on the farm you have to take things from one place to another. One of the most important machines is the tractor. This is a powerful vehicle with large wheels. It has replaced the horse as a source of power almost everywhere in the West. Tractors are used to pull the ploughs that work the land, and the seed drills that plant the seeds. The tractor, with its trailer, carries heavy loads around the farm.

Preparing the soil

Farmers prepare their soil carefully before they plant their seeds. First, they turn over the soil with ploughs. This buries the weeds. Then they break up the big lumps of earth left by the plough with cultivators or harrows. Harrows are like large rakes which are pulled over the soil. They leave it smooth ready for sowing. A seed drill plants the seeds in long, straight rows and covers them with soil at the same time. All these machines are pulled by a tractor.

Harvesting

Harvest time, when the crops are gathered, is the busiest time on many farms. Special machines have been made to harvest different types of crop. The combine harvester cuts the corn and separates it from the stalks, all in one large machine. Other crops like hops, potatoes and peas are picked by machines. Pea harvesters also separate the peas from the pod. These machines are complicated and expensive, but they save the farmer a lot of time and hard work.

Other farm machines

Milking machines can milk cows twice a day. Very complicated machines, controlled by computers, also provide just the right amount of food for the animals at feeding time. Machines are used to dry corn in the barn after harvest and to grind it into meal to feed the animals. The land itself must be fed with manure and fertilizers before it can grow good crops. These fertilizers are spread evenly over the land by machines. ■

See also
Agricultural revolutions
Farming

1826 First practical reaper for cutting crops, designed by the Reverend Patrick Bell.

1902 First petrol-driven tractor, the Ivel.

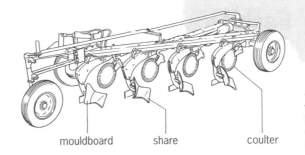

◀ A plough pulled by a tractor. The coulter cuts into the soil, the share digs it up and the mouldboard turns it over.

mouldboard   share   coulter

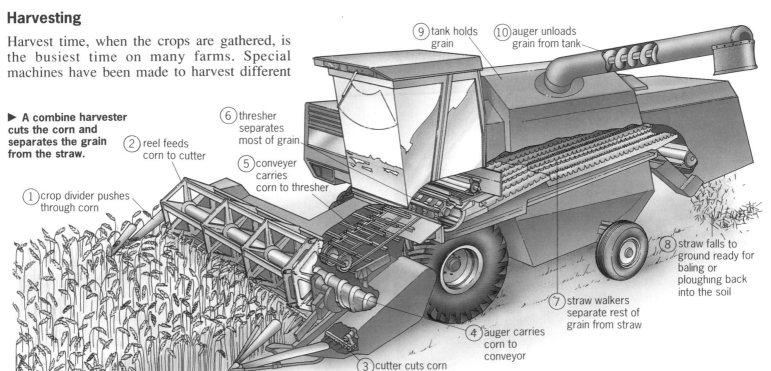

▶ A combine harvester cuts the corn and separates the grain from the straw.

① crop divider pushes through corn

② reel feeds corn to cutter

③ cutter cuts corn

④ auger carries corn to conveyor

⑤ conveyer carries corn to thresher

⑥ thresher separates most of grain

⑦ straw walkers separate rest of grain from straw

⑧ straw falls to ground ready for baling or ploughing back into the soil

⑨ tank holds grain

⑩ auger unloads grain from tank

Festivals

These are just a few of the many thousands of festivals celebrated all over the world. Different regions and countries use their own calendars, and dates change in many cases from year to year, so these pages can only show roughly when they happen.

- Christian
- Jewish
- Buddhist
- Hindu
- Sikh

▼ Festive flames

Autumn

Harvest festival
Churches are decorated with fruit and vegetables in thanksgiving.

Rosh Hashanah
New Year's Day commemorates the creation of the world.

Yom Kippur
Day of Atonement for fasting, prayer and asking forgiveness.

Navaratrami or Durga Puja or Dussehra
Celebration of the Goddess Durga and the triumph of good over evil.

Simchat Torah
Rejoicing in the Law by parading and even dancing with the scrolls in the synagogues.

Kathina Day
The end of the rainy season retreat when new robes are offered to monks.

All Saints or All Hallows Day
1 November.
Celebration of the lives and work of all the saints.

Diwali
Hindus and Sikhs light lamps indoors and outdoors, give presents and send cards.

Remembrance Day
The Sunday nearest to Armistice Day on 11 November, which was the end of World War I. People remember those who died fighting in both World Wars.

Thanksgiving
The fourth Thursday in November in the United States; the second Monday of October in Canada. A celebration of the harvest of the first settlers.

Guru Nanak's Birthday
Sikhs celebrate the birthday of their founder by going to the Gurdwara to sing hymns and hear teaching about his life.

Have a Happy Thanksgiving

Winter

Christmas Day 25 December
Catholic and Protestant Christians celebrate the birth of Jesus.

Christmas 6–7 January
Eastern Orthodox Christians celebrate the birth of Jesus.

Yuan Dan
Chinese New Year's Day, celebrated with fireworks, the Lion Dance, and giving presents of flowers and sweets.

▲ With every good wish for Christmas and the New Year

▼ Best Wishes for a Happy New Year

KUNG HAI FAT CHOY

Deng Jie
The Chinese Lantern Festival marks the lengthening of days.

Shrove Tuesday
Pancake Day, when leftovers of rich food are eaten before Lent. In many Catholic countries, Carnival is celebrated.

▲ May your home be filled with the special blessings of a very happy Passover Season

Spring

Holi

A spring festival in India. There are processions, games and bonfires and people throw coloured water over each other.

Mothering Sunday

Traditionally Christians visited their mother church and took gifts to their mothers.

Palm Sunday

Commemorates the arrival of Jesus in Jerusalem at the beginning of Holy Week. Palm branches were laid on the ground and waved to welcome him.

Passover or Pesach

Jews remember the Exodus (going out) of their ancestors from slavery in Egypt and also celebrate the barley harvest. A special meal with symbolic food is eaten at home.

Easter Sunday

Christians celebrate the resurrection of Jesus after his death on the cross the Friday before, which is called Good Friday.

◄ Happy Easter

Baisakhi or Vaisakhi

Guru Gobind Singh gave the Sikh community the 5 'Ks', which are symbols of Sikh identity. This remembers that day in 1699.

Whit Sunday (Pentecost)

Christians remember how the Holy Spirit came to Jesus' followers six weeks after Easter. This gave them the courage to go out and teach his message.

Wesak

Theravada Buddhists celebrate the birth, enlightenment and death of Gautama Buddha.

Summer

Raksha Bandham

Sisters tie threads of red and gold round their brothers' wrists as a protection from harm. The brothers give them presents in return.

Janamashtami

Hindus celebrate the birthday of Krishna by making an image of the baby Krishna, singing songs about his life, dancing and sharing sweets.

▲ Vaisakhi Greetings

See also

Carnivals
Christmas
Diwali
Easter
Eid
New Year Celebrations
Passover
Saints

Biography
Buddha
Gobind Singh
Jesus
Muhammad
Nanak

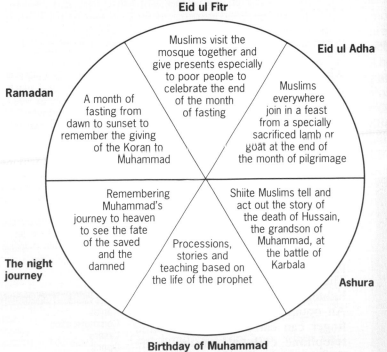

Eid ul Fitr — Muslims visit the mosque together and give presents especially to poor people to celebrate the end of the month of fasting

Eid ul Adha — Muslims everywhere join in a feast from a specially sacrificed lamb or goat at the end of the month of pilgrimage

Ashura — Shiite Muslims tell and act out the story of the death of Hussain, the grandson of Muhammad, at the battle of Karbala

Birthday of Muhammad — Processions, stories and teaching based on the life of the prophet

The night journey — Remembering Muhammad's journey to heaven to see the fate of the saved and the damned

Ramadan — A month of fasting from dawn to sunset to remember the giving of the Koran to Muhammad

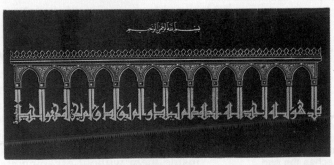

Muslim festivals

Muslim festivals do not take place during the same season each year. Muslims use a lunar calendar (based on the Moon) and their year is shorter than those adjusted to the movements of the Sun. Each festival is earlier than it was the year before.

▲ Best Wishes for the Happy 'Eid'

Fish

Fish are animals with backbones and gills. They all live in water and may be found in unpolluted swamps, ponds, lakes and rivers. Some live in the cold and darkness of cave streams, and a few kinds can even survive in hot springs. But most fishes live in the sea, especially in the shallows close to land, or in the surface waters over the great ocean depths.

Sharks and their relatives are known as the cartilaginous fishes, for they have a gristly skeleton. The rest, which are called the bony fishes, have a skeleton made of true bone. Most of them also have an armour of overlapping scales, which are made of very thin plates of bone.

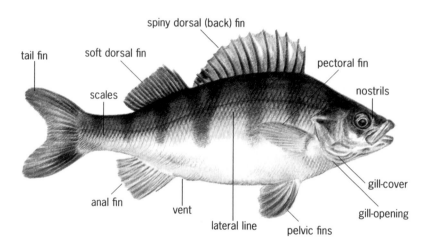

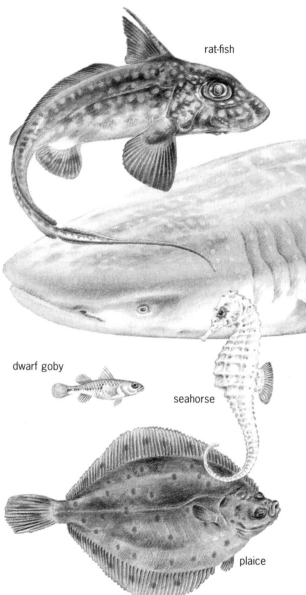

▲ Fish are covered with protective scales and are streamlined so they move easily through water. Their tail fin pushes them forwards, and the other fins are for steering and keeping upright.

The shape of fish

Water is about 800 times as dense as air, so fish have to work hard to swim through it. Those that go fastest, like mackerel and tunny fish, are very streamlined, with a crescent-shaped tail. Slower-moving fish, like tench and carp, have deeper bodies and squarer tails. Fish living in coral reefs are usually very narrow from side to side. This probably helps them to find safety between the branches of coral. Some kinds of fish, like rays and turbot, live on the sea-bed. They have flattened, camouflaged bodies, and so are hard to see.

When they swim, most fish use powerful zigzag muscles which move their bodies and tails from side to side. Only very few kinds paddle along with their fins. Fins are mainly used for balancing, stabilizing and braking.

Most kinds of fish are helped by a swim bladder: a gas-filled bag which acts like an internal lifebelt

and holds the fish up in the water. Watch a goldfish in a tank. It does not sink, even when it is totally still. When it wants to swim, all of its energy goes to pushing itself forwards through the water. Other kinds of swimming creatures must use some of their energy to stay at the same level in the water. Compared to the speed of most land animals, fish move quite slowly. But if they are frightened they can accelerate quickly away.

The life of a fish

A few kinds of fish are born alive, but most hatch from eggs. Usually there is a definite breeding season, which is triggered by the right temperature and amount of light. Some fish,

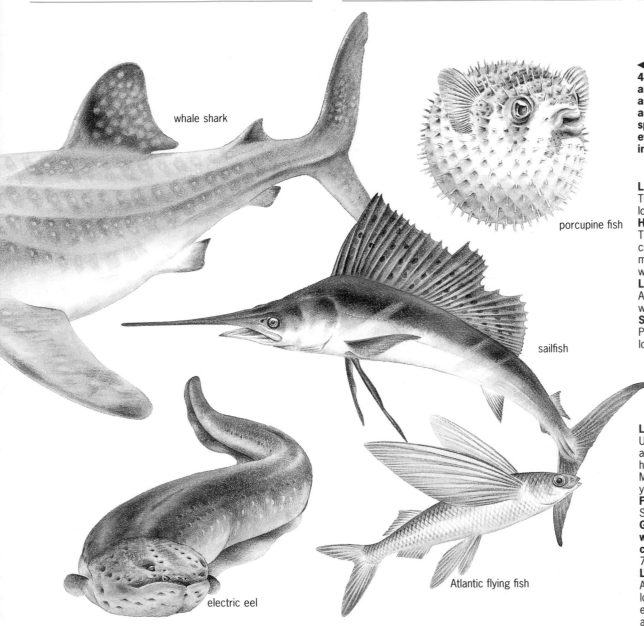

whale shark

porcupine fish

sailfish

electric eel

Atlantic flying fish

Largest fish
The whale shark, up to 18 m
long, weighs over 40 tonnes
Heaviest bony fish
The ocean sunfish, nearly
circular in shape, may
measure 4 m long and
weigh over 1,500 kg
Largest freshwater fish
Arapaima, up to 3 m long;
weight up to 200 kg
Smallest fish
Pygmy goby, up to 11 mm
long; weight 4–5 mg

Lifespan
Unknown for big fish,
although some sturgeon
have lived over 80 years.
Many fish live only about a
year, or even less.
Fastest
Sailfish, about 109 km/h
**Greatest depth from
which a fish has been
caught**
7,130 m
Largest number of eggs
An ocean sunfish, 1·24 m
long, contained an
estimated 300 million eggs;
a large codfish may lay
about 9 million eggs

Subphylum Vertebrata
Class Cyclostomata
(lampreys and hagfish)
about 62 species
Class Chondrichthyes
(cartilaginous fishes) about
800 species
Class Osteichthyes
(bony fishes) about 20,000
species (most of these
belong to a group called the
teleosts, or modern bony
fishes)
Number of species More
than 21,000

like eels and salmon, migrate long distances to reach the best place to spawn (produce eggs). Most fish are unable to move from sea water to fresh water.

Most kinds of fish lay huge numbers of eggs. These are almost always fertilized outside the body of the female. It is unusual for fish to take any care of their young, although there are some which produce smaller families and look after them. Among these it is often the male, rather than the female, that protects the babies until they are big enough to be independent.

Fish which live in fresh water or near the seashore usually lay eggs that sink to the bottom, where they may be hidden among plants. Open-sea species generally lay very tiny eggs which float. When these hatch they become part of the sea plankton. Very few of these tiny fish survive, as they provide food for many other animals. When they grow a little bigger, some young fish may avoid enemies by taking shelter among the stinging tentacles of some kinds of jellyfish.

As they grow, many kinds of fish live in schools, which contain fish of the same age and species. A school of fish behaves as a single unit. If danger threatens they swim close together, twisting and turning like one fish.

Some kinds of fish do not live in schools, but occupy and defend territories. This can be seen in coral reefs, where a single head of coral will be defended by several fish. Some other species are territorial only during the breeding season. The male stickleback, for instance, protects a small area in which he makes a nest. He entices females to lay their eggs in it, and drives away all other males.

► Male stickleback defending his nest against an attacker. In this case the 'attacker' is a harmless snail.

Most fish grow throughout their lives. In many fish it is possible to tell how old they are by looking at their scales, or at some bones, called otoliths, in their ears. These grow at different speeds at different times of the year, so they form rings, like tree rings, which can be read off to give the age of the fish.

The senses of fish

Fish have the same basic senses as we do: sight, hearing, touch, scent and taste.

Most fish have eyes on the sides of their heads. This gives them all-round vision, which they need because a fish is unable to look behind by turning its head. Most fish see best when they are looking forward, and many seem to be long-sighted when looking sideways. Many fish have good colour vision. This is important in the courtship of some species, and in the species which can change their colour to match their surroundings.

Fish do not have ears that they can twitch, for their ears are inside their skulls. Like those of other vertebrates, a fish's ears function as organs of balance as well as for hearing. Sounds travel very well under water, and many fish make noises to communicate with each other. Usually these are drumming or grunting notes, made by muscles which twang against the swim bladder.

Many fish live where there is not much light, and their sense of touch helps out their sense of sight. Some have finger-like projections called

► Shoal of sardines. The light reflected off their silvery scales acts to confuse predators that swim into the shoal.

barbels round the mouth. With these the fish can explore the sea or river bed.

More important is the *lateral line system*. This is a series of very sensitive nerve endings lying just below the skin along the side of a fish. Any movement in the water makes underwater waves which cause changes of pressure in all directions. The lateral line system detects them, and the fish knows that there may be an enemy or a possible meal near by.

Most fish have a very good sense of smell. Many use it to find their prey. Some, if they are injured, release a special substance from their skin into the water. When other members of the school smell this, they are aware of the danger and swim quickly to safely. Salmon have another use for their sense of smell. They probably use their smell memory to migrate back to the stream where they were born to lay their eggs in the same place.

The sense of taste is related to the sense of smell. Some fish have large numbers of taste buds, in and around the mouth.

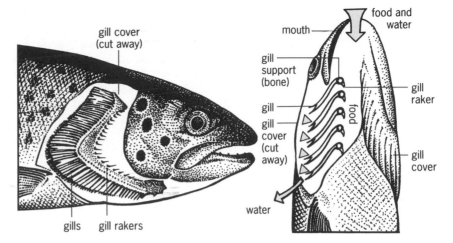

The food of fish

Freshwater fish eat all sorts of food, including water plants, snails, worms, insects and their larvae, and other fish. Some fish, like grey mullet, are called detritus feeders. They suck up mud from the river bed and digest from it the huge numbers of tiny organisms living there.

In the open sea, where there are no rooted plants, most fish are carnivores (flesh-eaters). Some feed on plankton and are called filter feeders.

▲ Gill cover cut away to show gills and gill rakers. Gill rakers are like combs attached to the bone supporting each gill. They let water, but not food, pass out through the gills.

◀ Cleaner wrasse busy at work in the mouth of the fierce moray eel. The wrasse feeds on parasites on the skin of other fish, which in return do not harm it.

The fish takes a mouthful of water containing plankton, closes its mouth and pushes the water out over its gills. The plankton is filtered out as the water goes through, and the fish then swallows it. This saves energy, as the fish uses the same action to breathe and feed. Even some very large fish, such as basking sharks, are filter feeders. Other species eat shrimps, squid, or other fish.

Some of the strangest of all fish are those which live deep in the ocean. Most have huge mouths and teeth and some can swallow creatures bigger than themselves, as they have few chances to feed and may not eat again for months. ■

👁 See also

Aquariums
Eggs
Fishing
Fishing industry
Oceans and seas
Plankton
Ponds
Respiration
Rivers
Sharks
Streams
Swimming
Vertebrates

Fishing

Fishing is the most popular sport in many countries. In Britain there are about 4 million active anglers. In Japan the figure is nearer 20 million. In Australia there are about 5 million. There are three main types of fishing: coarse fishing, game fishing and sea fishing.

Coarse fishing

Coarse fishing is the cheapest, easiest and most popular form of fishing. The word 'coarse' refers to the type of fish; many of those caught are not edible.

Roach, perch, dace, chub, bream, pike, tench and several other varieties abound in many rivers, canals, ponds or lakes and are often quite easy to catch. To do so you need some food or bait to tempt them to bite.

For most coarse fish your bait could be things you eat yourself, like bread, cheese, sweetcorn or luncheon meat. These fish also fancy food you do not like, such as worms or maggots.

All you need to be properly equipped is a simple rod, a reel and line, and some hooks, weights and floats. Later you may learn other methods like spinning or ledgering.

Spinning uses metal shapes, known as 'spoons' or 'spinners', as bait. Ledgering is a way of catching bottom-feeding fish. A weight close to the bait anchors it down on the river bed.

reel

floats

weights

hooks

landing net

keep net

Game fishing

Game fishing is often said to be the most entertaining form of angling because of the fish and methods involved. Salmon, sea trout, brown trout and rainbow trout are beautifully coloured fish and good to eat. Char and grayling are also game fish. Once hooked, these fish will often put up a long fight before they are finally caught.

A main method of catching them is fly fishing. This means using hooks dressed as artificial flies to imitate the natural insects on which these fish feed. Dressing such flies is an art in itself.

You use a floating line and dry flies for fish seen feeding on the surface, a sinking line and wet flies for those below. These artificial flies attract fish by appearing as food and by their bright colours.

You fish with a rod which will cast a fly. This requires a rhythmical action, lifting the rod sharply straight above your head and then propelling the line forward to land gently on the water.

casting

reel

dry fly floating on surface of water

wet fly sinks below surface of water

flies (hooks)

Sea angling

Catching sea fish in nets has provided people with food for centuries. Sea angling for fun, however, is a recent form of the sport, which started with fishing off piers, using tackle and methods similar to simple types of coarse fishing.

You can also cast from the beach or rocks, since many species live close to the shoreline. Many more anglers fish from anchored boats or troll bait behind moving ones. There is an immense variety of sea fish and most of them are good to eat, especially cod, bass, whiting, flounder and mackerel. The fish swim at different depths, and some, like flatfish, you will only catch on the sea-bed.

Sea fish range from tiny to huge, so there are many different types of tackle and bait for catching them. You can use anything from a simple hand-line with hooks up to very heavy tackle indeed for sharks or swordfish.

Safety

Fishing is a safe sport if you are sensible. Like all water sports, however, it has its dangers. Be especially careful when in a boat or wading in fast water, and preferably wear a flotation waistcoat or other buoyancy aid. Hooks can catch people as well as fish, so protect your eyes with glasses when learning to cast. Carbon rods are excellent electricity conductors, so do not touch live wires with them or use them when lightning is flashing near by.

In the 20th century fishing rods have become lighter but stronger with the use of materials like fibreglass and carbon fibre. Lines are stronger too when they are made from synthetic materials like nylon.

Conservation

Respect close seasons for catching freshwater fish. These vary for different species and are designed to protect fish when spawning (laying eggs). Preserve fish stocks also by releasing the fish you take, or limiting your catch of fish to eat.

In America bait fishing is called still fishing. Ice fishing is also very popular there. Holes are cut in a frozen river and baited hooks are dropped beneath the ice.

Help fight the pollution which kills fish. Do not discard nylon line which can entangle birds, or use lead shot which may poison swans. Coarse fishermen often use keep-nets to retain all their catch before releasing the fish at the end of the day. Be careful not to overfill keep-nets, and set them up in deep water to avoid harming the fish.

Fishing competitions are held in many countries. Sometimes anglers compete to catch the heaviest weight of fish. In other competitions they compete to see who can cast the greatest distance or with the most accuracy.

Flashback

The earliest record of fishing for fun is almost 2,000 years old. One of the world's all-time best-selling books is Izaak Walton's *The Compleat Angler*, written in 1653. It has been translated into many languages and been printed in more than 400 editions. For the fifth edition (reissue), Charles Cotton added a second part on fly fishing in clear streams. The final words of the book give good advice for enjoying this tranquil sport: 'Go angling. Study to be quiet.' ∎

⊙ See also
Fish
Fishing industry
Prehistoric people

Fishing industry

The fishing industry employs more people than those simply catching fish. There are also the people who make and repair equipment, and those who process and sell fish.

Inshore fishing

Inshore fishing boats do not sail very far from the coast. The fishermen may use rods and lines or small nets. They usually return to sell their catch the same day. Almost every coastal village in the world has some fishermen to supply daily needs. Boats very often sail together in fleets. The boats often leave before sunrise and return in the evening. On some Caribbean islands, you can buy flying fish caught that day directly from the fisherman, who sells his catch from the sands when he returns. In other parts of the world the fish are caught at night. Fish are attracted to lights shining from the boats. The catch is sold fresh in the morning when the boats return to shore.

Deep-sea fishing

Most of the world's fish catch comes from the deep oceans, too far from land for ships to catch and return the same day. Deep-sea fishing ships are bigger than those that fish inshore. The Japanese are great fish-eaters and Japanese fishing fleets catch more fish than those of any other country. Japanese fleets catch fish all over the world, far from Japan in the seas of the North and South Atlantic, the Antarctic, the Pacific and the Caribbean. The ships can stay at sea for months; many trawlers feed their catches into a 'factory ship' where the fish are processed

while still at sea. In the factory ship the fish are cleaned, gutted and frozen. The fish are caught in one of the three types of net shown below, the different types being used for different fish, some near the ocean surface, others much deeper. The nets of some modern ships are too heavy to be dragged on board, so some have great pipes, like vacuum cleaners, that suck up the catch from the net into the hold while the net is still in the water.

The average world catch of fish is 92 million tonnes a year. The biggest fishing nations are:

Russia	12 million tonnes
Japan	12 million tonnes
China	10 million tonnes
Peru	6 million tonnes
Chile	6 million tonnes
USA	5 million tonnes

▶ Unloading fish from the net into the hold of a Russian trawler.

Fish farming is not a new industry. In the Middle Ages fish ponds were made in many parts of Europe. Some of the largest are in southern Bohemia (now Czechoslovakia).

See also

Fish
Fishing
Oceans and seas

▼ These are the three main types of net used to catch most of the world's fish. The drift and purse seine nets are used to catch fish near the suface, trawls catch fish near the ocean floor.

drifting   trawling   purse-seining

Overfishing

In some oceans fishing fleets have caught too many fish. More and more ships have fished the same waters and the holes in their nets are too small to allow younger fish to escape and keep breeding to make the next generation. This 'overfishing' has meant that certain stocks of fish are now in danger, such as the herrings of the north-east Atlantic and the Pacific Ocean perch.

Anchovies caught by Peruvian fleets used to be the largest single catch in the world, but since the early 1970s the numbers caught have declined dramatically. This may be partly due to overfishing, but it is also partly because of changes in the ocean currents.

Fish farming

China is the world's most important fish-farming country. Lakes, rivers and parts of the coast are stocked with fish which are bred just to catch and eat. This fish farming is also called 'aquaculture', and it is becoming more and more popular in many parts of the world. On many of Scotland's lochs (deep inland lakes) fish farms breed salmon. In coastal fish farms, sea-water fish, shrimps, crabs and lobsters can be reared, and are much easier to catch than at sea. ■

Fjords

Fjords are long, narrow, steep-sided inlets of the sea. The name is Norwegian, and the west coast of Norway has a series of spectacular fjords. They are long enough to show up on any map of Norway. Sogne Fjord is 183 km (114 miles) long, and yet its average width is less than 5 km (3 miles). In places, it is over 1,200 m (4,000 ft) deep.

Fjords are also found around the coast of Iceland and Greenland. The Nordvest Fjord, part of Scoresby Sound in east Greenland, is the longest fjord in the world, 313 km (195 miles) long. Around the Pacific Ocean, there are fjords in Alaska and western Canada, and also in southern Chile. The far south-west of South Island, New Zealand is called Fiordland. You can pick out the fjords if you look at the maps of these countries.

Where there are fjords the mountains reach right to the coast. In the past, all these areas had much more snow and ice. Glaciers filled the mountain valleys, scraping away the rocks of the valley sides and floors. Sea-level was lower than now, which helped the glaciers to dig even deeper. When the last ice age ended, most of the glaciers melted. The mountain valleys left behind by the glaciers were steep-sided and deep. As sea-level rose, the valleys were drowned, to become the long inlets of the sea called fjords. Some of these mountains are high enough and cold enough to have glaciers even today. ■

See also
Glaciers
Ice ages
New Zealand
Norway
Valleys

▼ Milford Sound in New Zealand is a fjord which shows how the high sides of the mountains drop down into the inlet, which is actually a drowned river valley.

Flags

cap   sleeve

width

length

hoist rope

flagstaff

Flags are flat pieces of material that can be flown from a staff or pole. They are used as symbols of a nation or other group of people.

The flag itself may bear a symbol. For example, the maple leaf on the Canadian flag represents a type of tree that is common in Canada. The Israeli flag uses Jewish symbols: the stripes from the Jewish prayer shawl and the six-pointed Star of David. Even flags that do not bear obvious symbols come to represent the group by their design and choice of colours.

Very few flags have words on them, because words cannot be read from both sides.

Other types of flags have symbols that send special messages. A red flag means danger and a white flag means peace. The International Signal Flags used on ships represent letters and numbers that can be combined in different ways. Today, radio is a more common way to send messages at sea.

The study of flags is called vexillology.

A flag is flown at half mast as a sign of mourning for someone who has died. Flags may be dipped or lowered as a salute, a sign of respect.

Flashback

Symbols that can be held high to identify a person or a group have been in use for centuries and in many cultures.

The Romans used carved standards and cloth flags. There was a standard bearer attached to each century (a unit of 120 foot soldiers). A legion (several thousand soldiers) followed a bronze standard in the shape of an eagle. In later times flags were decorated with Christian symbols such as the cross of St George.

See also
Heraldry
Symbols

The kings and noblemen of Europe in the Middle Ages had complex flags based on their heraldic symbols. Many were hard to recognize at a distance. When international shipping increased in the 16th century, simpler flags were developed to be used on ships. By the 18th century, nations were creating their own national flags in simple, striking designs. Today nearly all national groups have a distinctive flag of this kind. ■

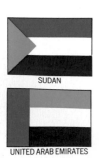
SUDAN

SWEDEN

SWITZERLAND

SYRIA

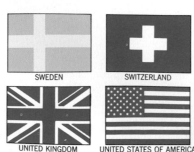
UNITED ARAB EMIRATES

UNITED KINGDOM

UNITED STATES OF AMERICA

URUGUAY

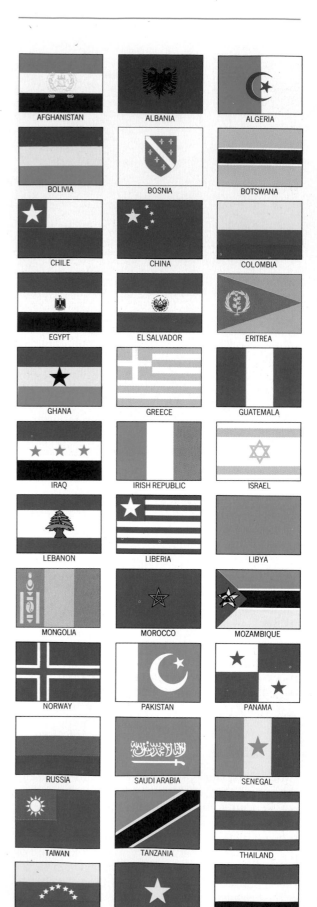

AFGHANISTAN   ALBANIA   ALGERIA

BOLIVIA   BOSNIA   BOTSWANA

CHILE   CHINA   COLOMBIA

EGYPT   EL SALVADOR   ERITREA

GHANA   GREECE   GUATEMALA

IRAQ   IRISH REPUBLIC   ISRAEL

LEBANON   LIBERIA   LIBYA

MONGOLIA   MOROCCO   MOZAMBIQUE

NORWAY   PAKISTAN   PANAMA

RUSSIA   SAUDI ARABIA   SENEGAL

TAIWAN   TANZANIA   THAILAND

VENEZUELA   VIETNAM   YEMEN

ANGOLA	ARGENTINA	AUSTRALIA	AUSTRIA	BANGLADESH	BELARUS	BELGIUM
BRAZIL	BULGARIA	BURMA	CAMBODIA	CAMEROON	CANADA	CHAD
CROATIA	CUBA	CYPRUS	CZECHOSLOVAKIA	DENMARK	DOMINICAN REPUBLIC	ECUADOR
ETHIOPIA	FIJI	FINLAND	FRANCE	GABON	GAMBIA	GERMANY
HAITI	HONDURAS	HUNGARY	ICELAND	INDIA	INDONESIA	IRAN
ITALY	JAMAICA	JAPAN	JORDAN	KENYA	NORTH KOREA	SOUTH KOREA
MADAGASCAR	MALAWI	MALAYSIA	MALI	MALTA	MAURITANIA	MEXICO
NAMIBIA	NEPAL	NETHERLANDS	NEW ZEALAND	NICARAGUA	NIGER	NIGERIA
PAPUA NEW GUINEA	PARAGUAY	PERU	PHILIPPINES	POLAND	PORTUGAL	ROMANIA
SIERRA LEONE	SINGAPORE	SLOVAKIA	SOMALIA	SOUTH AFRICA	SPAIN	SRI LANKA
TRINIDAD AND TOBAGO	TUNISIA	TURKEY	UGANDA	UKRAINE		
YUGOSLAVIA	ZAÏRE	ZAMBIA	ZIMBABWE	UNITED NATIONS		

Fleas

▼ The rabbit flea, shown here feeding on a rabbit's ear, is the major cause of the spread of myxomatosis, a disease which has killed millions of rabbits in Britain and Australia.

All fleas are parasites and live on mammals or birds. They are perfectly shaped for such a life. Their wingless bodies are flattened from side to side, so that they are narrow enough to creep between the hairs or feathers of their hosts. They also have long, backward-pointing hairs and sharp claws, so that they are difficult to dislodge if the host tries to scratch them away. They can walk, but do so rather slowly. If they need to move fast, they jump, using their large back legs.

Fleas feed on blood, which they suck up with narrow, tube-like mouthparts. Blood clots when it comes into contact with the air. To prevent this from happening, when it has located a blood vessel beneath the skin of its host, the flea pumps in a tiny amount of anti-clotting saliva before it begins to feed. Fleas can pass diseases to their hosts in their saliva when they feed. A flea bite itches, because the body reacts against the protein from another animal.

Fleas lay their eggs in the nests or beds of their hosts. The young that hatch out are worm-like and feed on scraps of skin and other waste. Some fleas breed at the same time of year as their hosts, so that when their young are born there is a crop of fleas ready to live on them. ■

Fleas have been recorded as jumping a distance of more than 30 cm, which is about 200 times the length of its body.

Phylum
Arthropoda
Class
Insecta
Order
Siphonaptera
Number of species
About 1,100

⊙ **See also**
Insects
Parasites

Flesh eaters

Flesh eaters are called carnivores. Plant eaters are called herbivores.

▼ The red piranha is not a large fish, but it has razor-sharp teeth and strong jaws and travels in large shoals. Piranhas will attack wounded animals.

All animals have to feed. Carnivores eat the flesh of other animals. Herbivores, which eat plants, are the chief food of the carnivores, so there are, for instance, always more rabbits than foxes, and more antelopes than lions.

Among mammals, most carnivores are active hunters. They usually have good senses of smell, hearing and sight and are intelligent, so that they can outwit their prey. Generally, each type of carnivore feeds on a few sorts of prey, usually smaller than itself. But carnivores such as lions or wolves, which live in groups and hunt together, can tackle prey bigger than themselves.

Flesh is easier to digest than plant material, so carnivores feed quickly, bolting down huge pieces of meat. Meat is also very nutritious, so flesh eaters do not need to spend large amounts of time feeding as the plant eaters do. Most large carnivores do not need to feed every day. Many small carnivores feed on the flesh of insects and other invertebrates, including some other carnivores.

To kill their prey, most carnivores have sharp claws or teeth, although a few small or slow animals such as spiders use poison to subdue prey which may be faster or more active than themselves. In either case, the kill is almost always made quickly.

Most carnivorous animals do not kill more than they need at any one time. Those that do so usually make a store of the surplus, which they eat. ■

A few sorts of animals such as human beings, rats, pigs and cockroaches eat almost everything. These are called omnivores.

The largest land carnivore is the polar bear. The two smallest mammals in the world, a shrew and a bat, are both flesh eaters. They eat very small animals, such as slugs and insects. The largest of all flesh eaters is the blue whale, which feeds on the flesh of small shrimp-like animals called krill.

⊙ **See also**
Food chains and webs
Lions
Poisonous animals
Wolves

Flies

Flies are among the commonest of insects, and many people think of them as being dirty and spreading disease. Although some are harmful to humans in this way, most are not. Flies live in a great variety of ways. Some of these seem to us to be unattractive, but even flies that live on decaying plants and animals are important. These are recyclers, which means they help change dead things into chemicals which plants need to grow, so that the plants may use them over and over again. Others are pollinators, as they carry pollen from flower to flower. Many kinds of animals and birds feed on flies.

Flight

All flies use only one pair of wings to fly with. Their back wings, which are very small, are used only to balance them as they fly. The movement of the wings is very fast in many flies. Houseflies beat their wings about 200 times each second, mosquitoes about 600 times and some of the smallest midges at a rate of over 1,000 times a second.

Shapes

Flies vary a lot in shape. One big group, that includes all the mosquitoes and midges, have slender, soft bodies. The daddy-long-legs, which is easy to see because it is so large, also belongs to this group. It is harmless, but many of the adults in this group have biting and sucking mouthparts and the females feed on the blood of mammals or birds.

A second group, which includes the horseflies and clegs, have short, hard bodies. The females also feed on blood, although the males feed only on plant juices. The third and largest group of the flies is the one which includes the houseflies and hoverflies. All of these have short,

well armoured bodies, and most feed on liquids of various kinds. A very small number of these flies feed on blood.

Grubs

Flies spend the first part of their lives as larvae, also called grubs or maggots. The larvae live in many different ways. The blind maggots which live in the flesh of dead mammals or birds are the most familiar. Other kinds live in the soil, hunting small animals. The larvae of some hoverflies are useful to farmers and gardeners as they eat greenfly and other aphids. Others live in water. One of the strangest of these is the rat-tailed maggot of one of the hoverflies. This can survive in polluted water, for it pushes a long tube, like a snorkel, up to the surface to breathe. Some larvae are harmful to cattle and other animals, as the adults lay their eggs on the skin and the larvae burrow in to become parasites. ■

▲ The robber fly feeds on other insects. It has dagger-like mouthparts for piercing and sucking the blood of its prey, which can be insects as large as dragonflies, grasshoppers, bees and wasps.

Largest fly
Australian robber fly, *Phellus glaucus*, body-length 5 cm

Phylum
Arthropoda
Class
Insecta
Order
Diptera
Number of species
At least 85,000

◄ Hoverflies are important pollinators as they feed on nectar.

See also
Insects
Larvae
Mosquitoes
Parasites

Flowering plants

There are about 235,000 species of flowering plants. The smallest is a tiny duckweed called *Wolffia*, scarcely a millimetre across. The tallest is a type of eucalyptus tree which grows to over 100 m in height. These trees are so wide at their base that it would take ten people holding hands to encircle one.

▶ **Flowering plants consist of a shoot and a root. The shoot bears leaves and flowers containing the plant's reproductive organs. Eventually the flowers produce fruit and seeds.**

The green chlorophyll in leaves can use the energy from sunlight to make food materials out of water and the carbon dioxide gas in the air.

Flowering plants are the most advanced and complicated group in the plant kingdom. They have flowers which contain sex organs that produce fruits and seeds. A seed is a tiny plant enclosed in a protective coat with a store of food so that, when conditions are right, it quickly forms a new plant.

The best-known flowers have brightly coloured petals. But many, such as grasses and some trees, have no petals at all, and a few, like the hellebores, have petals which are green like leaves.

Structure of a plant

Flowers contain a plant's reproductive organs. The female part, the ovary, is in the centre and contains ovules which later become seeds inside a fruit. The male parts, the stamens, usually surround the ovary, although sometimes they are in a separate flower. They produce pollen grains to fertilize the ovule (pollination).

Stems contain tubes which carry liquids around the plant. One set of tubes carries water and mineral salts from the soil to the leaves for photosynthesis. Other tubes carry liquid food, made in the leaves by photosynthesis, to the growing parts of the plant and to food storage organs such as tubers. Stems are usually stiff and upright, but some stay underground and may grow sideways through the soil. Stems may be hairy, spiny, smooth, furrowed, or rough, like tree bark.

Leaves need light to make food by photosynthesis, so they are arranged on the stem to receive as much light as possible. The veins of a leaf join up with the tubes running up and down the stem. Water is lost by evaporation from stomata (pores) on the leaf underside, so desert plants that must conserve water, such as cacti, often have very reduced leaves or spines.

Roots anchor a plant and absorb water and minerals from the soil. Fibrous roots consist of many fine branches which go out in all directions. Tap roots go straight down into the soil and may also store food, as in a carrot.

Types of flowering plant

Flowering plants can survive in many different places. Some grow in water, which gives them more support than air, so their stems tend to be weak and their leaves feathery. Shrubs and trees are land plants with tough, thick stems made of

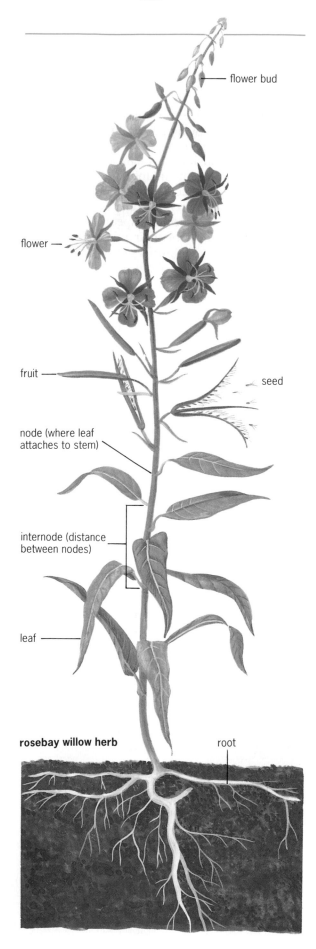

flower bud

flower

fruit

seed

node (where leaf attaches to stem)

internode (distance between nodes)

leaf

rosebay willow herb

root

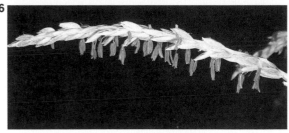

wood. Non-woody land plants, called herbaceous plants, are supported by water pressure in their stems and leaves, which is why they wilt in a drought. Many desert plants have leaves reduced to tough, hard spines, and thick fleshy stems full of stored water. Some plants, such as mistletoe, are parasites on other plants; some, such as pitcher plants, have ways of catching insects and a few, such as some tropical orchids, sit high in tree branches with long roots trailing to the ground.

Life cycles of flowering plants

Each growing season a plant increases in size and weight, and stores food until it has enough to produce flowers and seeds. **Annuals** are plants which are completely exhausted after flowering, so they die, leaving only their seeds to survive the winter. **Biennials** have a two-year life cycle. During the first year they grow and make food, which is stored, usually in the roots. The shoot dies but the root survives through the winter underground. The second year the plant uses this food to grow a new shoot and make flowers and seeds, then it dies completely. **Perennial** plants continue flowering year after year. Each year they can make enough food to produce fruits and seeds and still have some to spare. This is stored for growth the following year. ■

▲ These are the flowers of
1 Bougainvillaea
2 Waterlily
3 Cactus plant
4 Horse-chestnut tree
5 Bell heather
6 Grass

◄ **Annual plants have a one-year life cycle. They grow from seed in the spring, flower in the summer, produce new seeds and die.**

◄ **Biennial plants have a two-year life cycle. In the first year they grow leaves and roots. In the winter the leaves die. The roots survive and new leaves, flowers and seeds are produced in the second year. Flowers and seeds grow. The plant then dies.**

◄ **Perennial plants produce roots that store food. Food is also sometimes stored in bulbs, corms and tree trunks. The roots survive the winter and the plant produces leaves and flowers year after year.**

first year | second year

Flowers

Flowers contain a plant's reproductive organs. They produce fruits and seeds which give rise to the next generation of plants. Not all plants have flowers with brightly coloured and scented petals. Grasses have no petals, and some trees have petals so small you hardly notice them. Flower parts are arranged in rings on the end of a flower stalk. These parts come in many shapes and sizes, but they all have the same functions.

Parts of a flower

Sepals form the outermost ring of a flower. They are often green and look like small leaves. They cover and protect the flower at the bud stage of growth, and when the flower opens they usually bend back close to the stem.

Petals can be coloured and scented, with a tiny cup at the base called a nectary which produces sugary nectar. Petals like this attract insects which, when they come to collect nectar, transfer pollen from flower to flower. The majority of flowers have petals.

Stamens are a flower's male sex organs. Each consists of a stalk supporting a pair of anthers. An anther is a sausage-shaped bag containing pollen grains. Pollen grains contain the plant's male sex cells. Anthers open by splitting along their length and the two sides curl back to expose the pollen.

Carpels are a flower's female sex organs. Each has a swollen base, called the ovary, containing one or more ovules. These contain the plant's female sex cells. The top of a carpel forms a style, which ends in a pointed or flattened area called the stigma. Pollination is the transfer of pollen from anthers to stigmas. After pollination the ovary becomes a fruit and the ovules inside become seeds.

▲ The biggest flower in the world is *Rafflesia*. It grows up to 1 m across and is produced by a parasitic plant which lives on the roots of lianas in the tropical rainforests of south-east Asia. It flowers once every ten years.

Natural oils are extracted from the flowers of rose, jasmine and orange and used in perfumes.

Some flowers are used as spices. Saffron comes from a Greek crocus. It has to be hand-picked and up to a quarter of a million flowers are needed to make one pound of this spice. It is the most expensive spice grown. Cloves are the dried flower buds of a tropical tree from Indonesia.

Flower buds such as those of cauliflower, calabrese, broccoli and globe artichokes are eaten as vegetables.

The flowers of hops are put into beer to give it a bitter flavour.

▶ A flower contains a plant's reproductive organs. The male parts are called stamens and they produce pollen. The female parts are called carpels, and after fertilization they produce fruits and seeds.

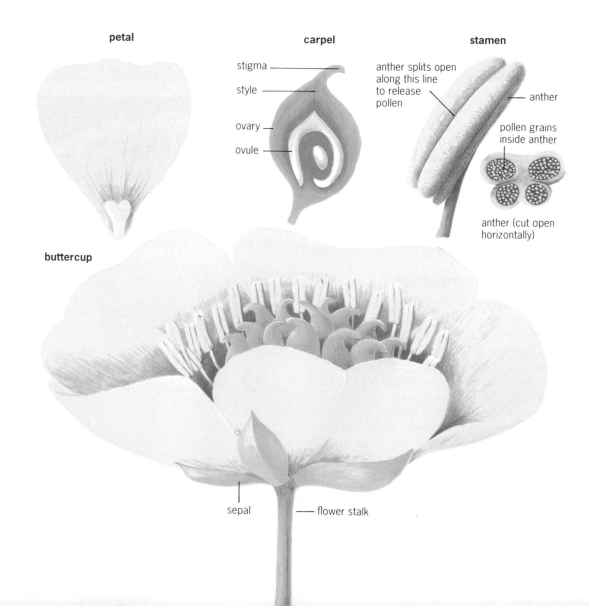

petal

carpel

stamen

stigma
style
ovary
ovule

anther splits open along this line to release pollen

anther

pollen grains inside anther

anther (cut open horizontally)

buttercup

sepal

flower stalk

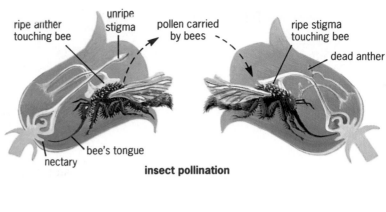

insect pollination

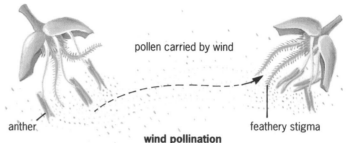

wind pollination

Pollination and fertilization

Most flowers have developed ways to ensure that pollen from one flower is carried to the stigma of another flower of the same kind. This is called cross-pollination. There are two main ways this takes place: by insects and by wind.

Insect pollination occurs because insects are attracted to a flower by its colour, smell, nectar and sometimes its pollen. White or cream flowers (such as honeysuckle and night-scented stocks) are pollinated by night-flying moths, which are also attracted by strong perfumes. Petals form a landing platform and many have special markings, called honey guides, to show the insect where the nectar is to be found. Some honey guides are invisible to us but can be seen when photographed in ultraviolet light, which insects' eyes can see. While the insect is searching for nectar, pollen grains cling to its body. These stick to the stigma of the next flower the insect visits.

Wind pollinated flowers need to be in a position to catch the breeze. Some, like grass flowers, grow above other plants on long stems. Others, like catkins, hang below the leaves or grow before leaf buds open. Pollen grains are small and light to float on the slightest breeze. They are produced from anthers dangling on long stalks, in huge quantities, because each grain has a very slight chance of reaching a stigma. Spreading, feathery stigmas act like nets to catch pollen drifting past.

Once a pollen grain sticks to a stigma of the same kind of flower it grows a tube down the style into an ovule in the ovary. The nucleus of a sex cell in the pollen grain moves down this tube and joins a nucleus in the ovule. This is called fertilization and starts the ovule developing into a seed, and the ovary into a fruit.

Wild and garden flowers

You can find wild flowers growing in any place where the soil is not cultivated. Look along waysides, hedgerows, river banks, and in woodlands, old meadows and waste ground. Many wild flowers have been bred for colour, size and smell to become garden flowers. It is sometimes possible to find the wild relatives of garden flowers growing in the countryside.

Arrangement of flowers

Many plants have one flower on the end of a stalk, but some have flowers arranged in groups. The simplest arrangement is a spike with the oldest flower at the bottom and the youngest bud at the top. Umbrella-like arrangements, called umbels, have flower stalks of equal length at the end of a stem so the flowers form a flat head. Sunflowers, dandelions and thistles have 'flowers' made up of many tiny flowers called florets. Some florets are short tubes, like those at the centre of a sunflower. Others have strap-like petals like those at the edge of a sunflower. ■

▲ Pollination is the transfer of pollen from the anthers of one flower to the stigmas in another flower of the same kind. This can be done by insects or the wind.

See also
Flowering plants
Fruit
Gardens
Grasses
Herbs
Reproduction
Seeds
Spices
Trees
Vegetables
Weeds

◄ The simplest arrangement of flowers on a stem is one flower on the end of a stalk. But flowers are also arranged in other ways. The daisy type looks like one flower but is actually made up of many tiny flowers (florets).

spike
foxglove

simple umbel
cowslip

compound umbel
cow parsley

daisy type
ox-eye daisy

Fluoride

Fluorides are chemicals formed by fluorine. One of these, calcium fluoride, occurs naturally in drinking water in some parts of the world. It dissolves as the water flows over certain rocks. Scientists have discovered that tooth decay is less common in these areas. They have found that the fluoride strengthens the white enamel of the teeth, especially in children.

Putting fluorides in water

Fluorides are sometimes deliberately added to drinking water to prevent tooth decay. Many toothpastes also contain fluoride for the same reason. Not everyone agrees that water should be fluoridated like this, since too much fluoride can be harmful.

Linings and lubricants

Some fluorides are very tough but slippery substances. One, known as 'Teflon', is used to coat non-stick saucepans and frying pans. Others are used as lubricants. ■

See also
Dentists
Fluorine
Teeth
Water supplies

Fluorine

Fluorine is a yellow-green gas, one of the most active of all the elements. It will eat away most metals. When combined with hydrogen to make an acid it will even dissolve glass, so it is very difficult to store. The acid is used by some artists to etch pictures on glass.

When combined in a special way with carbon and chlorine to form chemicals called 'CFCs' (chlorofluorocarbons), it seems to become harmless. Because they were thought to be harmless, CFCs were used as the circulating gas in refrigerators and the propellant (the gas that produces the pressure) in aerosol cans. Now scientists know that they produce holes in the ozone layer. ■

Safer kinds of propellants can now be used.

See also
Aerosols
Elements
Fluoride
Ozone

Fog

▲ **Cars and headlights in thick fog in Germany.**

Fog is like a cloud on the ground. You cannot see very far in fog and it is wet. This is because fog is made of lots of water droplets in the air.

All air has some water in it. Most of this water is a gas called 'water vapour'. You can see water vapour forming if you boil a kettle and the steam disappears into the air. If this water vapour is cooled it becomes droplets of water and makes fog.

Early in the morning the ground cools down and so the cool earth lowers the temperature of the air above it, forming fog. If there is a strong wind a fog does not form, but gets blown away. When the sun gets up it warms the air and the fog turns back into a gas.

When fog forms in big cities it mixes with pollution in the air to form smog: half fog, half smoke. Up until the 1950s Londoners called them 'pea soupers' because it was like trying to see through a thick pea soup. ■

In 1956 the Clean Air Act made it illegal to use coal for fires in central London. Factories were also required to reduce the smoke from chimneys. Smog no longer formed.

See also
Pollution
Water

Folk dance

A folk dance is special to the part of the world it comes from. Each country, each area, has folk dances of its own. In Britain, morris dancing is probably the best-known type of folk dance. There are morris dancing troupes in most towns and cities. They perform outside in good weather, and send round a hat to collect money from their audience. Other British folk dances include Highland dancing and Lancashire clog dancing. Nowadays most such dances are for entertainment, but centuries ago the dancers had more serious purposes.

What were folk dances for?

Some folk dances were performed to bring good luck and ensure good crops. Many became part of religious ceremonies. In the Far East, people dressed as dragons or lions danced to frighten away evil spirits. The Maori performed war-dances to delight the gods of war and terrify the enemy. People in dry areas, for example the Aborigines in Australia and the plains Indians of North America, performed rain-dances to please the sky-gods and bring rain. The dance movements imitated the swelling of the clouds and the flow of falling water.

Other folk dances began as celebrations. People literally 'danced for joy'. In many parts of the world, dancers performed to celebrate a successful harvest. Their movements imitated the action of ploughing, sowing and gathering.

In eastern European countries, people still dance at weddings, baptisms, and other family

◀ Morris dancing is a very ancient tradition. It may be that the sound of the bells on the dancers' legs and the waving of handkerchiefs was intended to frighten away evil spirits. The leaping in the air was probably to make the crops grow.

▼ In Africa music and dance go together and celebrate every stage of the human life cycle. This dancer is from Zambia in southern Africa.

occasions. In Africa, there are dances for just about every social event. In Britain and the USA children play games such as 'Ring a Ring o' Roses' or 'Oranges and Lemons'. Although we seldom think of such games as folk dances, that is what they are.

Folk-dance troupes

Until the end of the 19th century, folk dances, like folk songs, were little known outside their own country or local area. But just as some late 19th-century collectors began rescuing and publishing folk songs, so other people collected dances. They visited country areas, watched the dances and noted down the steps. ■

◀ Men and women dancing in a circle in Lemnos, a Greek island. Round dances are common in the Balkans and in eastern European countries.

⊙ **See also**
Dance
Folk music
Hornpipe
Nursery rhymes

Folk music

Cecil Sharp (1859–1924) was a lawyer who became a music teacher. He collected folk songs and folk dances in Britain and America. Songs he heard in the Appalachian Mountains in the USA turned out to be British folk songs which had been taken to America by early emigrants.

Alan Lomax later toured America with a tape recorder discovering folk songs and their singers. He later put great folk and blues singers like Huddie ('Leadbelly') Ledbetter, Josh White and Woody Guthrie on the radio.

Folk music is also heard in other parts of the world. African 'high life' and Latin American 'tango' music are both forms of folk music.

Classical composers like Dvorak and Holst have written music based upon the folk songs of their day.

Some modern folk musicians
Joan Baez
Bob Dylan
Fairport Convention
Steeleye Span
The Dubliners

▶ **Photograph of an English folk musician playing the violin in the early years of this century.**

▶ **Street musicians playing in County Kerry, the Irish Republic.**

◔ **See also**
African music
Nursery rhymes
Singing and songs

Biography
Beethoven
Dvorak

Pop and rock special
Dylan

A lot of the music that we know from past times has been preserved by being written down. But the music and words of folk songs have been passed from person to person down the generations by listening and copying. Nursery rhymes and musical games such as 'The Farmer's in his Den' are types of folk song.

Modern folk music

Some kinds of popular music written today are considered to be folk songs. Modern folk groups try to use traditional instruments, to give the music a more 'folky' style. Some artists have made their own version of traditional folk tunes, such as Simon and Garfunkel's version of 'Scarborough Fair'.

What are folk songs about?

Many folk songs began in country areas. They were made up to help the day's work along, or to enjoy when the work was done. Some tell of events in ordinary people's lives. Others are season-songs, about the work people do in winter, spring or harvest time. There are story songs, cradle songs, nature songs, riddles, songs about war, and sailors' songs. Some modern folk songs are 'protest' songs. Their words are about such things as poverty, racism and nuclear war. In fact almost anything you can think of has inspired a folk song.

Flashback

In the 19th century, huge numbers of people moved from the country into towns and cities. Folk songs were in danger of being forgotten, so throughout Europe, musicians and other interested people began to 'collect' them so that they would not be lost. The collectors asked people who remembered folk songs to sing them, and then wrote down the words and music. As more and more songs were collected, people began to realize that they were finding the same songs in slightly different versions in different places. ■

Folk tales and fairy tales

No one knows who first makes up a folk tale. People (the folk) pass them on by telling them. Each teller adds ideas of his or her own, and so the tale grows. Some folk tales, such as the Anansi stories from Africa, or the Arabian Nights stories from the Middle East, are very old. Others are recent, like the story of a monster stalking a local wood or marsh, or the tale of the hitch-hiker who turned out to be the ghost of somebody killed in a car crash. But old or new, the stories still change and grow in the same way, each time they are told.

People enjoy two kinds of folk tales most of all. First, they like stories about ordinary people like themselves. Many folk stories are about poor people who use brains or bravery to win good luck, or greedy, wicked or foolish people who come to grief. There is the story of the brave little drummer-boy who terrifies the enemy by playing march-beats in the middle of the night, and the tale of the three drunks who try to catch the moon's reflection in a pond. Such stories are like gossip about unusual goings-on among our own relatives or neighbours.

Second, people like folk tales involving magic. Magic animals in such tales as Puss in Boots cast spells and talk. Giants roar that they bake their bread from flour ground from human bones. Elves steal human babies, and fairy godmothers promise three wishes to good little boys, and

beings set out on magical adventures, killing giants, riding dragons, outwitting wizards and discovering fairy gold. In stories like these, poor young men or women often leave home to seek their fortune, and end up marrying princesses or princes and living happily ever after.

Fairy tales

Properly speaking, a 'fairy tale' ought to be a story containing fairies. Many do. There are countless stories like Rumpelstiltskin (about a battle of wits between a girl and a spiteful elf) or Cinderella (where the heroine is helped to happiness by her fairy godmother). But many 'fairy tales' are nothing of the kind. In France in the late 17th century, there was a fashion for retold folk tales. The writers called them *contes des fées*, 'stories of fairies'. When the stories, which are about giants, wizards and other magical beings as well as fairies, were translated into English, they were called *fay tales* or 'fairy tales', and the name has stuck. This is why some of the best-known folk tale collections of all, such as the stories retold by Perrault, the Grimm brothers, Hans Andersen and Andrew Lang, are often known in English as 'So-and-so's Fairy Tales'. ∎

◀ **The Prince of The Ebony Isles and his Magic Horse, from the Arabian Nights.**

Cinderella
A story similar to that of Cinderella was written down in China in the 9th century. In Europe there is no written version before the 17th century but the story had probably been told orally for centuries before that. The Cinderella story is found in Egypt and India as well.

Chapbooks
Fairy stories were printed in England in the 17th and 18th centuries in chapbooks. These were little books of 16 or 24 pages, often illustrated by woodcuts and sold by travelling pedlars. These pamphlets were not written and published especially for children but many children enjoyed them. *Tom Thumbe, His Life and Death* was published in 1630.

Many collections of fairy stories were published during the 19th century. Perrault's Tales were translated from French and Grimms' Tales from German. Irish fairy tales were published in the 1820s and in the 1840s Hans Andersen's tales were translated from Danish. By the end of Victoria's reign there were books containing stories from many cultures including Norse, Russian and Indian.

◀ **A scene from Briar Rose (another version of The Sleeping Beauty story), taken from Grimms' Nursery Tales. The illustration is by Arthur Rackham.**

⊙ See also
Anansi
Arabian Nights
Fairies
Giants
Pantomimes

Biography
Andersen
Grimm brothers

Food

Food supplies you with energy, and with the materials your body needs for growth, repair of wounds, wear and tear, and staying healthy.

Energy is needed for everything that goes on in the body. Your muscles use energy when you move and your brain uses it when you think. Energy is needed for thousands of chemical changes that take place throughout the body every second. You use energy even when you are completely relaxed or asleep. This energy keeps your body warm, your heart beating and your lungs breathing.

The smallest amount of energy that you need to keep you alive is called your basal metabolic rate (BMR). Your BMR depends on your age and sex. The average adult BMR is between 6,000 and 7,000 kJ per day (the kilojoule is a unit used to measure energy content). The amount of energy you need on top of your BMR, when you wake up and start moving, also depends on your age and sex and what you are doing. A baby uses much less energy than an adult, and a young athlete or road worker uses far more energy than an elderly retired person. The more energy you use, the more food you need to supply it.

Nutrients for energy

Foods are mixtures of useful nutrients, together with things that the body cannot use. There are five types of nutrient: carbohydrates, fats, proteins, vitamins and minerals. Carbohydrates are found in sugary foods such as sweets, honey, jam and treacle, and starchy foods such as bread, potatoes and rice. Carbohydrates are our main source of energy.

Fatty foods include butter and cream, which come from animals, and also oils from plants such as olive oil, sunflower oil or maize seed oil. Fats can supply twice as much energy as carbohydrates. Instead of using them straight away, the body keeps some of them as an energy store. Fat is mostly stored under the skin.

Nutrients for body repairs and maintenance

Protein occurs in almost all foods, but some foods have much more protein than others. Vegetables such as lettuce and cabbage have a very small amount. Foods which are high in protein include meat, especially liver and kidney, cheese, eggs, fish, milk, beans (including tinned baked beans) and peas.

There are many different kinds of proteins in food from animals and plants. Most people get protein from both animal and plant food. Vegetarians do not eat meat, but they can stay healthy with proteins from plants.

Your body is built mainly of proteins, and you need proteins to help it replace damaged and worn out parts. Growing children and people

Kilojoules and calories are the units used to measure the energy content of food.

Some books and magazines use the word 'calories' to measure energy from food: 4·2 kilojoules = 1 calorie.

▼ The chart shows roughly how much food and energy is needed by different groups of people. But a chart like this can only show averages. People of the same age, sex and build may have quite different needs.

Birth to 1 year	8 years	11 years		15 years		Adult (light work)	
Energy used in 1 day							
0–3 months 2,300 kJ 3–6 months 3,200 kJ 6–9 months 3,800 kJ 9–12 months 4,200 kJ	Active children 8,800 kJ (both sexes)	Males 10,500 kJ	Females 9,600 kJ	Males 12,600 kJ	Females 9,600 kJ	Males 11,550 kJ	Females 9,450 kJ
Diet							
At least 2 g of protein are needed per kg of body weight from 0–6 months and 1·6 g per kg from 6–9 months, gradually reducing to 1 g per kg. Weaning usually begins at about 4 months.	At least 30 g of protein a day, but 53 g are recommended.	80–100 g of protein per day and 60% of this should be first class protein. About 300 g of carbohydrate per day except for those doing heavy work who should eat far more.		Sugar should not be eaten in large quantities as it increases tooth decay. About 100 g of fat should be eaten per day.			

recovering from an illness or injury need plenty of protein, but healthy adults need it too. This is because bodies are rebuilding themselves all the time. The liver and kidneys, for example, are completely replaced by new material every 20 days.

Vitamins and minerals are nutrients which you need in small amounts but which are essential for good health. Vitamins take part in many important chemical changes in the body. Most vitamins come from food, but the body can make vitamin D if the skin gets enough sunlight. You need minerals such as iron for healthy red blood cells, and calcium and phosphorus for healthy bones and teeth and to make your muscles and nerves work properly.

Fibre

You also need to eat food that the body cannot digest but which helps it to get rid of waste products. This is why fibre is so important. Fibre is the parts of food plants which humans cannot digest. Fruit and vegetables, wholemeal bread and pasta, brown rice, peas and beans all contain plenty of fibre. The fibre absorbs water as it passes through the body, and this helps make the solid waste in the gut bulky and soft. The body can then easily get rid of the waste as faeces through the anus.

If people do not eat enough fibre, the faeces become hard and compact and take longer to pass through the body.

	Kilojoules per 100 g	Types of food
meat and fish	600 to 1,200 kJ	Mostly protein with a lot of fat and oil. Many vitamins, especially in fish oil.
dairy produce	300 to 3,000	Mostly fat, especially butter and cheese. Eggs have a lot of protein and many vitamins.
cereals	1,000 to 1,600	Mostly starchy carbohydrate with a little protein. Some vitamins in wholemeal bread.
vegetables	40 to 350	Contain a lot of water, some carbohydrate and protein. Very little fat. Very rich in vitamins.
fruit	100 to 300	Contain a lot of water with some carbohydrate and a little protein. Rich in vitamin C.
sweets and cakes	1,000 to 2,300	Mostly carbohydrate, especially sugar, with some fat and a little protein. No vitamins.

▲ The energy supplied by food is measured in units called kilojoules (kJ). Different foods supply different amounts of energy, as the food chart shows.

Adult (moderate work)		Adult (heavy work)		Pregnant and nursing mothers		Elderly retired people
Males 12,100 kJ	**Females** 10,500 kJ	**Males** 15,000 to 20,000 kJ	**Females** 12,600 kJ	**Pregnant** 10,000 kJ	**Nursing** 11,300 kJ	8,000 to 9,000 kJ
				Pregnant women should eat about 85 g of protein per day increasing to 100 g during breast feeding, together with increased amounts of food containing calcium, iron, and all vitamins.		Old people should avoid eating too much fat, oil and sugar as these will quickly make them overweight. They should eat plenty of fruit and vegetables for vitamins and minerals, and fish and lean meat for protein.

Football

▶ Dave Beasant, team captain and goalkeeper for Wimbledon, lifting the FA Cup after his team had beaten Liverpool 1–0 in the 1988 final. For many football fans knock-out competitions, such as the FA Cup, produce the most dramatic and exciting football.

In the qualifying matches for the 1992 European Championships, the tiny Faroe Islands (population about 48,000) surprised the footballing world by beating Austria (population about 7·5 million) 1–0. Upsets such as this, when an unfancied team beats more famous and successful opponents are often known as 'giant-killing acts'.

There are several different games called football, played with a variety of different-shaped balls. The best-known, by far, is Association Football, or 'soccer', the most popular game in the world.

It is also the simplest. In its most basic form any sort of ball and two coats for a goal are all you need to have a game.

A full-sized game has two teams of eleven, two goals, and a full-sized ball. The object is to score a goal by kicking or heading the ball into the goal. Teams progress by passing or running with the ball (dribbling). Tackling must be directed at the ball (no hacking or tripping the player!). Only the goalkeeper is allowed to handle the ball, and only within his penalty area.

The story of football is the story of great players and great teams, great games, exciting goals, and spectacular saves. There is general agreement that the greatest player of all was Pelé, who played for Brazil, possibly the greatest team of all, in three World Cup Finals.

▼ The football pitch, with the teams preparing for kick-off. Another modern formation is 5–3–2. This is known as the 'sweeper' system, because the extra defender plays slightly behind the rest of the defence and collects or 'sweeps up' the ball when it is played past the other defenders.

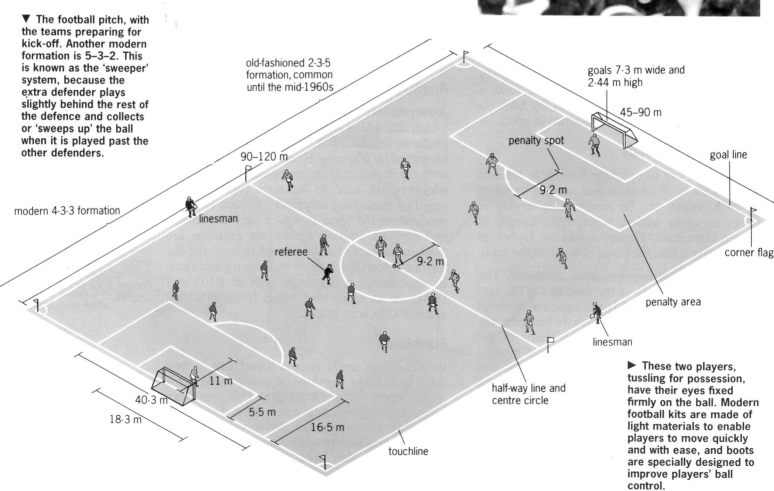

old-fashioned 2-3-5 formation, common until the mid-1960s

goals 7·3 m wide and 2·44 m high

45–90 m

penalty spot

goal line

9·2 m

90–120 m

corner flag

modern 4-3-3 formation

linesman

referee

9·2 m

penalty area

linesman

11 m

40·3 m

5·5 m

half-way line and centre circle

18·3 m

16·5 m

touchline

▶ These two players, tussling for possession, have their eyes fixed firmly on the ball. Modern football kits are made of light materials to enable players to move quickly and with ease, and boots are specially designed to improve players' ball control.

The World Cup

The World Cup is the most important international competition in soccer. It takes place every four years. Over 120 countries enter the regional qualifying rounds, with 24 going on to the finals in a particular host country. Brazil and Italy have each won the World Cup three times. The competition is dominated by European and South American countries, but African and Asian teams are growing stronger and they want more places in the finals.

Other major competitions

Other major international tournaments are the European and South American Championships. Famous club competitions include the European Cup (for the champion clubs of each country), the English Football League and the FA Cup. Over 500 clubs enter the FA (Football Association) Cup. It is a knock-out competition, with the first games taking place in August and the final being played at Wembley in London in May.

Fans

By the end of the 19th century, top games were attracting big crowds. In Britain, the largest crowd for one match was the 149,547 at the Scotland versus England game at Hampden Park in 1937. Attendances remained high during the late 1940s and 1950s, but since the 1960s they have declined. The reasons include hooliganism and the fact that there are many other things for people to do. But football worldwide is still the most popular spectator sport, and many more follow the game through TV and newspapers, keeping up a keen interest in a particular club.

Fans have been involved in major tragedies. In Britain, people died in disasters at Bolton in 1946 and Ibrox Park, Glasgow, in 1971. In 1985, 50 were killed by fire at Bradford, and in 1989, 90 Liverpool fans were crushed to death at Hillsborough, Sheffield, during an FA Cup Semi-Final. In 1985, a riot at Heysel Stadium, Brussels, involving Liverpool and Juventus fans at a European Cup Final left over 40 dead, and resulted in English clubs being banned from European competition. Similar tragedies have happened around the world.

Flashback

A similar game to football was recorded in China 2,500 years ago, and there are references to the game throughout the Middle Ages in Europe. The modern game as we know it began in the public schools of southern England in the 19th century. The rules were written in 1863. The FA Cup was first awarded in 1872; the first British competition, with the first international, England versus Scotland, was played at the end of the same year. Professionalism and the Football League arrived in the 1880s. In 1904 FIFA, the international organizing body, was set up.

⊙ See also
Hurling
Rugby

Biography
Sports special

FIFA is the abbreviation for the French title: Fédération Internationale de Football Association (the international federation of association football).

The most goals scored by one player in an English League season is 60 in 39 games by William Ralph 'Dixie' Dean for Everton in the 1927/28 season. In Scotland the record is 66 in 38 games by James Smith of Ayr United in the same season.

▼ Goal-mouth action from an FA Cup match in 1931. The game is Crystal Palace versus Everton at Selhurst Park and the player on the far left is 'Dixie' Dean, one of the most famous forwards of the time. The players look different in their big boots and baggy shorts, but the excitement was the same.

Forests

In a rainforest there may be as many as 750 species of tree in an area of 1 sq km.

A forest is a large area of land covered mainly with trees and undergrowth. Some forests, such as the great Amazon rainforest, have existed for thousands of years. Although vast areas of forest have been destroyed by human activity, 20 per cent of the world's land remains covered in forest, both natural and specially planted.

Forests can grow wherever the temperature rises above 10°C (50°F) in summer and the annual rainfall exceeds 200 mm (8 in). Different climates and soils support different kinds of forests; for example, coni-fer forests grow in cold climates, and rainforests grow in the humid tropics.

▼ Autumn in a deciduous forest.

▼ El Junque rainforest in Puerto Rico.

The forest environment

Forests create their own special environments. The crowns of the tallest trees cast a shade on the forest floor. Where a large tree falls, the new patch of light encourages lush growth of vegetation, including the seedlings of more trees.

There is little wind inside a forest. Trees draw up water from the soil, and some later evaporates from their leaves. So the air in a forest is still and moist.

The trees shield the forest interior from the full strength of the Sun's rays, and also prevent heat being lost into the sky at night. So the temperature inside the forest does not vary so much as outside. The days are cooler, and the nights warmer, making the forest a sheltered place for wildlife.

The structure of a forest

A forest has a definite structure. The larger tree species have branching crowns which form an almost continuous canopy over the roof of the forest, allowing only small shafts of sunlight through. In tropical forests, a few very tall trees, called emergents, grow through the canopy into the sunlight above. Below the canopy are smaller trees and the young saplings of taller trees. These form the understorey. Below them are shrubs and briars, and on the forest floor a layer of smaller shrubs and plants. In some forests, vines and lianas trail from one layer of the forest to another in dense tangles.

▶ **Emergent trees rise through the canopy. It is windy here, so the wind will spread their seeds.**

▶ **The canopy of spreading treetops is so dense it may be 8 m thick in places.**

▶ **The understorey is darker than the canopy as less light penetrates. It provides shelter for many forest animals.**

▶ **The shrub layer. If the canopy is very dense there will be few shrubs.**

▶ **The forest floor is so dark that few plants can grow. It is where the forest decay takes place.**

60 m

40 m

20 m

0 m

Tropical rainforest

Here temperatures are high and the air is moist all year round. The rainforest has such a dense tangle of vegetation that it is often difficult to distinguish the various layers. Plants, such as orchids, even grow on the trunks and branches of trees and fallen logs.

There are so many different kinds of trees that there may be two or even three layers of understorey, formed by different species. Climbing figs, vines and lianas dangle from the branches high in the canopy. Herbs and shrubs carpet the forest floor.

Deciduous forest

These forests are found in temperate climates. The main tree species are deciduous, which means that they shed their leaves in winter, or in the dry season. For part of the year the forest floor receives plenty of light, so herbs may flourish there. These forests have strong seasonal patterns of producing leaves, flowers, fruits and nuts. The understorey may include occasional evergreen trees and shrubs, such as holly and yew. Ivy, honeysuckle, clematis and other shrubs and herbs may climb or twine up the trees towards the light.

Coniferous forest

Coniferous forest is found further north and higher up mountain slopes than any other kind of forest. The main trees are conifers (cone-bearing trees) such as pines. Most are evergreen, with narrow leaves coated in shiny wax to reduce water loss, which would otherwise be high on windswept mountain slopes. They can also survive drought and the freezing of soil water in winter. Their branches slope downwards, so snow easily slides off. The dense canopy lets very little light through, so few plants grow beneath it, and there is a thick layer of dead leaves.

The world's largest forest is coniferous. It is in Siberia and covers an area of 11 million square km.

The largest rainforest is Amazonia in South America. It covers an area of about 6.5 million square km.

Forest life

Forests provide shelter and food for many animals. Leaves, flowers, fruits, seeds and nuts are food for insects, birds and small mammals, such as squirrels and mice, which in turn are food for larger birds and mammals. The moist forest soil has its own community: worms, centipedes, beetles, ants, and the eggs and larvae of many insects. Hollow trees, crevices under roots and bark, and the moist soil provide sites for nests and burrows. The forest is a noisy place, because visibility is poor among the trees and animals use calls and smells to communicate with each other.

▼ Creatures such as this millipede thrive in the humidity of the rainforest.

Dense tropical rainforest in Queensland (above), and mangrove swamp in Kenya (left). Both provide habitats for numerous plant and animal species.

Different layers of the forest have their own special communities. Birds, squirrels and, in tropical forests, monkeys roam the canopy. Some animals have long tails which help them to balance as they leap from branch to branch. South American monkeys, mice, rats, and some small marsupials and lizards use their tail as a fifth limb, curling it around the branches.

Anteaters, lizards and bears have strong claws for climbing. Sloths and koala bears have slow life-styles needing very little energy, so they live by feeding on the leaves that have few nutrients, which other animals do not want. At night, bats hunt insects or forage for nectar and fruit.

Lower down are creatures that nest in holes, such as owls, toucans, starlings, woodpeckers and parrots. On the forest floor live burrow-dwellers such as badgers, stoats, mice, foxes and armadillos; foragers like wild pigs and deer; and large predators such as tigers, pumas and wolves. Snakes lie in wait among the dead leaves.

Ants live at all levels, collecting leaves or seeds, or preying on other insects.

Rot and decay

Most of the food available in the forest is locked up in the bodies of the trees themselves. When trees die or are blown down, or when leaves, twigs, flowers or fruits fall, they quickly rot. Woodpeckers drill holes in soft rotting trunks, and bark beetles excavate tunnels under the bark, allowing fungi to enter. Fungi dissolve the tree's tissues and absorb the nutrients.

When the fungi die, they in turn are broken down by bacteria. The dead plant material gradually crumbles into the soil, where more animals and plants, many too small to see, set to work. These include worms, ants and termites. scavenging beetles, slugs and snails, soil fungi and bacteria.

As the once living material breaks down into smaller and smaller particles, the food it contained escapes into the soil, to be taken up by growing plants. Without rot and decay, the forest soils would soon become too poor to support trees.

A similar process acts on dead animals. Vultures, crows and other scavengers tear up the flesh, and flies lay their eggs in it. Their maggots clean the flesh off the bones. These processes happen much faster in the warm humid climate of tropical forests, where corpses can almost disappear in a few days.

Forest economics

Every year the world consumes 3 billion cubic metres (100 billion cubic feet) of wood. For large areas of the world, firewood is the main source of energy, the only source the poor can afford. Timber is used for house frames, ship-building, paper, packaging, fencing and many other structures. It may be extracted directly from natural forest, or grown in plantations or managed forests. The fruits and nuts of forest trees provide food and spices. Forest trees also provide oils for cooking and industry, syrups, resins, varnishes, dyes, rubber, latex, kapok, fibres, insecticides and drugs, including anti-biotics. Many of these come from rainforest trees, and there are probably thousands of species of rainforest trees with uses as yet undiscovered.

Forests have other important functions. A forest acts like a giant sponge, absorbing rainfall and preventing it from running away into rivers. It then releases the water slowly by evaporation from its leaves. This helps to stabilize the rainfall of areas downwind from the forest. Forest cover also prevents the soil being eroded (worn away) and silting up rivers and lakes. By holding the water back, the forest prevents disastrous flooding further downstream.

Secondary forests

When original, 'virgin' forest is cut down, trees and shrubs soon colonize the new space. This new forest growth is called secondary forest. It has fewer species and its plants and animals are much less varied than those of virgin forest. The first colonists are plants with easily dispersed seeds, which can live in areas with wind and bright light. Fast-growing species shade slower-growing ones, which then die out, so the plants gradually change. If the clearing is small enough and the disturbance not too great, this secondary forest will eventually turn back into virgin forest. But if the disturbance continues, or not enough untouched forest remains, some species may be unable to move back, or the first pioneer species may get too strong a hold, offering too much competition. Most of the woodland we see in cooler countries and the cultivated tropics today is secondary forest.

Disappearing forests

Many rainforests grow on very poor soils, and there may well be more foods locked up in the plants than there are in the soil. When rainforest is cut down and burned, the remaining soil is often too poor to support crops for long. With its cover of vegetation gone, soil is easily washed away in the tropical rains, and it silts up lakes and reservoirs. With no trees to trap the rainfall, the area may even turn to desert, and areas downwind of the destroyed forest also become drier and do not support growth so well. Because more water runs freely off the soil, it causes flooding further downstream.

Like all green plants, trees produce their own food by photosynthesis. They absorb carbon dioxide, one of the gases responsible for the 'greenhouse effect', and release oxygen. Forests are major suppliers of the world's oxygen. In the late 1980s an area of about 200,000 sq km (80,000 sq miles) was burned down every year, releasing 7,600 million tonnes of carbon dioxide. Scientists and others are campaigning to stop this destruction of the Earth's resources. ■

◀ Loading timber at a logging station in Canada.

▼ Road being cut through Brazilian rainforest. Destruction of rainforests not only destroys the habitats of many plants and animals, bringing some near to extinction, but it may also ultimately affect the world's climate.

Foster children

Foster children are the children in a family whose own parents are unable to look after them for some reason. Foster parents offer to look after children because they are fond of children and would like to have more in the family. In Britain foster parents are paid money by the local Social Services Department to cover the cost of extra children in their family.

Children are asked about the kind of family they would like to live in. Great care is taken to match the children to a family that is right for them, but even so, moving into a new family can be difficult. A social worker visits regularly to check that everyone is happy with the arrangement. Sometimes foster children stay only a short while with their new family, but sometimes they spend most of their lives there.

Children are fostered because their parents have asked the Social Services to arrange this, perhaps while one parent is ill, or sometimes because their parents have neglected or ill-treated them and the court has ordered them to be taken into the care of the Social Services Department. Arrangements are usually made for foster children's parents and family to visit them. ■

See also
Families
Social workers

Biography
Barnardo

Foxes

Foxes are small members of the dog family. Most foxes live alone, although cubs born in the spring remain with both parents through the summer. The red fox is found over more of the world than any other carnivore (flesh-eater). It can survive from the Arctic tundra through grassland to temperate forests, and has recently discovered that it can make a good living in towns and suburbs, close to human beings.

The red fox can survive on a wide variety of foods, such as small rodents, rabbits, insects, earthworms and carrion. It also eats fruit, and in season wild berries, apples and rosehips can make up 90 per cent of its diet. Some foxes do a lot of damage killing game birds and raiding hen runs, but most do not, and their usefulness in killing pests generally outweighs any harm. In spite of this, they are hunted and trapped in many areas. But they often escape, and because of this they have a reputation for intelligence and cunning. They have very good sight, hearing and sense of smell, and can also run fast (up to 48 km/h or 30 mph) over long distances, jumping obstacles and swimming through water.

Most other species of fox live in more specialized environments, but are similar to the red fox. ■

Distribution
Red fox in most regions north of the tropics and in Australia, where it was taken by settlers during the last century. Arctic foxes in the Arctic. Other species in Africa, Asia, America.
Largest
Small-eared dog, head and body length up to 100 cm; weight 9 kg
Smallest
Fennec fox, head and body length as little as 24 cm; weight as little as 0.8 kg
Number of young 4 or 5
Lifespan Up to 6 years in the wild, up to 13 in captivity

Subphylum Vertebrata
Class Mammalia
Order Carnivora
Family Canidae (dog family)
Number of species 21

▲ The Arctic fox, with its smoky grey summer coat, which turns white in winter, is more sociable than other foxes. Sometimes they travel huge distances in search of food.

◄ Red fox cubs are reared by both parents, who feed them and guard them while they play. They sometimes bring injured animals so the cubs can learn to make a kill.

See also
Dogs   Wastelands
Jackals   Wolves

Fractions

Fractures

Fraction comes from a Latin word meaning 'breaking', because the whole number is broken up into parts.

Vulgar used to mean 'of the ordinary kind', which is what vulgar fractions were when decimals were a new invention. Improper fractions are ones that are not written in the standard 'proper' form.

The ancient Egyptians used fractions like $\frac{1}{4}$ and $\frac{1}{5}$ with numerator 1, and they had a special sign for $\frac{2}{3}$, but they had no other fractions. They had to write
$\frac{1}{2} + \frac{1}{10}$ for $\frac{3}{5}$,
$\frac{1}{2} + \frac{1}{5} + \frac{1}{10}$ for $\frac{4}{5}$,
$\frac{1}{2} + \frac{1}{4} + \frac{1}{14} + \frac{1}{28}$ for $\frac{6}{7}$,
and so on.
To multiply a fraction by 2 might be quite a difficult mathematical problem, as in the example quoted in the margin of the article on Algebra, which calls for
$2 \times 100 \times \frac{1}{13}$.

If you measure something the answer will not always be a whole number of units. Fractions allow you to divide up the gap between whole numbers so that a more accurate measurement can be given, such as in motorway distance signs (exit $\frac{1}{3}$ mile) or shoe sizes ($6\frac{1}{2}$).

There are two standard ways of writing fractions. One way is to write one whole number over another like this: $\frac{3}{4}$. This is called a **vulgar fraction**. $\frac{3}{4}$ means that you are dividing the gap between 0 and 1 into four equal steps, and then going up just three of them.

Vulgar fractions are sometimes written as percentages. 75 per cent (75%) really means $\frac{75}{100}$. The other way of writing fractions is to use a decimal point, as in 0·75. You can find out more about decimals and percentages in separate articles.

In a vulgar fraction like $\frac{3}{4}$, the top number is called the numerator and the bottom number is the denominator. Sometimes, the numerator may be bigger than the denominator, as in $\frac{5}{4}$. A fraction like this is called an **improper fraction**. It is a way of writing a number larger than one. $\frac{5}{4}$ is exactly the same as four quarters plus an extra one quarter, so it is another way of writing $1\frac{1}{4}$.

Fractions are easy to add provided they have the same denominator. Say you want to find the answer to $\frac{1}{2} + \frac{1}{4}$. The fraction $\frac{1}{2}$ is exactly the same as $\frac{2}{4}$, so your sum can be written as $\frac{2}{4} + \frac{1}{4}$. As the denominators are the same, you can add the numerators. So:

$$\frac{2}{4} + \frac{1}{4} = \frac{3}{4}.$$

The use of calculators has meant that in many cases we now use decimal fractions rather than vulgar fractions, preferring 0·85 to $\frac{85}{100}$ or $\frac{17}{20}$. Fractions are still used mathematically; for example in probability. ■

See also
Arithmetic
Decimals
Numbers
Percentages
Probability

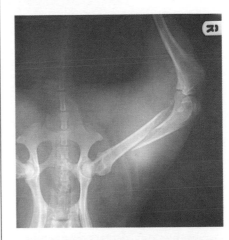

◀ **X-ray photograph of a Border collie's femur (thigh bone) fractured in an accident.**

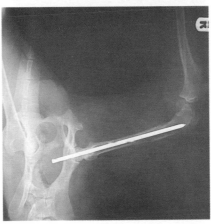

◀ **X-ray photograph showing the steel pin inserted to set the fractured bone.**

A fracture is a broken bone. Bones are very strong, but if you are hit or fall awkwardly you may fracture one. There are many different kinds of fractures. In some the skin surface is not broken. In others the broken bone may tear the skin and show through. This is called a compound fracture. Greenstick fractures are common in young children. The bone bends but does not break.

With a fracture, the affected part of the body is very painful and difficult to move. The skin may be discoloured and swollen. If you suspect a fracture you must go to the hospital. An X-ray will show how badly the bone is broken. If it is a simple fracture you may not need treatment. If it is a bad break, the doctor fits the edges of the bone together and may put a plaster cast on the limb to hold the bone in position until it heals. ■

See also
Bones
First aid
Skeletons
X-rays

Area
547,026 sq km
(211,208 sq miles)
Capital
Paris
Population
55,600,000
Language
French, Breton, Basque
Religion
Christian
Government
Parliamentary republic
Currency
1 franc = 100 centimes

The Tour de France is one of the world's famous cycle races. The route includes sections in all the mountainous areas of France, where the competitors face long, steep hill-climbs.

▶ **Tourists visiting a nuclear power-station. France produces over 65 per cent of the electricity it needs by nuclear power.**

The Monte Carlo Rally is a famous motor-racing event which is held in January. The drivers are tested on the snow and ice in the beautiful mountain scenery of south-eastern France.

▶ **Men of all ages play boules (a form of bowls) with heavy metal balls and a smaller 'jack'. The game can be played on any piece of flat ground.**

France

France is the largest country in Western Europe and has many different landscapes and ways of life. High mountains provide the borders with Italy and Spain. The Alps include peaks like Mont Blanc and their snowfields attract many skiers in winter. There are National Parks in the Alps and also in the Pyrenees where some wild bears still roam.

France's longest river, the Loire, rises in the high plateaux of the centre. Here are extinct volcanoes which form the conical peaks of Auvergne and deep gorges where the River Tarn cuts through dry limestone uplands known as Causses. Smaller uplands include the forested Vosges in the east and the moorlands of Brittany in the north-west. Elsewhere there are wide plains, most extensive in the Paris Basin and in Aquitaine around the city of Bordeaux.

Most of Europe's climate types are found within France. Brittany benefits from the warm Atlantic Gulf Stream and its mild, damp weather contrasts with the varied temperatures of interior plains such as Alsace. The Mediterranean south has hot, dry summers, and the spiny, deep-rooted plants growing there can resist drought.

Food and farming

Her large size and variety of physical conditions make France the leading agricultural producer in the European Community. A lot of wheat is grown, especially on the large farms of the

northern plains, providing flour for the crusty bread which the French buy daily. Maize is grown mainly to feed livestock, and in summer many of the fields are yellow with sunflowers which provide both food for animals and oil for cooking.

France has some famous breeds of cattle including the pale-coated Charolais and the rich brown Limousin, which are exported to many other countries. Dairy cows, most numerous on the lush pastures of the north-west, produce milk for the cities and for cheeses such as Brie and Camembert for which France is famous. Roquefort is a cheese made from the milk of sheep.

Vines flourish in many parts of France. The most extensive vineyards are in the south, but some of the best-known wines come from grapes grown on the sunny slopes of Burgundy and Champagne. Great skill goes into the blending and maturing of these wines, which are sold throughout the world. The south also produces many other fruits and vegetables, but irrigation water is needed in the dry summer.

Towns and industry

France possesses only limited resources of coal and other fuels. Huge quantities of electricity are generated from nuclear power-stations and at hydroelectric dams in the mountains and on the rivers Rhône and Rhine. Loss of jobs in steel-making and textiles has created employment problems in the older industrial regions of the north-east. New science-based industries flourish in Toulouse, Grenoble and other cities of the south. Concorde, Airbus, the Ariane space rocket and high speed trains (TGV) are typical products of French technical skills.

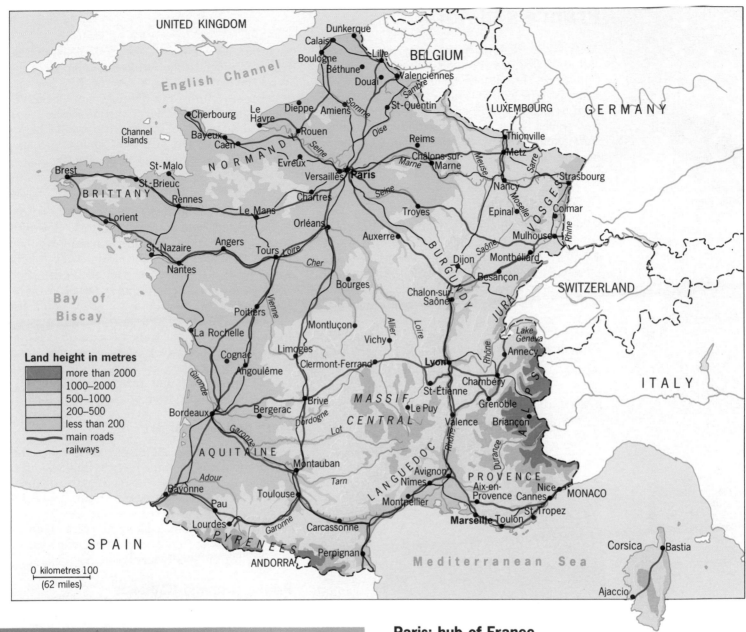

Land height in metres

- more than 2000
- 1000–2000
- 500–1000
- 200–500
- less than 200
- main roads
- railways

0 kilometres 100
(62 miles)

UNITED KINGDOM

English Channel

Channel Islands

BELGIUM

LUXEMBOURG

GERMANY

Dunkerque
Calais
Boulogne
Béthune
Lille
Valenciennes
Douai
St-Quentin
Le Havre
Dieppe
Amiens
Somme
Cherbourg
Bayeux
Caen
Rouen
Evreux
NORMANDY
Reims
Marne
Châlons-sur-Marne
Thionville
Metz
Sarre
Strasbourg
Brest
St-Malo
St-Brieuc
Versailles
Paris
Seine
Nancy
Moselle
VOSGES
Colmar
Epinal
BRITTANY
Rennes
Chartres
Troyes
Mulhouse
Rhine
Lorient
Le Mans
Orléans
Auxerre
Meuse
Saône
Montbéliard
Dijon
Angers
Tours
Loire
BURGUNDY
Besançon
St-Nazaire
Cher
SWITZERLAND
Nantes
Bourges
Chalon-sur-Saône
JURA
Bay of Biscay
Poitiers
Vienne
Montluçon
Allier
Vichy
Loire
Lake Geneva
La Rochelle
Cognac
Limoges
Clermont-Ferrand
Lyon
Annecy
Rhône
Angoulême
Gironde
MASSIF
St-Étienne
Chambéry
ALPS
ITALY
Brive
CENTRAL
Le Puy
Grenoble
Bordeaux
Bergerac
Dordogne
Valence
Briançon
Lot
Garonne
Durance
AQUITAINE
Montauban
Avignon
PROVENCE
Adour
Tarn
Nîmes
Aix-en-Provence
Nice
Bayonne
LANGUEDOC
Montpellier
Cannes
MONACO
Pau
Toulouse
Marseille
Toulon
St-Tropez
Lourdes
Garonne
Carcassonne
SPAIN
PYRENEES
Perpignan
Corsica
Bastia
ANDORRA
Mediterranean Sea
Ajaccio

Paris: hub of France

Almost one-fifth of the population of France live in the city and suburbs of Paris, the capital. Main roads and railways converge here and this helped the growth of manufactures such as car-making and fashion clothing. Many more people are employed in offices and shops. The cathedral of Notre-Dame (Our Lady) stands on an island in the Seine where Paris was founded. Other famous buildings include the Eiffel Tower, the Arc de Triomphe and the church of Sacré-Coeur (Sacred Heart) on the hill of Montmartre where artists have their studios. ■

◄ The Eiffel Tower in Paris stands 300 m (984 feet) in height, and was for years the world's tallest structure. It was designed by Alexandre Eiffel for the World's Fair of 1889.

See also

Europe
France's history

France's history

▲ Astérix, the cartoon Celtic hero.

Some of France's famous cathedrals took hundreds of years to build. The cathedral of Notre Dame in Paris was begun in 1163 but was not finished until 1340. On the other hand, the main part of Chartres Cathedral was completed in just 30 years in the 13th century.

Astérix is an imaginary character, but a warrior called Vercingetorix really lived in the 1st century BC. He was a fierce leader of the Celts in what is now called France. The Celts were wealthy people, selling iron, and farming wheat and grapes. After a long, hard struggle against Vercingetorix, Julius Caesar conquered them, making their lands part of the Roman empire for 500 years.

Clovis the Frank

When, in the 5th century, Goths and Visigoths attacked the Romans, they left Gaul, which was soon invaded by tribes from the east. Among these were the Franks, who conquered much of Gaul. Their king, Clovis, became a Christian and settled in Paris. His reign gave France her name, her religion and her capital city.

Charlemagne

By the end of the 8th century, a king called Charles, a clever soldier, finally ruled all of France except Brittany. He won so many victories, especially against the Saxons, that he captured much of the old Roman empire of the West, taking Christianity wherever he went. It was on his return from fighting with Charles in Spain that the legendary warrior Roland was killed at Roncevaux. The Pope crowned Charles as Emperor in the year 800 and he became known as Charlemagne, Charles the Great.

Chivalry and cathedrals

After Charlemagne it was many centuries before French rulers held so much territory. Powerful lords, like the Dukes of Normandy, of Burgundy and of Brittany, were their rivals. They fought for or against the king, or with each other, and went on crusades. The ordinary people worked long hours on the land to grow food for themselves and their lords. Skilful stonemasons built beautiful cathedrals in Chartres, Paris, Reims and other cities. They were like great books in stone and glass meant to teach those people who could not read about God. The Middle Ages was a time of great faith.

Wars and Joan of Arc

In the later Middle Ages, plague, famine and war brought misery to the French. English kings, descendants of William of Normandy, claimed most of northern and western France, and from 1337 to 1453 the two countries fought each other for more than a hundred years. Joan of Arc is still remembered because she helped drive the English out of France.

Protestants and Catholics

French seamen, including Jacques Cartier, joined in the voyages of discovery in the 16th century, and her explorers and traders learned a great deal about North America. Writers and painters were interested in the Renaissance in Italy. But Protestant ideas from Calvin in Geneva brought civil war to France. Catholic and Protestant nobles fought bitterly to win over each other's followers. This went on into the 17th century and made it hard for French kings to control their country.

The Sun King

The Sun King changed all that. Instead of relying on the nobles to help him, Louis XIV paid officials to rule the country. He persuaded the nobles, by letting them off taxes, to live in his great palace at Versailles. There they hunted,

► This painting was made in the 15th century, towards the end of the Middle Ages. It is one of twelve illustrations showing the months of the year. This is June. Peasants are harvesting with scythes and pitchforks. The illustration was done for an illuminated manuscript called Les Très Riches Heures du Duc de Berry.

gambled and intrigued for the chance to ask the king for favours. France stayed Catholic, but Louis allowed some Frenchmen to be Protestants for a time. Able men led his armies and France won victories, becoming the largest, richest and most learned country in Europe. Painters, musicians and writers worked for Louis, and some people admire the playwright Molière almost as much as Shakespeare.

The Sun seemed a fitting symbol for a king who brought glory to France, but there were clouds too. War was expensive. Poor French people paid higher and higher taxes. Louis's successors were weak and by the 18th century both rich and poor in France were discontented.

French Revolution

In Paris, there is a busy area called Bastille Square. Two hundred years ago a huge fortress stood there. Many poor people lived in its shadow and were angry because bread was so expensive that they could scarcely afford enough to eat. On 14 July 1789 crowds marched through the streets and stormed the prison. King Louis XVI had had a bad day's hunting and wrote in his diary 'July 14 – Nothing'. He was wrong. That day marked the start of the French Revolution, during which Louis XVI, his wife Marie Antoinette and many nobles and others had their heads cut off.

Liberty, Equality, Fraternity

After storming the Bastille, people formed a National Assembly (a parliament) so that they could lower the price of bread and stop businessmen, peasants and workers being kept down and overworked by the nobles. Their slogan was 'liberty, equality, fraternity' and it has inspired many ordinary people in other countries to attack rulers who treat them unfairly.

Terror

After the king was executed, the members of the National Assembly quarrelled among themselves about how to run the country. Many parties and leaders emerged. The best-known were the Jacobins, led by Robespierre. There followed a reign of terror when thousands of people were guillotined. It is said that women sat knitting with the hair of victims as the tumbrels (carts) passed and the heads rolled. The Reign of Terror lasted from 5 September 1793 until 27 July 1794. During these months, 300,000 people were arrested. 17,000 of those were executed but an unknown number died in prison before being brought to trial.

Even so, the revolutionaries helped to improve the lives of ordinary people, and their struggle is still remembered in the words of the French National Anthem, the 'Marseillaise'.

▲ A painting depicting the storming of the Bastille, the huge prison in Paris. There were few prisoners inside, but the act of capturing it symbolized the destruction of the once powerful monarchy.

◀ The painter has depicted Louis XIV in all his splendour with a crown on the table beside him. Louis once said in a speech 'L'État c'est moi' (I am the state). He believed that the monarch had absolute power over his subjects.

▼ The tricolore (three-coloured), one of the symbols of the Revolution, has been the French flag ever since.

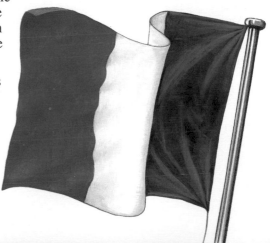

After a four month siege of Paris by the Germans the Parisians set up their own government called the Commune in 1871. When this revolution was put down, 20,000 people were killed and 7,000 were deported from Paris.

After the Revolution

The revolutionaries went to war against the kings and queens of Europe to help their subjects to be free. A young general, Napoleon Bonaparte, won victories in battle in Italy, Germany, Russia and Austria. He made himself Emperor of France and passed laws (the Civil Code) to make sure people were treated fairly. He took these ideas to the lands he conquered and for some time he ruled much of Europe except Britain and organized trade for the benefit of France. Many countries turned against him and he met his last defeat at Waterloo in 1815.

Right through the 19th century, French politics were a battle between the enemies and the supporters of the Revolution. Some brought back kings; others overthrew them. A nephew of Napoleon became Emperor Napoleon III for a time, but fell when France was defeated by Germany in 1870 and the people of Paris called again for revolution.

La Belle Epoque

Meanwhile the lives of the French were changing. Railways made it easier to travel and to transport goods. Farmers found new markets and grew more and better food. Peasants left the countryside to find better-paid work in the towns, but they found it was more uncomfortable to live there than on the land. The people who owned the railways and other companies, however, grew very rich. They welcomed visitors to stylishly furnished salons and showed off their fine clothes at the theatre and the opera. Paris became famous for fashion. No wonder this became known as *La Belle Epoque* (The Beautiful Era). Towards the end of the century, artists like Monet and Renoir, and musicians like Debussy and Ravel, whose music is still enjoyed today, lived there. The Folies Bergère and Moulin-Rouge music halls were popular. France made progress in science and technology too. Marie and Pierre Curie discovered radium and Louis Pasteur found out about the causes of disease and developed vaccination. The Lumière brothers worked on cinema techniques and Blériot improved aviation.

The 20th century

By the 20th century, France's population was falling and Germany was taking the lead in industry and trade. The two countries had been rivals for centuries and fought again in World War I. France and her allies won, but her people were exhausted. Her population did not grow, and like other countries, she suffered during the depression of the 1930s.

In World War II she fought the Germans again but was defeated, and in 1940 was occupied by the armies of Hitler. Some Frenchmen joined the Vichy Government in collaborating with the Germans, but many joined the resistance movement. In 1944, with the help of the British and Americans and the Resistance, General de Gaulle liberated France. Later he became President and ruled France throughout the 1960s. De Gaulle insisted that France should have its own nuclear bomb and not rely on NATO for its defence. He also wanted France to be a powerful member of the European Community and vetoed Britain from joining.

▼ **General de Gaulle on Bastille Day, 1968.**

France 'marries her century'

The shock of the war, a rise in the population, help from America and some clever planning by French politicians led to an 'economic miracle'. France grew strong and rich, and workers' incomes doubled in twenty years. French films were much admired in the 1950s and 1960s, but they sometimes criticized the new France, saying her people were selfish and too interested in material things, instead of caring about people less fortunate than themselves. In 1968 students and workers who were dissatisfied with the government of de Gaulle went on demonstrations and strikes in Paris. Afterwards improvements were made in education and the social services. France in the 1980s still had problems. There was high unemployment in the cities and poverty among small farmers and immigrants from North Africa. But for the majority of the French, the standard of living was much higher than it had been thirty years ago. ■

Frescos

◄ Ceiling of the Sistine Chapel, Rome. Michelangelo worked for four years in a twisted bent-over-backwards position on top of a 20m-high scaffolding to paint a massive series of ceiling frescos. This illustration is just one of very many ceiling panels. It shows God giving life to Adam. The story comes from Genesis in the Bible. Michelangelo suffered from physical pain throughout this time. He wrote in 1510, 'My beard toward Heaven, I feel the back of my brain upon my neck.'

Fresco has been called the most difficult painting technique. It is used for large-scale wall paintings. The wall surface is first coated with a rough layer of plaster, followed by a second smoother layer. The design is drawn on this smooth second layer. A final thin layer of wet plaster is applied, fine enough to let the drawn lines show through. Quickly, before the plaster dries, the artist must paint the picture with pigments mixed with water, adding deeper colour with layers of quick-drying glazes. When the colours dry they become lighter, and the artist has to make allowances for this fact.

The paints immediately soak into the plaster. As the plaster dries, the painting becomes permanently bonded into the wall. As the picture is now part of the structure of the wall, the paint cannot flake off the surface. This is why fresco is so long-lasting.

Because the plaster dries so fast, a whole wall cannot be painted at once. So the picture design is divided into sections, called *giornata* in Italian, meaning 'one day's worth'. Often artists have to work on scaffolding. They always begin at the top of the wall and work down, to prevent drips.

Fresco is a very ancient painting technique and was used in by the Minoans in Crete 1,000 years before Jesus lived. Later it was used in China, Greece, India and Italy. It is not suitable for a damp and humid climate, and so the frescos attempted in Britain did not last. In Mexico frescos by modern artists such as Diego Rivera have been very successful.

Wet fresco, called 'buon' fresco or 'true fresco', is the most common. But there is another kind: fresco 'secco' ('dry' fresco) involves painting onto lime-soaked plaster. Lime-resistant pigments are painted on this surface, so producing a pale matt, chalky appearance. These colours are not completely absorbed by the surface and they may flake off in time.

The most beautiful examples of fresco painting are in Italy. These were painted between 1300 and 1600. There are many different styles and types, but since they were painted in the Middle Ages and during the Renaissance, they mostly tell stories of the life of Jesus and the saints, or events from the Old Testament of the Bible. Luckily many have survived in good condition, due to the long-lasting nature of the technique. ■

Fresco is an Italian word meaning fresh.

See also
Minoans
Paintings
Biography
Giotto
Michelangelo
Rivera

Friction

Meteorites entering the Earth's atmosphere from outer space are burnt up by the heat generated from friction with the air.

When two surfaces rub, a force called friction opposes the movement. A skater moves easily because there is little friction between ice and skates. There is more between shoes and the floor. Friction makes it possible for us to walk. Without friction we would slide about. Friction between rubber tyres and the road allows wheels to grip. Friction between brake-pads and wheels means we can slow and stop machines. Sometimes it can be wasteful. The force needed to overcome friction often creates heat, unwanted sounds and wear.

▼ **When you ride a bike, some friction is helpful and some is a nuisance.**

Friction helps ...

friction helps your hands grip the handlebars

friction stops you when you put the brakes on

friction helps your feet grip the pedals

friction helps the tyres grip the road

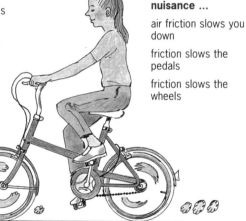

Friction is a nuisance ...

air friction slows you down

friction slows the pedals

friction slows the wheels

Reducing friction

Spacecraft experience enormous heating when re-entering the Earth's atmosphere due to friction with the air. The front of the spacecraft has a special shield which heats to several thousand degrees centigrade; it melts and then 'boils off'. This protects the spacecraft and crew from overheating.

Lubricants such as oil provide a thin layer of liquid between surfaces and cut down friction. This can reduce wear in moving parts of machines. The bearings in machines often have a lubricant sealed inside. Oiling hinges stops them squeaking and makes them move easily. A layer of air can reduce friction. This is why a hovercraft can move easily. Some surfaces, like PTFE plastic used on non-stick pans, cause very little friction. Ball-bearings reduce friction by changing a sliding action to a rolling one. Try pushing a book across a table. Now put marbles between the book and the table and try again. ■

See also
Brakes

Frogs

▲ The colourful red-eyed leaf frog from the rainforests of Costa Rica.

◄ Leopard frog launched from the water by its powerful hind legs.

▼ Poison from the arrow poison frogs of South America is used by local people to tip their arrows.

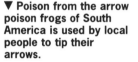

Distribution
Widespread in moist habitats throughout the tropical and temperate zones. They cannot live in salt water.
Largest
Goliath frog from West Africa measures 80 cm fully stretched out, and weighs 3 kg
Smallest
A Cuban frog measures only 8·5 mm
Greatest jumper
South African sharp-nosed frog, less than 10 cm long, can average 3·1 m a leap.
Most poisonous
Golden dart-poison frog from South America. One adult frog contains enough poison to kill 2,200 people.

Subphylum Vertebrata
Class Amphibia
Order Anura (frogs and toads)
Number of species
About 2,600 frogs and toads

◉ See also
Amphibians
Feet and hands
Metamorphosis
Newts
Poisonous animals
Salamanders
Tadpoles
Toads

Frogs are amphibians (able to live in water and on land). They have long powerful hind legs for jumping. Many also have webbed feet for swimming. Frogs have large bulging eyes to help them spot prey. Adult frogs live on land and feed on worms and insects, which they catch with their long sticky tongues.

At a certain time of year, frogs travel to a pond to mate. The male frogs croak to attract the females. Some frogs have pouches under their throats which they can blow out to make a louder sound. Frogs mate and lay their eggs in water. The eggs (frog-spawn) hatch into tiny fish-like tadpoles, which gradually change shape, lose their tails and develop legs as they grow.

Most frogs match their background, so their enemies cannot see them easily. They have slime on their skin which can make them taste bad. Many frogs have poisonous flesh or skin. If an animal eats them, it will feel very ill, and will avoid eating frogs in future. Poisonous frogs often advertise the danger with bright yellow, orange, red and black patterns, so they are easy to avoid. ■

Frost

You may have seen on clear, cold mornings the pretty white sugar-like coating on grass and trees. And if it has been very cold in the night, windows sometimes have a delicate ice-flower pattern on them.

Frost forms at night when the temperature of the air falls below the freezing point of water (0°C, 32°F). Moisture in the air freezes into tiny ice crystals where the air touches blades of grass and branches of trees.

Frost can do a great deal of damage to plants, especially new shoots and buds. When water freezes it expands and pushes outwards. Plants are made up of small packets, or cells, which mainly contain water. A sharp frost freezes the plants quickly, the water expands and breaks the cell walls. That part of the plant is destroyed. When frost freezes the water in mountain rocks they will also break apart. Soil is also broken by the action of frost.

Frost-bite

Very cold air can damage our noses, fingers and ears if they are not well wrapped up. In severe cases of frost-bite the blood does not travel to that part of the body and it may die. ■

In the 17th and 18th centuries there was a widely held view among scientists that frost patterns on windows were a form of vegetation, growing in a similar way to ferns.

The danger of frosts is reduced if the soil is very moist. Some farmers in America have protected their crops by flooding the fields so that a layer of light mist forms over the fields preventing them from cooling rapidly.

◉ See also
Cold
Dew
Ice
Snow
Water

Fruit

When we think of fruit we tend to think of apples, oranges and pears and the other fruits we eat. But 'fruit' is also used to describe the special part of a flowering plant in which seeds develop. Some fruits have a succulent flesh to attract animals which will then spread the seeds after eating the fruit. Others grow wings or hairy parachutes to help them float when carried away by the wind. Each fruit has developed a successful way to spread its seeds and make sure the plant survives.

Development of a fruit

Seeds developing in a fruit produce a special chemical called a 'growth hormone'. This causes the ovary to grow into a fruit.

Pollination and fertilization are described in the article called Flowers.

You can watch this development in the growth of a tomato. After pollination and fertilization the flower petals wither and drop off and the ovary swells into a round green fruit. A tiny brown point on the surface of the fruit opposite the stalk marks the position of the style. If you cut through a tomato and look at one half you will see that each seed is attached to a swollen central part called the placenta. When the tomato has grown to full size it ripens by changing colour from green to red and developing a sweet flavour. It is now ready to spread its seeds.

▼ Tomato developing from fertilized flower.

◀ Plums have a fleshy outer layer surrounding a woody 'stone'. Inside is the kernel, the seed of the plum. This type of fruit is called a drupe. Peaches and apricots are also drupes.

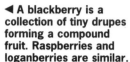

◀ A blackberry is a collection of tiny drupes forming a compound fruit. Raspberries and loganberries are similar.

◀ In false fruits the fleshy part is not formed from the ovary wall. In apples and pears, for instance, the stalk swells out around the ovary to form the fruit.

◀ Pineapples are unusual fruits, as the stalk grows around the fertilized flowers to become the fruit. The dead flower parts become completely enclosed and are removed when you peel the fruit for eating.

◀ Bananas and some grapes have been bred to produce fruit without seeds. As no seeds are produced, new plants can only be obtained by taking cuttings of the parent plant.

◀ Some fruits, such as the fruit of the cuckoopint, 'lords and ladies', are poisonous. Fruits that are poisonous to people are not necessarily poisonous to other animals, which help to spread the seeds by eating the fruit.

Dispersal of soft fruits

Many soft fruits are eaten by animals, especially birds. The seeds inside the fruit pass through the animal's gut without being digested and fall to the ground in the animal's droppings. The seeds are now ready to grow surrounded by suitable fertilizer! The same happens when we eat a tomato, which is why there are always tomato plants at sewage farms. Some fruits, such as those of the parasitic plant mistletoe, are very sticky. The seeds cling to birds' beaks, and are then wiped off into cracks in the bark when the birds clean their beaks. The seed germinates and a new mistletoe plant grows from the crack in the bark.

▲ Yellow-necked mouse with rosehip. The mouse eats the rosehip but it is unable to digest its seeds. These will pass unharmed through the mouse's gut, to germinate in the mouse's droppings.

◄ Lupin seeds are dispersed by 'explosion'. The pod (fruit) splits open and the two halves twist up, shooting out all the seeds.

◄ Burdock seeds are dispersed by animals. The 'burs' catch in an animal's fur, matting the hairs together. These are removed later when the animal grooms its fur.

▲ Coconuts are dispersed by water. The ripe coconut falls into the sea to be carried by the currents and washed up on another beach where it may germinate.

Dispersal of dry fruits

Some fruits use wind to carry them away from the parent plant. Sycamore, field maple and ash all have winged fruits called keys. You could collect some, throw them into the air and watch them spin down like tiny helicopters. In dandelion and thistle, parachutes of hairs support the fruits in the wind. Poppies and orchids produce tiny, lightweight seeds which are scattered when the fruits sway in the breeze.

Plants growing near water, like the coconut palm, may use it to carry their fruits. In waterlilies each seed has its own float to support it when

carried away by the current. Other fruits like balsam explode, scattering their seeds great distances. On a hot day you may hear the popping of the dry pods on broom as they suddenly twist open and fling out their seeds.

Animals spread fruits when they collect them for their food stores. Squirrels may hide hazelnuts underground, and if they are forgotten they are already planted for the next growing season. Other fruits, like cleavers, have hooks which catch in the fur of a passing animal. These are spread when the animal grooms itself and tosses away the fur ball around the fruit. ■

▲ Dandelions are dispersed by the wind. Each fruit is attached by a stalk to a ring of hairs which acts like a parachute.

◉ See also

Flowers
Fruit farming
Nuts
Seeds

Fruit farming

▲ Oranges are grown in groves in straight rows and are usually harvested in winter. As citrus fruits are grown in both the northern and southern hemisphere we can buy them all year round.

Different kinds of fruit grow well in different places according to the climate they need.

Deciduous fruits

Apples are the most important fruit for farming in temperate lands. The trees are grown in large orchards in rows and are harvested by hand and packed into boxes, often sorted into different sizes. Apples last a long time and travel well. Those not sold for eating may be made into cider, a fermented drink, in England and northern France. In northern France they also make calvados, a stronger drink. Pears are less popular as a fresh fruit because they do not store so well, and most are canned. Like apples, plums, peaches, apricots and cherries, they grow on trees. Raspberries, gooseberries, and currants grow on shrubs, and strawberries on the ground; these are 'soft fruits' which perish easily.

Citrus fruits

Oranges, lemons, grapefruit, tangerines and limes are all citrus fruits, and these are grown in large quantities in many parts of the world including the Mediterranean region, and California and Florida in the USA. An orange bought in Britain may have been grown in Spain or Morocco or Israel and brought to Britain by ship. Orange juice drunk in New York may have been made with oranges either from Florida or Brazil. One type of orange grown in Spain is called a 'Seville orange' after the region where they were first grown. Seville oranges are used to make the best type of marmalade.

Tropical fruits

Many fruits grow well only in the warm, wet climates of the tropics. They include mangoes, avocados, pineapples, bananas, papayas and the durian. It is sometimes possible to grow these fruits in other climates in a greenhouse, but frost and cold temperatures will kill the plants. Some pineapples are sold to eat fresh, but many are canned or used for juice. Bananas are the most important export for some of the countries of Central America, such as El Salvador, Honduras and Panama. Most are exported in container ships to the USA. ■

▶ Pineapples growing in Hawaii. These plants need a warm climate and plenty of rain so they grow best in tropical countries. The part we eat is the swollen stem. The diamond-shaped segments of skin are the fruitlets which fused with the stem after they flowered.

See also
Fruit

Fuel

A fuel is a material that is used to produce heat or other forms of energy. Energy is vital to almost every human activity, from cooking to building a skyscraper.

Fossil fuels

Nearly all fuels produce heat by being burned. Most of the world's energy comes from the so-called 'fossil fuels': coal, oil and natural gas. These are the remains of plants and animals that lived millions of years ago. Fossil fuels will not last for ever. It is estimated that the world's supply of oil will only last for between another 30 and 60 years, and coal for 250 years. Fossil fuels will eventually run out. There is an urgent need to develop something to replace them.

Wood as a fuel

At present about 14 per cent of the world's energy is believed to come from burning wood. Wood is the main fuel for about 2 billion people, most of them living in the Third World. In some areas whole forests have been cut down for fuel. Unlike coal, oil or natural gas, new wood can be grown quite quickly. Unfortunately, not enough trees are being planted. Trees are being cut down faster than new ones can grow, causing a severe shortage of wood.

Nuclear fuels

At present only 4 per cent of the world's energy comes from sources other than wood and fossil fuels. Nuclear energy is the most important of these, and so it is the most obvious power source to expand. However, nuclear power-stations are extremely expensive. If an accident occurs at one there can be great dangers, as was shown by the fire at the Chernobyl reactor in the Ukraine (then part of the USSR) in 1986. Getting rid of nuclear waste materials is very costly, and it can lead to serious pollution.

New fuels

There are a number of new fuels which could be developed. Many countries simply bury their household rubbish. In Britain, for example, 70 million tonnes of household rubbish are thrown away every year. This rubbish contains the same amount of energy as 20 million tonnes of coal. A number of cities, including London, Amsterdam, Frankfurt and Paris, now have power-stations that burn household rubbish to produce electricity.

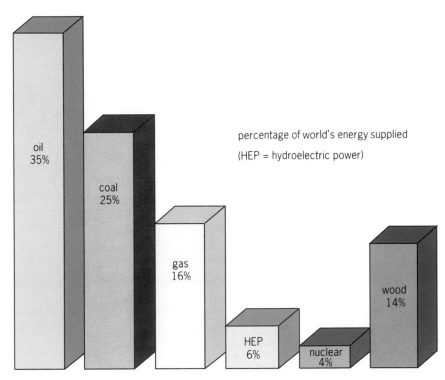

percentage of world's energy supplied

(HEP = hydroelectric power)

▲ How the world gets its energy. Oil provides more of the world's energy than any other fuel. But wood is the most widely used fuel for cooking and heating.

Many plants, such as maize, cassava and sugar cane, are rich in sugars. It is possible to collect these sugars and turn them into alcohol. Alcohol is a valuable concentrated fuel. Brazil is one country that has been trying to reduce its oil imports by growing these plants. Many Brazilian cars use alcohol instead of petrol.

Fuel cells

Fuel cells are quite a new way of producing electricity. They change the chemical energy in hydrogen and oxygen into electrical energy. A fuel cell power-station has been built in New York. It takes oxygen from the air and uses various fuels such as alcohol and natural gas to provide hydrogen. The electricity produced is fed into the city's supply. Most fuel cells are expensive and quite large. Some are already in use in the United States Space Shuttle and in space laboratories.

Making fuel go further

The other way of making existing supplies of fuel last longer is to use them more efficiently. Petrol and diesel engines are being developed which are lighter in weight and which use fuel more efficiently. Insulating homes and factories reduces heat loss and means that less fuel is needed to warm these buildings. Even switching off electric lights conserves fuel. ■

See also
Coal
Electricity supply
Energy
Forests
Insulation
Nuclear power
Oil

Biography
Diesel

Funerals

Saying goodbye to a person who has died is very important. A funeral is the last rite of respect by families and friends, and everyone tries to be there. Religious people teach that death is not the end of life and that it is wrong to be completely miserable when a person dies. So funerals are often a mixture of sadness and hope, loss and celebration.

There are different traditions about what should be done with the body of a dead person. Hindus, Buddhists and Sikhs prefer cremation (burning). Hindus like to scatter the ashes of the person on the River Ganges if this is possible. They believe that all life is one and that returning the remains of a person to a sacred river is a good end for them.

Jews and Muslims prefer to bury their dead. Jews teach that everyone should have the simplest coffin available because all men and women are equal before God. For the same reason Muslims are buried in simple white robes. Jews are buried facing Jerusalem and Muslims face towards Mecca.

Christians nowadays can choose burial or cremation. The words in most Christian funeral services remind people of the central Christian teaching of the resurrection of the dead.

'Earth to earth, ashes to ashes, dust to dust: in sure and certain hope of the resurrection to eternal life through our Lord Jesus Christ, who died, was buried, and rose again for us.' ■

See also
Burial mounds
Death

Fungi

Moulds, mildews, yeasts and mushrooms are all fungi. Fungi live either on the dead remains of animals or plants, or as parasites on living things.

Yeasts have only one cell, but all other fungi are made of fine threads of cells called hyphae. These form a tangled mass called mycelium. Mushrooms are made up of interwoven hyphae and grow from a network of mycelium underground.

Fungi reproduce by making millions of microscopic spores in special reproductive hyphae. Mushrooms are reproductive hyphae. Each spore can make a new mycelium, which is why fungi are so common. Fungi grow so fast that a single spore can produce more than 1 km (^{2}/$_3$ mile) of hyphae in 24 hours.

Decomposers

Fungi which decompose (rot) dead plants, animals and their wastes, break them down into chemicals which soak into the soil, keeping it fertile for plants.

Disease carriers

Many fungi cause disease when they grow on living things. Athlete's foot is a fungus which infects skin between the toes, and farmer's lung fungus can infect vital organs causing serious harm. Rusts and smuts are fungi which cause plant diseases. In the 1840s a fungal disease called potato blight wiped out the Irish potato crop causing a million deaths from starvation, and a mass migration to the USA. Over 5,000 types of fungi attack crop and garden plants. Fungi can attack an incredible number of different materials: cloth, paint, leather, waxes, jet engine fuel, wire insulation, photographic film and even the coating of camera lenses.

Useful fungi

For centuries yeasts have been used in breadmaking and brewing. A mould produces penicillin, which stops bacteria growing. This was the first antibiotic to be discovered. Other antibiotics are also produced by moulds. ■

Over 100,000 species of fungi are known but it is thought that as many as 200,000 have yet to be discovered.

The hyphae of some rainforest fungi can spread for up to 500 m in the soil.

▶ **Bracket fungus growing on a dying tree. You can only see part of the fungus. The rest, the mycelium, is growing inside the tree.**

See also
Antibiotics
Ecosystems
Mushrooms
Penicillin
Spores
Yeasts

Biography
Fleming

Fur

The African naked mole rat is probably the most unusual mammal without hair. They live in shallow tunnels underground and remain hairless all their lives.

Fur is the name given to the coat of hair found on almost all mammals. Only some very unusual mammals like whales, dolphins and ourselves are not covered in fur. Human beings have only small patches of hair instead of a complete fur coat like monkeys and apes. But most mammals are born without any fur.

Fur is made up of at least one layer of hairs which grow out of a mammal's skin. All hairs are made of a tough protein called keratin. Feathers and scales are also made of this protein.

The hairs of fur are tightly packed together to make a dense layer that traps air. It is the fur and air together that act as a warm, insulating blanket. Without the fur it would be very difficult for mammals to keep up their temperature.

Often, fur is composed of two layers of hair. An under layer of shortish hairs forms the main pelt, while longer 'guard' hairs stick out further. Both types of hair may be coloured. The normal range of colours is from white through buffs, browns and reddish browns to black. White is due to a lack of colouring, while the other shades are caused by differing amounts of the dark brown pigment, melanin.

◄ The striped fur of a skunk acts as a warning to other animals. The striped skunk is the most common species of skunk in the USA.

The colour and patterning of fur are often important for camouflage or display. The spots on a leopard break up its outline in the dappled sunlight of a forest. The striking black and white patterns of a skunk are a warning to other animals. ■

See also
Camouflage
Feathers
Fur farming
Hair
Skin

▼ Fur can be made up of two layers. The longer guard hairs cover the much shorter under hairs.

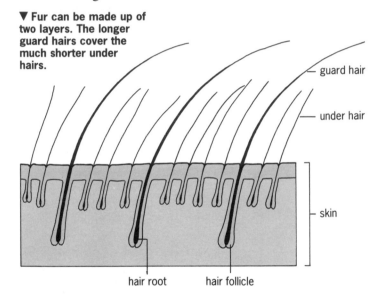

guard hair

under hair

skin

hair root   hair follicle

Fur farming

Animal fur has long been used by people for clothing and rugs. In Siberia, for example, some tribes kept reindeer, whose fur was used as rugs to lie on in their shelters. Gowns of reindeer fur reached down to below the knee, and long boots of deer-skin were tied about the ankle with leather thongs. Squirrel tails were tied around the head against the cold.

In the modern world fur is still used for clothing in very cold climates.

The fur is often taken from animals kept on fur farms. The animals are kept in cages. They are fed and reared until their fur is ready to be used. Then the animal is killed and skinned and the fur used to make a fur coat. One large coat of mink fur, one of the most expensive, may be made from the pelts of 100 animals.

Many people consider fur farming to be cruel. Some groups of campaigners for animal rights have released animals from cages as a form of protest. ■

Fur farming is carried out in Canada, Russia and the USA.

A pelt is an animal skin with the fur still on it.

See also
Inuit
Reindeer

Furniture

Furniture is useful in various ways:

- for sitting on (stools, benches, chairs)
- for putting things on (tables, stands, desks)
- for sleeping on (beds)
- for storing things (chests, cupboards, wardrobes)

Some furniture, such as a sofa bed, performs more than one function. Other furniture is designed to meet a specialized need, such as a cabinet to hold a TV or video recorder.

Like clothes, furniture has to be chosen to meet our needs: we use it every day and it needs to be comfortable. The designers of school furniture design chairs, tables and work tops to fit children of different sizes. This is important, as sitting on a chair that is too big or too small can be tiring. However, furniture can sometimes be too comfortable. Scientists are finding that people who spend too much time in easy chairs can develop back pains in later life. Such discoveries have led to a science called ergonomics, which studies how furniture and lighting can best be designed to suit our life-style.

Furniture makers use wood, glass, cork, cane, metal, plastic and a variety of other materials, even folder cardboard. Strong, lightweight furniture can be made from such materials as hollow metal tubing, laminated woods and fibreglass. Foam rubber and new spring devices make possible thin, but hard-wearing upholstery.

The first pieces of furniture were made in prehistoric times of slabs of stone and chunks of wood. The village at Skara Brae in Orkney built in the New Stone Age includes sleeping places and benches built into the walls.

In time, people tried to make furniture that was beautiful as well as useful. Wealthy Egyptians had fine carved and painted beds, chairs and tables as long as 4,000 years ago. Egyptian styles influenced much of the ancient world including the Greeks and the Romans, who used marble, bronze, terracotta, ivory and bone in their furniture. For thousands of years all fine furniture was designed to suit the tastes of the nobility and other wealthy people: comfort and practical use were not really important.

In western Europe during the Middle Ages (1100–1500) people spent much of their time outdoors, except when they ate and slept, and so needed little furniture except tables, chests, and benches. Beds and chairs were for the privileged rich.

Since the end of the Middle Ages many different styles of furniture have been made. Early furniture was often sturdy and heavy. As tastes changed and furniture makers learnt new methods, furniture became lighter, more elegant and showed finer craftsmanship. The story of fine furniture can be seen as a series of styles becoming popular for a time and then falling from fashion. Designers sometimes revived earlier styles and adapted them to fit the tastes of the time. By the end of the 18th century, some of the best designers had become famous, although the furniture named after them was made by other people who copied their designs.

As ordinary people's standard of living improved from about 1800 onwards, so did the demand for furniture. Eventually this demand was met by mass-producing furniture in factories. Most 20th-century furniture has been machine-made. Recently, furniture designers have chosen clean, simple shapes, often using new materials, to try and reflect the world we live in.

In the Middle Ages, landowners and church officials travelled frequently and usually took their furniture with them on long journeys. It was quite common for visitors to bring along their own beds and other pieces of furniture.

An antique is an object many years old that has artistic value. Most antique collectors believe that antique furniture should be at least 100 years old. Others add that it must be made in a historical style that is no longer in use, and that it must have been made while that style was in fashion.

Famous furniture makers
Thomas Chippendale
1718–1779
Robert Adam
1728–1792
Thomas Sheraton
1751–1806

◀ This photograph shows the dining room of a successful sugar merchant's house in Bristol, England, as it would have looked around the end of the 18th century. Its fine furniture, glassware and decoration tell of the owner's wealth and were probably intended to impress visitors.

▲ This photograph shows a Puritan living room as it would have looked in New England, USA, in the 17th century. The furniture reflects the Puritan belief that God wanted people to live simply, without wasteful, showy ornamentation in their homes. The room also has a bare, harsh feel about it, reflecting the struggle that faced early European settlers.

Furniture developed differently throughout the world, depending on the needs of the people in a particular country or region. Chinese furniture, for instance, was carved so expertly that the wooden joints fitted together tightly without glue, screws or pegs. This allowed the wood to expand and contract as the temperature changed. The Japanese traditionally used few pieces of furniture. Because of the threat of earthquakes they lived in light, one-storey buildings. These included movable partitions that could be used to create different arrangements of space inside a house, so any furniture had to be small and portable. Furniture consisted of screens, storage chests, writing tables and head- and arm-rests. People sat on the floor and slept on mats, so beds and chairs were unnecessary. ■

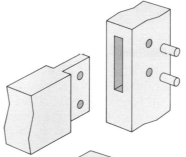

▶ A mortise and tenon joint with dowels to give extra strength. Chairs frequently use this joint.

▲ The lounge of a typical 1930s suburban house. It is furnished and decorated in a style known as Art Deco, after the styles exhibited at the *Exposition des Arts Décoratifs* held in Paris in 1925. This was a popular fashion before World War II.

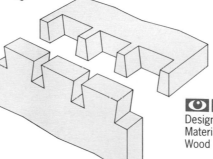

▶ A dovetail joint is used in making drawers. The wedge shapes prevent it being pulled apart.

See also

Designers
Materials
Wood

Gabon

Area 267,667 sq km
(103,347 sq miles)
Capital Libreville
Population 1,151,000
Language French, Fang,
others
Religion Christian, Muslim,
Traditional
Government Republic
Currency 1 African
Financial Community (CFA)
franc = 100 centimes

See also
Africa

Gabon is a hot and wet African country. It has a narrow coastal plain, but high plateaux and mountains covered by thick forest make up most of the country.

Gabon has a wide variety of wildlife, including elephants, gorillas and leopards. Most of the people are farmers, but the country's wealth comes from its minerals, including oil, manganese and uranium.

In 1849, France founded Libreville, now capital of Gabon, on the coast. Libreville, which means 'free town', was a home for freed slaves. Gabon was later ruled by France, but it became independent in 1960. ∎

Galapagos Islands

The islands belong to Ecuador.

See also
Tortoises

Biography
Darwin

These islands are in the Pacific Ocean, 1,000 km (600 miles) west of South America and almost on the Equator. There are thirteen main islands and more than 40 small ones. All the islands are volcanic, some of them still active. There is hardly any fresh water because the climate is so dry. Very few people live permanently on the islands, but thousands of tourists visit them every year.

The biologist Charles Darwin studied the plants, birds and animals of the islands in 1835, and found many species which were different from those on the mainland. These discoveries supported his theory of evolution by 'natural selection'.

The islands are now a National Park, and the Darwin Research Station is on Santa Cruz. ∎

▼ The Galapagos Islands have many unique species of plant and animal life, including the giant tortoise which gives its name to the islands (galápagos is the Spanish word for 'tortoises').

Galaxies

Our Sun and all the stars you can see in the night sky belong to a giant family of stars that we call our Galaxy. On a dark night, the Milky Way looks like a hazy band across the sky. It is the light from countless stars in the Galaxy.

If you could go far out in space to look at the Galaxy, you would see a flat, circular shape with a bulge in the middle and a pattern of spiral arms. Between the stars there are giant clouds of gas and dust, some of them shining brightly and some dark. Beyond our own, there are many more galaxies scattered all through the Universe.

Kinds of galaxies

Ours is a spiral galaxy, about 100,000 light years across. Many large galaxies have beautiful spiral shapes. There are also elliptical galaxies that are just flattened balls of stars. The third kind are irregular, which means they have no particular shape. Some are very strange and look as if they have exploded or might be two galaxies colliding. Many of these galaxies send out strong radio waves that can be picked up by radio telescopes. Galaxies tend to cluster together in space. Our own Galaxy belongs to a cluster that we call the Local Group.

Some well-known galaxies

The nearest galaxies to us are the two Magellanic Clouds. They look like little clouds of stars and can be seen only from the southern hemisphere. They are about 180,000 light years away. The biggest galaxy in our Local Group is called the Andromeda Galaxy. It can just be seen by eye as a misty patch. It is a spiral 130,000 light years across. One of the biggest galaxies that astronomers have studied is an elliptical one called M87. It is a million light years across and 50 million light years away. ∎

▶ The spiral galaxy in Andromeda is just over 2 million light years away and is our nearest big galaxy. There are two small elliptical galaxies close to it.

▶ An elliptical galaxy, called M49, photographed with a large astronomical telescope. This giant ball of stars is 42 million light years away and measures 50,000 light years across.

See also
Cosmology
Light years
Milky Way
Stars
Universe

Gambia

Gambia is the smallest country in Africa. It stretches for 320 km (200 miles) along both banks of the River Gambia, but it is only about 35 km (22 miles) wide.

There are two ferries but no bridge across the river. One is at Banjul, and the other upstream where the trans-Gambia highway links northern and southern Senegal. Elsewhere dug-out canoes and other small boats carry passengers, often balancing a bicycle or a motor bike.

Gambia has two seasons; a long dry season from October to May, and a short, hot, wet season. The natural vegetation is savannah and there is swamp forest near the river. But most of the land has been cleared for farming. Groundnuts (peanuts) are the main crop.

Banjul, the capital, was once a port for the slave trade. Now hotels for tourists lie to the south of the town. The Gambia was a British colony from 1843 to 1965 when it became an independent member of the Commonwealth. Gambians speak English as well as several African languages spoken by their neighbours in Senegal. ■

Area 11,295 sq km
(4,361 sq miles)
Capital Banjul
Population 695,886
Language English, Malinke, Wolof, Fulani, others
Religion Muslim, Christian, Traditional
Government Republic
Currency 1 dalasi = 100 butut

See also
Africa
Parks
Senegal
Slave trade

Gambling

Gamblers try to win money by predicting the future before it happens. Gambling is common in games such as roulette, poker and backgammon, where chance has a part to play.

People gamble on the results of sporting events such as horse races, boxing matches and football matches. When they do the pools, they try to predict which football matches will be drawn next Saturday.

When someone places a bet, the money they pay over is called their stake. In horse racing, the amount which can be won depends on the odds set by the bookmaker. Odds of 10 to 1 mean that if someone bets £1 on a horse, and it wins, the bookmaker will pay them £10 plus their original £1 stake. If the horse loses, the bookmaker keeps the £1. A horse with a better chance of winning will have lower odds on it, for example 2 to 1.

People who gamble almost always end up losing money, because the odds are calculated so that bookmakers, casinos and amusement arcades always make a profit. ■

Gambling machines are sometimes called 'one-armed bandits'. Most people lose money on them, but people do become addicted to playing them.

See also
Probability

Game birds

Subphylum
Vertebrata
Class
Aves
Order
Galliformes
Number of species
About 245
True pheasants
48 species varying in size
from 40 to 235 cm
Partridges
84 species from 16 to
72 cm
Old World quails
10 species from 14 to
20 cm
American quails
36 species from 18 to
36 cm

Lady Amherst's pheasant

golden pheasant

peacock

▶ **Pheasants and their
relatives have some of the
most attractive and exotic
feathers in the bird world.**

The largest feathers in the
world belong to the crested
argus, a pheasant with tail
feathers over 15 cm wide
and 150 cm long.

Most grouse have feathered
legs and feet.

Throughout history birds have been hunted
for food or sport. Those more commonly hunted
in Europe and North America are pheasants,
partridges and grouse, which are often called game
birds. Bustards, quails and some wading birds,
such as snipe and woodcock, are also traditionally
game birds, as are turkeys and guineafowl in
some parts of the world.

Ducks, geese and swans, which have also been
hunted for centuries, are generally called wildfowl
and not game birds.

▶ **A male and female red
jungle fowl with their
young. Despite their
name, jungle fowl have
been domesticated for
many centuries.**

Many game birds are carefully protected and even
reared by gamekeepers to ensure there are
sufficient numbers available for the next shooting
season. Hunting is also usually controlled by law
so that shooting does not take place when the
birds are nesting.

Pheasants

Members of the pheasant family are heavy,
ground-living birds with short, rounded wings
and strong feet and claws for scratching at the
soil to find food. There are pheasants, or their
relatives, in most parts of the world, yet most
never travel far.

The family includes the partridges and the
tiny quails, some of which make amazingly long
migrations. True pheasants are popular birds and
are often kept in captivity because many of them
have beautiful feathers, especially in their long
and wonderfully marked tails. Peacocks and jungle
fowl are close relatives of the true pheasants.

While pheasants nest and find their food on the
ground, many will fly into trees and bushes to
sleep safe from predators at night.

◉ **See also**
Ducks, geese and swans
Wading birds

common pheasant

Grouse

Some grouse are found in dense forests, others on snowy mountain tops. Those species that live on mountains or in the north are often called ptarmigan and they moult into a white winter plumage for camouflage in the snow.

Although grouse are at home on the ground, they will also feed on trees, eating fresh shoots. All male grouse defend territories they have chosen. In spring, a red wattle above the eyes of the male becomes larger. Some have elaborate displays which often take place at leks, 'dancing grounds' where males strut around showing off to females.

Jungle fowl

Scientists believe that the red jungle fowl is the ancestor of our domestic fowl or chicken. It is a forest bird which lives wild in south-east Asia. It has a long tail and a red 'comb' along the top of its head. Like other pheasants it has horny 'spurs' on its legs which it uses when defending its territory. Jungle fowl have been domesticated since the 5th century BC and possibly even earlier. ■

Ganges

The Ganges is a large river that rises in the foothills of the Himalayas in northern India and flows south-eastward into the Bay of Bengal, a distance of about 2,506 km (1,557 miles).

In India it is considered a sacred river, and thousands of Hindu pilgrims travel each year to holy cities along its banks.

For most of its length the Ganges flows across the broad, flat Gangetic Plain as a wide, sluggish, meandering river. As it crosses Bangladesh, the Ganges is joined by the great Brahmaputra River, and together they form the largest delta in the world, 300 km (200 miles) across.

The rich sediments deposited by the river have made the Ganges delta and the Gangetic Plain two of the most fertile and densely populated regions in the world. ■

The Hindi word for the river is *Ganga*.

The most famous holy city on the Ganges is Varanasi.

See also
Bangladesh
Hindus
India
Rivers

Gangs and gangsters

Criminals often work in gangs (groups organized to carry out crime on a large scale). There are underworld gangs in every major country of the world. Many of the biggest gangs are in the USA.

Some modern gangsters are involved in the illegal drugs trade, smuggling and selling cocaine, heroin and other drugs.

Probably the most notorious time for gangs and gangsters was during the Prohibition period in the USA. Between 1920 and 1933 a change to the American constitution banned the manufacture and sale of alcoholic drinks. The ban did not stop people wanting to drink, and gangs were formed to supply liquor. They ran illegal drinking dens, called speakeasies.

The best-known of the prohibition gangsters was Al Capone, of Chicago. He became a multimillionaire.

During the days of the American Wild West, many outlaws such as Jesse James and Billy the Kid ran gangs. In Australia the most famous gang leader of the last century was Ned Kelly.

Gangs operated in England in the past, too. For almost 150 years the smugglers of England's south coast, mostly in Kent and Sussex, imported silk and brandy, gin, tea, tobacco and other goods, until customs duties were made so low in the 1840s that smuggling ceased to be profitable. ■

See also
Drugs
Mafia
Outlaws
Smugglers
Biography
James, Jesse
Kelly

Gardens

▶ Garden of Tofukuji Temple in Kyoto, Japan. The rocks and the patterns in the sand are carefully designed to make a calm and peaceful place.

The Muslims designed formal gardens with pools and narrow canals which ran through patios and courtyards. They introduced these features to Spain during the centuries when they ruled there. The Mughal emperors of India made similar gardens.

◉ See also
Flowers
Herbs
Market gardens

▼ This cottage garden in Surrey, England is densely planted with perennial flowering plants. Foxgloves and Canterbury bells are blooming. The tall hollyhocks on the left are in bud.

From prehistoric times, once people stopped wandering from place to place and set up permanent settlements, they began to control the wild ground on the doorstep. At first gardens were simple clearings in the forest, where food crops could be grown, and domestic animals such as chickens and pigs could be watched over in safety.

Gradually food growing and livestock rearing expanded to full-scale farming, and the ground immediately around the home became a real garden, where special plants were grown. In the medieval garden the main plants were herbs. Some, such as parsley, thyme, rosemary and sage, were grown to flavour food. Others, such as comfrey and feverfew, were grown to make medicines for treating sickness.

Gradually, gardeners grew more and more flowers, and now most gardens are a mixture of decorative plants and crops, in a sheltered, private space next to the house.

Traditional gardens

There are many different styles of garden. The English cottage garden is packed with all kinds of flowers, fruit and vegetables, all grown for use in the house, but combining to make a colourful display.

By contrast, the Japanese traditionally have gardens which are designed to strict rules, and which use such things as raked sand, rugged rocks, and clipped shrubs to create a kind of miniature landscape, the ideal setting for quiet meditation. In the hot countries around the Mediterranean, water is an important feature of gardens, used in still, reflecting formal canals and pools, or as sparkling, cooling fountains.

Most of the big houses, mansions and stately homes of the past had very extensive gardens. If the climate was harsh, there would be high walls built for protection. In colder regions, glasshouses and conservatories would often be built, so that more delicate plants such as grape vines and peach trees could be grown. Large numbers of gardeners would be employed to mow the lawns, cultivate the soil, clip the hedges and sweep leaves from the paths.

Modern houses have much smaller gardens, and most are now designed to make them easy to care for. Neat tidy lawns are a common feature, because they are quick and easy to maintain with lawnmowers. Weeds are controlled with chemical weedkiller, and chemicals are also used to kill harmful insects and other pests.

Wildlife gardens

Now that people are becoming more concerned about the state of the environment, disappearing wildlife, and pollution, some people are beginning to create another new style of garden. Instead of killing weeds and pests, they are encouraging more living things to share their garden. They are gardening organically, which means they have stopped spraying chemicals. They are also planting flowers that will attract more insects, and provide food for the birds. Many of them are making ponds to provide a home for wildlife, and doing everything they can to bring nature closer to their homes.

Lots of schools are making wildlife gardens too, so that children can study nature right outside the classroom. ■

Gases

Gases are all around us, for we live surrounded by air which is a mixture of gases. We have to breathe air to stay alive. Air, like all gases, spreads out to fill any container in which it is placed. Solids and liquids do not do this. Many gases, like those in the air, are invisible and have no smell or taste.

Air: a mixture of gases

Air is a mixture of at least nine different gases. These gases have many important uses in industry. Large amounts of oxygen, for example, are used in making steel from iron. Oxygen is blown through molten iron to burn up the impurities in the iron and turn it into steel. Sometimes oxygen is mixed with another gas called acetylene and burned. The oxy-acetylene flame, as it is called, is so hot that it can melt steel and so can be used to cut steel or weld (join) pieces of steel together.

Nitrogen makes up 78 per cent of air. It is very hard to make things burn in it, so nitrogen is often used to fill the containers where explosives and oil are stored. But the main uses of nitrogen are in making fertilizers, explosives, dyes and drugs.

Carbon dioxide and fires

Carbon dioxide is used for fire extinguishers. When the gas leaves the fire extinguisher, it forms a 'blanket' over the fire as it is heavier than air. This cuts off the air and helps to put the fire out. Large quantities of carbon dioxide are used in making fizzy drinks by dissolving the gas in the drink under high pressure. When the cap of the bottle is removed, the carbon dioxide bubbles up.

▲ Welding two pieces of metal together using an oxy-acetylene flame.

Helium is very light and does not burn. It is used to fill weather balloons and modern airships. Hydrogen was once used for airships, but unfortunately it burns too easily. Nowadays hydrogen is mostly used in making margarine and, together with nitrogen, in making fertilizers. Tubes filled with neon or other rare gases glow when electricity flows through them. They are used for making advertising signs that light up at night.

Gases as fuels

Natural gas, the gas burned in cookers or central heating boilers, was formed from the remains of plants and animals that lived millions of years ago. ■

◉ See also
Air
Balloons and airships
Fertilizers
Helium
Iron and steel
Neon
Oxygen

Biography
Boyle
Priestley

Geiger counters

Radioactivity can be detected with an instrument called a Geiger counter. Some substances are radioactive and send out tiny, invisible particles called alpha and beta particles. The Geiger counter measures the amount of radioactivity by counting these particles. Each particle produces a little electric current that can either be seen as a reading on a meter or heard as a click through earphones or a loudspeaker. The level of radiation is given by the number of clicks. High levels of radiation can be very dangerous, and so it is important to detect them quickly. With a Geiger counter you do not need to keep looking at the meter because you can easily hear when you are approaching danger. ■

The Geiger counter was invented in 1912 by Hans Geiger, a German scientist.

◀ The Geiger counter is also known as the Geiger-Müller counter, because Geiger improved his invention in 1928 with the help of another German scientist, Walther Müller.

◉ See also
Radiation

Geological time

How old is the Earth? How long ago did the dinosaurs live? Did human beings live with the dinosaurs? These are all questions to do with geological time: the way in which Earth scientists divide up the record of the rocks. The amounts of time involved are huge: millions of years, and even thousands of millions of years.

Relative dating

Geologists (Earth scientists) realized a long time ago that the Earth was very ancient. They could see great piled up layers of rocks that had been laid down slowly on the ocean floor. They could see the effects of great movements in the Earth's crust which lifted great masses of rock up, folded them, or turned them over. They could see the great changes that had taken place through time in the fossil record.

It soon became clear to these early geologists, men such as James Hutton (1726–1797) and Charles Lyell (1797–1875), that layers of sedimentary rocks, such as mudstones, sandstones and limestones, could be arranged in sequences. The oldest rocks were usually at the bottom of the pile, and the younger ones at the top. They saw the layers of rock like the layers in a great cake. If you look at a high cliff made from sedimentary rocks, you can often see this pattern.

The first rule of relative dating then, was to assume that the oldest rocks in an area were the lowest ones in the sequence. The second, very important rule was that the fossils in these rocks could give the age. It soon became clear that the history of the Earth could be divided into hundreds of time units, each represented by a different set of fossils. Particular fossils, or groups of fossils, could be used as guides to the age of rocks in any part of the world. These techniques of relative dating are still used in the oil industry to identify the ages of rocks from boreholes. Even a tiny sample with some small fossils can pin down the age to within a few million years.

Absolute dating

But how can geologists talk about ages in terms of so many million years? The absolute, or precise, ages can be obtained from particular kinds of rocks which crystallized rapidly with some radioactive materials in them. These are mainly igneous rocks which form under conditions of high temperature. The basis of absolute dating is the fact that radioactive elements decay, or break down, at a constant rate. The rate of this decay is known. For example, it would take 4,510 million years for half of a sample of uranium-238 to break down to become lead-206. By measuring the exact proportions of these two elements in a rock sample, geologists can get a measurement of how long ago the crystals formed. ∎

▲ Grand Canyon National Park, Arizona, USA. The canyon is the deeply eroded course of the River Colorado. The river has cut down through 2 billion years of rock layers.

▶ Cliffs at Hunstanton, Norfolk, England showing three layers of rock, each formed at different times in the Cretaceous period. The ginger brown sandstone at the bottom is about 130 million years old, the white chalk at the top about 75 million years old.

Era	Period	Epoch	Millions of years ago		Evolution and events
CAINOZOIC	QUATERNARY	Holocene			
		Pleistocene	2		The Great Ice Age. Modern humans appear
	TERTIARY	Pliocene			
		Miocene			Many mammals appear
		Oligocene			Alpine earth movements create Alps, Himalayas and Rockies
		Eocene			
		Palaeocene	66		
MESOZOIC	CRETACEOUS				Dinosaurs die out
					Chalk deposited
			135		
	JURASSIC				Many dinosaurs
			205		
	TRIASSIC				First dinosaurs and mammals
			250		
PALAEOZOIC	PERMIAN				Continents move together to form
			290		the giant landmass Pangaea
	CARBONIFEROUS				Great coal swamp forests
			355		
	DEVONIAN				Caledonian earth movements. Ferns and fish
			412		
	SILURIAN				First land plants
			435		
	ORDOVICIAN				Animals without backbones
			510		
	CAMBRIAN				Trilobites. First shellfish
			550		
PROTEROZOIC	PRECAMBRIAN				First jellyfish and worms. Algae

See also
Dinosaurs
Earth
Evolution of living things
Fossils
Geologists
Rocks

Georgian Britain 1714–1830

The Pretenders
There were two attempts by
the Stuarts to win back the
throne. The first, in Scotland,
1715, was led by James II's
son James, called the Old
Pretender because of his
pretence (claim) to the
throne.
The second, in 1745, was
led by James's son Charles
Stuart, the Young Pretender,
Bonnie Prince Charlie. His
army was defeated at the
battle of Culloden, Scotland,
in 1746.

◀ **This painting of Robert Vernon Atherton and his family is by Arthur Devis. In the background is their fine country house, built in the Georgian, classical style. The park was an important feature of the homes of wealthy people in the 18th century.**

For more than a hundred years, from 1714 to 1830, the British throne was occupied by four kings named George. The century during which they ruled is often called the Georgian period. It was a time of both elegance and great poverty.

Politics

George I was the Elector (ruler) of Hanover in Germany. His grandmother had been a British princess and, after the death of Queen Anne, he was chosen to be King of the United Kingdom because he was a Protestant. George IV was his great-great-grandson. The Georgian period really extended through the reign of George IV's brother, William IV, who died in 1837.

George I spoke no English. As a result the real power passed into the hands of Britain's first prime minister, Robert Walpole, who used to talk to the king in French. Walpole remained prime minister into the reign of George II, who spoke English, but with a strong German accent. All through the Georgian period the powers of the kings grew less, and those of the prime ministers and Parliament grew greater.

None of the Georges was wise. George III in his later years had an unfortunate disease called porphyria that sent him mad, so his son, later George IV, had to rule on his behalf for nine years as Prince Regent. When the Georges did interfere in politics they were not very competent and tended to make a mess of things.

During the Georgian period Britain lost one empire, the thirteen North American colonies. But it was building up another in Australia and India before the period ended.

Country life

The backbone of the country was its country folk, the rich landed squires and the farmers and the ordinary people who worked on the land. The wealth of a typical country gentleman, whether he had a title or was just plain 'Mr', came from his large estates. The country gentleman lived in a very large house, and if he was rich enough he rebuilt it or added to it to make it larger still.

Usually the landowner was also the local Justice of the Peace, and he and his fellows virtually supplied the local government of the day. Sport, particularly hunting and shooting, was one of their main occupations. Landlords were very jealous of their rights when it came to preserving game, and poachers who were caught received very rough justice. Some, along with other criminals, were hanged. Many were transported to the colonies in North America. After those colonies were lost, they were sent to a new penal settlement in Botany Bay, Australia.

Landlords spent a great deal of time improving their estates. Some improvements brought better conditions for the workers. Others made their lives worse. This was the time of enclosures, when the old open field system gave way to more manageable farms, and of changes in farming techniques known as the agricultural revolution. In the Highlands of Scotland tenants were evicted and forced to emigrate to make way for sheep-grazing.

Rich and poor

The more fashionable rich people also had houses in London, and they went there and to Edinburgh in winter for 'the season'. Elegantly-dressed ladies and gentlemen attended a series of balls, parties and other social gatherings.

It also became the fashion to go to a 'watering place', in other words, a spa, where people could drink the mineral waters and recover from the rich meals and hectic life of London. Bath, Tunbridge Wells and Harrogate all developed as spa towns.

The state of the poor varied widely. Some were able to lead moderately comfortable lives, but many were housed in leaking, ramshackle cottages, and badly fed. Bread, cheese, peas, turnips, and later potatoes, were the mainstay of their diet. Meat was often too expensive for them to afford it.

In such homes and on such poor food about half the children died before they were five years old. People who were unemployed or unable to work were sent to the poorhouse, where they lived and died in appalling conditions.

For those poor children who survived there was little education, except for a few village schools. People with money could send their children to private schools, or engage governesses and tutors for them.

Trade and industry

Overseas trade brought wealth to merchants, bankers and businessmen. Some of that trade was in African slaves, which made the two ports, Bristol and Liverpool, extremely rich. Bristol was already an important city, but Liverpool grew from a little port with 5,000 inhabitants to a flourishing city.

From other ports Britain exported butter, cloth, corn, herrings, lead, tools, weapons and all kinds of utensils made in Birmingham, Manchester and other growing towns. British ships, protected by a powerful Royal Navy, returned with sugar from the West Indies and spices, fabrics, tea, indigo dye and other valuable materials from India.

Within England, travel and trade became easier and quicker. At the beginning of the century it took over three days to make the journey from London to Exeter or Manchester. By the 1780s you could get there in just over 24 hours by coach along the network of roads built by privately owned Turnpike Trusts. For transporting heavy goods, barges were best and towards the end of the century engineers constructed a system of canals that linked the larger rivers.

The 18th century was a boom time for builders, too. Georgian architects designed elegant terraces and spacious squares which are still admired in Dublin, Edinburgh, Bath, and other cities. This was a time of population growth and of enormous changes in the techniques of manufacturing textiles, iron and other goods. Georgian Britain saw the first industrial revolution. ■

Population of England
1700 5,000,000
1800 8,300,000

Many of the National Trust's 'stately homes' date from this period.

▲ Coach called 'The Star of Cambridge' leaving Ludgate Hill, London, at the beginning of the 19th century.

▶ Timetable for the Royal Mail at the General Coach office, Bath.

Geothermal power

Geothermal comes from two Greek words: *ge* meaning 'earth' and *therme* meaning 'heat'.

The centre of the Earth is very hot. In a few places the heat is close enough to the surface for people to use this 'geothermal' power.

Water which soaks down into the ground may be heated and then come to the surface as steam from cracks in the ground, or as geysers (hot springs). Such natural hot water is used for heating buildings in parts of New Zealand and Iceland.

A geothermal power-station uses steam from a borehole drilled a kilometre or more down into the hot rocks. If water is not there naturally then it is pumped down from the surface, through another borehole, to be heated by the rocks. The borehole takes the place of the boiler in a fuel-burning power-station. The steam drives turbines (special water wheels) which turn a generator to make electricity. Unlike most other types of power-station, geothermal stations need no fuel and do not pollute the atmosphere. ■

See also
Energy
Geysers
Hydroelectric power
Turbines
Water power

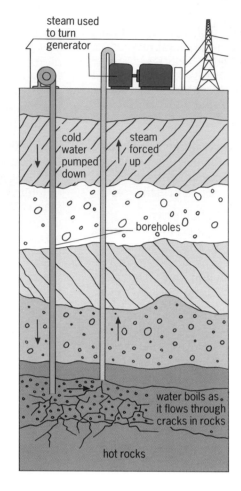

steam used to turn generator

cold water pumped down

steam forced up

boreholes

water boils as it flows through cracks in rocks

hot rocks

◄ Geothermal power-station. Cold water pumped down one borehole is heated by underground rocks. Steam coming up the other borehole is used to turn a generator.

Gerbils

Distribution
North Africa and Asia
Weight
About 130 g (male)
70 g (female)
Number of young
4 or 5
suckled for about 28 days
Lifespan
About 3 years

Subphylum Vertebrata
Class Mammalia
Order Rodentia
Number of species
56 true gerbils, 15 jirds

True gerbils are small rodents. Almost all of them live in very dry country on the edge of deserts in Africa and the Near East. They escape from the daytime heat in deep burrows and come out at night to feed on seeds and insects. Most are slender, sandy-coloured creatures, with long tails and very long hind legs. These enable them to leap over sandy ground, where feet adapted for running would sink into the soil.

There are many species of gerbil and of their close relatives the jirds and sandrats. Jirds are found in parts of Asia. These are rather stouter animals, with not quite such long hind legs as true gerbils. In the 1950s, some explorers took jirds from the cold desert region of Mongolia to America. At first they were used in laboratories, but later, people found that they made very good pets, so they are now kept in homes in many parts of the world. By mistake, they were known as gerbils. ■

See also
Albinos
Rodents

◄ Pet gerbils (jirds or Mongolian gerbils) all look much alike. They have been domesticated for so short a time that new varieties have not yet been developed. The two gerbils on the right are albinos. They are not a new variety; they were born with no colouring.

German history

There were already German tribes north of the River Rhine in Roman times. When the Roman empire collapsed, some of these tribes, the Franks, invaded Gaul. Their greatest king, Charlemagne, was crowned in AD 800. After he died, his empire was divided into West Francia (modern France) and East Francia or Franconia.

First German empire, the Holy Roman Empire

King Otto I of Franconia spread his power over all the German-speaking people of Europe, down the River Rhône and into Italy. He was crowned by the Pope in AD 962 and the Holy Roman Empire was born. Some of his descendants were strong emperors, especially Frederick II who joined southern Italy and Sicily to the empire. Others were weak and lost power to the dukes and princes of Germany.

Between 1452 and 1806, this empire was ruled by the Habsburgs from Vienna. Their greatest emperor was Charles V (1519–1556), but after his death the emperors gradually lost power. In the end the empire covered only what are now Austria, Czechoslovakia and parts of Hungary. The rest of Germany was ruled by 400 separate princes, dukes and bishops.

Second German empire

By the 19th century many German-speaking people wanted to be united in one country. In 1871 the German princes invited the King of Prussia to become Emperor of Germany. The first Chancellor (prime minister) was Otto von Bismarck. He tried to make life better for people by starting old-age pensions and payments for sickness and accident. People worked hard, building railways, new factories and a navy to make Germany very strong.

World War I and the Weimar Republic

Rivalry between Germany and other nations led to war in 1914. Six million of their people were killed or wounded and by 1918 many were starving. Some Germans blamed the emperor (Kaiser) for this, and he was overthrown. A republic was proclaimed in the city of Weimar. This republican government soon ran into trouble. By 1923 money was devalued. It took a whole basketful of notes to buy a loaf of bread, and people's savings had become worthless. Unemployment was rising and by 1932 there were 6 million people without work.

◀ William I of Prussia is proclaimed first emperor (Kaiser) of the German empire in January 1871. The ceremony took place in the Hall of Mirrors at Versailles, France after Prussia defeated France in the Franco-Prussian war. Bismarck is in white uniform.

The musician, Beethoven, and the writer, Goethe, both wanted a united Germany.

Third German empire: the Third Reich

In 1933 Hitler, leader of the Nazis, became Chancellor. He promised to unite all the German-speaking people into a new German empire (the Third Reich). Germans who opposed Hitler were silenced and many died in concentration camps. Jews were persecuted and those who could, migrated abroad. Hitler's armies took over Austria in 1938 and Czechoslovakia in the spring of 1939. When they invaded Poland later in 1939, World War II began.

Defeat, division and reunification

When allied troops defeated Germany in 1945, they discovered that 6 million Jews had been exterminated, most of them in death camps. Most German cities had been reduced to ruins by air raids and ground attacks. Money was valueless.

At the end of the war, Austria became a separate country again. Czechoslovakia and Poland were restored (with changed boundaries) and expelled at least 12 million Germans. Germany was divided into four zones of occupation; and Berlin into four sectors. In 1949 the Russian zone became the German Democratic Republic (East Germany), with the Soviet sector of Berlin as its capital. It was closely controlled by a dictatorial and centralized communist government.

The zones of the United States, Britain and France were combined to form the Federal Republic of Germany (West Germany). The three western sectors of Berlin formed an 'island' within East German territory. West Germany was a democracy, with a capitalist economy.

In October 1989 massive street demonstrations led to the fall of the communist government of East Germany. Free elections were held in March 1990, and Germany was reunited in October. ■

See also
European history
Holocaust
Nazis
World War I
World War II

Biography
Bismarck
Hitler
Marx

Artists
Dürer
Gropius

Composers
Bach
Beethoven
Brahms
Mendelssohn
Wagner

Reformers
Froebel
Luther

Scientists/inventors
Braun
Gutenberg
Humboldt
Kepler
Röntgen

Writers
Goethe
Grimm

By 1961 the East German economy was so much weakened by the loss of approximately 2·5 million people by migration to West Germany that the communist government erected a system of fortifications along the western boundary and encircling West Berlin (the Berlin Wall) to prevent escape. The wall divided Berliners until November 1989.

Germany

Germany lies in the middle of Europe between the Alps and Scandinavia. Although not as large as France, Spain, Sweden or Norway it has the biggest population of all European countries outside the Soviet Union.

Landscape

Much of Germany consists of the 'Central Uplands', a mixture of ancient block mountains with low hills and plains. Dark forests crown the hills, and castles look down across orchards and vineyards to fertile plains. In the Northern Lowland the sandy soil is not so fertile. Much of this land is covered with heath and pine forest, strewn with rock boulders left by glaciers of the Ice Age. In the far south lie the Alps.

The climate of Germany is temperate and allows crops such as wheat, maize and potatoes to grow well. Cattle graze in the damp and mild north-west and in the foothills of the mountains, but pigs, cattle and poultry are also kept in large battery units near to the cities, especially in the east. One reason for keeping animals indoors is that winters are sometimes very cold, with snow covering the ground for many weeks.

Area
356,945 sq km
(137,817 sq miles)
Capital
(Formal) Berlin
(Administrative) Bonn
Population
Over 79,070,000 (estimate)
Language
German
Religion
Christian, Muslim, others
Government
Federal Republic
Currency
1 Deutschmark = 100 pfennig
Highest mountain
Zugspitze
2,962 m in the Alps

▼ **Frankfurt is one of the largest cities in western Germany. It has the busiest airport and is the centre of German banking. Medieval buildings in the city centre were rebuilt in traditional style after World War II.**

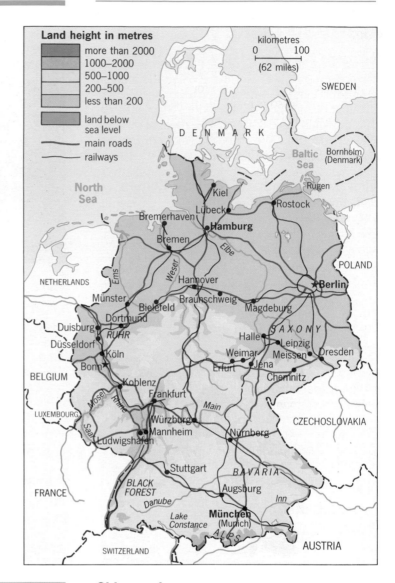

Cities and states

Germany is not dominated by a single huge city but has a network of large cities. Many of them, including Munich and Dresden, were formerly capitals of independent states such as Bavaria and Saxony that were united into the German empire in the last century. These cities inherited splendid palaces and art museums. In western Germany the cities have been well maintained and are prosperous, but in the east the communist government neglected older buildings. The state provided housing in the form of monotonous prefabricated blocks of apartments on the fringes of the cities.

Bavaria and Saxony are now two of the sixteen Länder (Federal States) which make up the modern Germany that was reunified in October 1990. These states vary greatly in size and population. But they are all important because the governments of the Länder have responsibility for education and other aspects of government.

People

Germans have a reputation for being busy and efficient. The day starts early for workers in factories and offices, and also for schoolchildren. There are few lessons in the afternoon but a great deal of homework. Even the youngest children carry books home in their large satchels.

The vast majority of Germans are German speaking; but there is a large minority (about 8 per cent) of people born outside Germany. West Germany has a high proportion of Turkish people who originally migrated as 'guest workers' to take jobs in factories when Germany was short of labour in the 1960s. The German constitution guarantees admission to all persons claiming German descent. The relaxation of frontier controls in the USSR and east Europe from 1989 onwards produced an inflow of hundreds of thousands of people from Polish Silesia, Hungary, Romania and the Soviet Union. The liberal immigration laws of the Federal Republic also produced an inflow of people claiming political asylum from countries such as Iran, Lebanon, Sri Lanka and Romania, the latter mainly gypsies.

Economy

Germany is the leading economic power in Europe, and one of the world leaders. West Germany is renowned for high-quality industrial products, such as machine tools, motor vehicles, electric and electronic equipment, chemicals and optical instruments. East Germany had a good reputation as a supplier of machinery, electrical equipment, chemicals and ships to the Soviet Union and other communist countries. But after the collapse of communist rule in eastern Europe in 1989 and the reunification of Germany in 1990, very few products from east Germany could compete in a free market. Factories closed and people faced unemployment and hardship.

Agriculture is not as profitable as industry in west Germany because of the large number of

small family farms. The farms of the formerly communist state of East Germany had been combined into huge co-operative (collective) units. After unification their sales suffered from poor marketing and packaging.

Roads and railways

In west Germany the *Autobahn* (motorway) system started by Hitler in the 1930s has been vastly improved and extended. West German railways are developing new high-speed lines, for example Hannover–Würzburg, which tunnel through hills and leap over valleys to keep an almost dead-level track, even in the mountains. West Germany also benefits from the Rhine, Europe's busiest waterway, which can take the large European barges laden with Ruhr coal and other heavy goods to above Basel. The condition of East German motorways, railways, canals and telecommunications after 45 years of communist rule was very poor.

Environment

West Germany had an excellent record environmentally. Power stations are equipped to remove pollution, and motor vehicles required to have catalytic converters. By contrast, East Germany relied for most of its electricity output on low-grade brown coal, which caused a high level of air pollution. Its salt, potash, uranium and chemical industries endangered lives of people living nearby, and also poured pollutants into the Weser and Elbe river systems leading into West Germany. Since 1990 many of the most polluting plants have been closed. ■

▲ Hohnstein is a typical village of Saxony, one of the five states which used to be part of the communist state of East Germany.

◀ Hand painting delicate porcelain at the Meissen factory near Dresden.

▲ On their first day at school, German children are given a Schultüte, a large paper cone filled with sweets.

See also
Europe
German history
Roads (photograph)

Germs

Microbes and micro-organisms are technical names for germs.

Germs are very simple microscopic creatures that cause disease. They must be magnified at least a hundred times by a microscope before you can see them. Bacteria and viruses are different types of germs.

Although bacteria and viruses are both called germs they are very different.

There are many types of bacteria. Some cause cuts to become infected and produce skin infections like boils. Others cause very dangerous diseases like tuberculosis, cholera and some types of food poisoning. Bacteria can be killed by antiseptics or antibiotics. Medicines called vaccines and serum can be used to protect people against germs. This is called immunization.

Germ warfare
Germs could be used as weapons to kill people, animals or crops. These would cause so much damage that in 1975 most nations agreed they would never use them.

Viruses are much smaller than bacteria. They cause a wide range of illnesses, from mild ones such as the common cold to fatal ones such as AIDS and rabies. Ordinary anti-biotics cannot be used to cure patients with viral diseases. A few anti-virus drugs are used, and people can be given vaccines to protect them against infection.

Bacteria and virus germs can cause diseases in animals and plants too, such as brucellosis (bacterial) in cattle and distemper (viral) in dogs. Plant viral diseases cause leaves to discolour and growth to stop. ■

See also
AIDS
Antibiotics
Bacteria
Diseases
Immunity
Living things
Vaccinations
Viruses

Biography
Lister
Pasteur

Geysers

A geyser is a natural jet of steam and boiling water which spurts out of the ground. Geysers only occur in some volcanic areas where water can seep down through layers of hot rock and collect underground. Here it is heated up under pressure, very much like water in a pressure cooker. The higher the pressure, the hotter the water must be to boil. When the water is superheated underground, it turns into high-pressure steam which spurts out of the ground as a geyser. When enough water has seeped back into the earth and heated up again, the display is repeated. ■

See also
Iceland

Ghana

Ghana is a country in West Africa. Most of southern Ghana has plenty of rain and thick forest grows. Large tropical hardwood trees, such as mahogany, are cut down for timber which is exported from the port of Takoradi on the Atlantic coast. Farmers earn money by growing cash crops such as cocoa, coffee and palm oil. Ghana exports more cocoa than any other country in the world and most of it goes to Britain to be manufactured into cocoa powder and chocolate.

As you travel northwards the scenery changes from thick forest to grass-land with some trees. In the far north there is hardly any rain between November and May. But peanuts (groundnuts), cotton and millet can be grown. Farmers also rear cattle, but the tsetse fly is a pest in much of Ghana because it carries a disease that kills cattle.

Flashback

From the 14th century, large states became powerful in the north and grew rich from trading in gold and salt. In the 18th and 19th centuries the Asante Confederacy was the most important state. The kings of the Asante ruled from their capital, Kumasi, until a British force invaded and destroyed it in 1874. The British established a colony, called the Gold Coast. In 1957 Ghana was the first black African state to regain independence. ■

Area
238,537 sq km
(92,100 sq miles)
Capital
Accra
Population
13,590,000
Language
English, Akan, Ga, Ewe
Religion
Christian, Traditional, Muslim
Government
Republic
Currency
1 cedi = 100 pesewas

The symbol of the Asante kings is the Golden Stool.

Anansi is a trickster-god of the Asante people, who tell many stories about him.

◄ **Traders displaying** *kente* **cloth. Asante weavers produce long, narrow strips in dazzling, complex patterns. Larger pieces are made by joining several strips edge to edge.**

See also
Africa
African history
Anansi
Slave trade

Biography
Nkrumah

40-395-3